THE
SIX
PILLARS
OF
SELF-ESTEEM

THE SIX PILLARS OF SELF-ESTEEM

Nathaniel Branden

BANTAM
NEW YORK   TORONTO   LONDON
SYDNEY   AUCKLAND

THE SIX PILLARS OF SELF-ESTEEM

A Bantam Book / March 1994

Book design by Kathryn Parise

For information address: Bantam Books.

LIBRARY OF CONGRESS CATALOGING-IN-PUBLICATION DATA
Branden, Nathaniel.
    The six pillars of self-esteem / Nathaniel Branden.
        p.   cm.
    Includes bibliographical references.
    ISBN 0-553-09529-3 : $22.95
    1. Self-esteem.   I. Title.
    BF697.5.S46B75   1994
    155.2—dc20   93-4491
                                                     CIP

Published simultaneously in the United States and Canada

Bantam Books are published by Bantam Books, a division of
Bantam Doubleday Dell Publishing Group, Inc. Its trade-
mark, consisting of the words "Bantam Books" and the por-
trayal of a rooster, is Registered in U.S. Patent and Trademark
Office and in other countries. Marca Registrada. Bantam
Books, 1540 Broadway, New York, New York 10036.

PRINTED IN THE UNITED STATES OF AMERICA

RRH   0 9 8 7 6 5 4 3

Contents

PART III EXTERNAL INFLUENCES: SELF AND OTHERS

To Devers Branden

THE
SIX
PILLARS
OF
SELF-ESTEEM

Introduction

My purpose in this book is to identify, in greater depth and comprehensiveness than in my previous writings, the most important factors on which self-esteem depends. If self-esteem is the health of the mind, then few subjects are of comparable urgency.

The turbulence of our times demands strong selves with a clear sense of identity, competence, and worth. With a breakdown of cultural consensus, an absence of worthy role models, little in the public arena to inspire our allegiance, and disorientingly rapid change a permanent feature of our lives, it is a dangerous moment in history not to know who we are or not to trust ourselves. The stability we cannot find in the world we must create within our own persons. To face life with low self-esteem is to be at a severe disadvantage. These considerations are part of my motivation in writing this book.

In essence, the book consists of my answers to four questions: What is self-esteem? Why is self-esteem important? What can we do to raise the level of our self-esteem? What role do others play in influencing our self-esteem?

Self-esteem is shaped by both internal and external factors. By "internal" I mean factors residing within, or generated by, the individual—ideas or beliefs, practices or behaviors. By "external" I mean factors in the environment: messages verbally or nonverbally transmitted, or experiences evoked, by parents, teachers, "significant others," organizations, and culture. I examine self-esteem from the inside and the outside: What is the contribution of the individual to his or her self-esteem and what is the contribution of other people? To the best of my knowledge, no investigation of this scope has been attempted before.

When I published *The Psychology of Self-Esteem* in 1969, I told myself I had said everything I could say on this subject. In 1970, realizing that there were "a few more issues" I needed to address, I wrote *Breaking Free*. Then, in 1972, "to fill in a few more gaps," I wrote *The Disowned Self*. After that, I told myself I was absolutely and totally finished with self-esteem and went on to write on other subjects. A decade or so passed, and I began to think about how much more I had personally experienced and learned about self-esteem since my first work, so I decided to write "one last book" about it; *Honoring the Self* was published in 1983. A couple of years later I thought it would be useful to write an action-oriented guide for individuals who wanted to work on their own self-esteem—*How to Raise Your Self-Esteem*, published in 1986. Surely I had finally finished with this subject, I told myself. But during this same period, "the self-esteem movement" exploded across the country; everyone was talking about self-esteem; books were written, lectures and conferences were given—and I was not enthusiastic about the quality of what was being presented to people. I found myself in some rather heated discussions with colleagues. While some of what was offered on self-esteem was excellent, I thought that a good deal was not. I realized how many issues I had not yet addressed, how many questions I needed to consider that I had not considered before, and how much I had carried in my head but never actually said or written. Above all, I saw the necessity of going far beyond my earlier work in spelling out the factors that create and sustain high or healthy self-esteem. (I use "high" and "healthy" interchangeably.) Once again, I found myself drawn back to examine new aspects of this inexhaustibly rich field of study, and to think my way down to deeper levels of understanding of what is, for me, the single most important psychological subject in the world.

I understood that what had begun so many years before as an interest, or even a fascination, had become a mission.

Speculating on the roots of this passion, I go back to my teenage years, to the time when emerging autonomy collided with pressure to conform. It is not easy to write objectively about that period, and I do not wish to suggest an arrogance I did not and do not feel. The truth is, as an adolescent I had an inarticulate but sacred sense of mission about my life. I had the conviction that nothing mattered more than retaining the ability to see the world through my own eyes. I thought that that was how everyone should feel. This perspective has never changed. I was acutely conscious of the pressures to "adapt" and to absorb the values of the "tribe"—family, community, and culture. It seemed to me that what was asked was the surrender of my judgment and also my conviction that my life and what I made of it was of the highest possible value. I saw my contemporaries surrendering and losing their fire—and, sometimes in painful, lonely bewilderment, I wanted to understand why. Why was growing up equated with giving up? If my overriding drive since child-hood was for understanding, another desire, hardly less intense, was forming but not yet fully conscious: the desire to communicate my understanding to the world; above all, to communicate my vision of life. It was years before I realized that, at the deepest level, I experienced myself as a teacher—a teacher of *values.* Underneath all my work, the core idea I wanted to teach was: *Your life is important. Honor it. Fight for your highest possibilities.*

I had my own struggles with self-esteem, and I give examples of them in this book. The full context is given in my memoir, *Judgment Day.* I shall not pretend that everything I know about self-esteem I learned from psychotherapy clients. Some of the most important things I learned came from thinking about my own mistakes and from noticing what I did that lowered or raised my own self-esteem. I write, in part, as a teacher to myself.

It would be foolish for me to declare that I have now written my final report on "the psychology of self-esteem." But this book does feel like the climax of all the work that preceded it.

I first lectured on self-esteem and its impact on love, work, and the struggle for happiness in the late 1950s and published my first articles on the subject in the 1960s. The challenge then was to gain public under-standing of its importance. "Self-esteem" was not yet an expression in widespread use. Today, the danger may be that the idea has become fashionable. It is on everyone's tongue, which is not to say that it is better understood. Yet if we are unclear about its precise meaning and about the specific factors its successful attainment depends on—if we are careless in our thinking, or succumb to the oversimplifications and sugar-coatings of pop psychology—then the subject will suffer a fate worse than being ignored. It will become trivialized. That is why, in Part I, we begin our inquiry into the sources of self-esteem with an examination of what self-esteem is and is not.

When I first began struggling with questions concerning self-esteem forty years ago, I saw the subject as providing invaluable clues to understanding motivation. It was 1954. I was twenty-four years of age, studying psychology at New York University, and with a small psychotherapy practice. Reflecting on the stories I heard from clients, I looked for a common denominator, and I was struck by the fact that whatever the person's particular complaint, there was always a deeper issue: a sense of inadequacy, of not being "enough," a feeling of guilt or shame or inferiority, a clear lack of self-acceptance, self-trust, and self-love. In other words, a problem of self-esteem.

In his early writings Sigmund Freud suggested that neurotic symptoms could be understood either as direct expressions of anxiety or else as defenses against anxiety, which seemed to me to be a hypothesis of great profundity. Now I began to wonder if the complaints or symptoms I encountered could be understood either as direct expressions of inadequate self-esteem (for example, feelings of worthlessness, or extreme passivity, or a sense of futility) or else as defenses against inadequate self-esteem (for example, grandiose bragging and boasting, compulsive sexual "acting-out," or overcontrolling social behavior). I continue to find this idea compelling. Where Freud thought in terms of *ego defense mechanisms*, strategies to avoid the threat to the ego's equilibrium represented by anxiety, today I think in terms of *self-esteem defense mechanisms*, strategies to defend against any kind of threat, from any quarter, internal or external, to self-esteem (or one's pretense at it). In other words, all the famous "defenses" that Freud identified can be understood as efforts to protect self-esteem.

When I went to the library in search of information about self-esteem, almost none was to be found. The indexes of books on psychology did not contain the term. Eventually I found a few brief mentions, such as in William James, but nothing that seemed sufficiently fundamental or that brought the clarity I was seeking. Freud suggested that low "self-regard" was caused by a child's discovery that he or she could not have sexual intercourse with Mother or Father, which resulted in the helpless feeling, "I can do nothing." I did not find this persuasive or illuminating as an explanation. Alfred Adler suggested that everyone starts out with feelings of inferiority caused, first, by bringing some physical liability or "organ inferiority" into the world, and second, by the fact that everyone else (that is, grown-ups or older siblings) is bigger and stronger. In other words, our misfortune is that we are not born as perfectly formed mature adults. I did not find this helpful, either. A few psychoanalysts wrote about self-esteem, but in terms I found remote from my understanding of the idea, so that it was almost as if they were studying another subject. (Only much later could I see some connection between aspects of that work and my own.) I struggled to clarify and expand my understanding chiefly by reflecting on what I observed while working with people.

As the issue of self-esteem came more clearly into focus for me, I saw that it is a profound and powerful human need, essential to healthy adaptiveness, that is, to optimal functioning and self-fulfillment. To the extent that the need is frustrated, we suffer and are thwarted in our development.

Apart from disturbances whose roots are biological, I cannot think of a single psychological problem—from anxiety and depression, to under-achievement at school or at work, to fear of intimacy, happiness, or success, to alcohol or drug abuse, to spouse battering or child molesta-tion, to co-dependency and sexual disorders, to passivity and chronic aimlessness, to suicide and crimes of violence—that is not traceable, at least in part, to the problem of deficient self-esteem. Of all the judgments we pass in life, none is as important as the one we pass on ourselves.

I recall discussing the issue with colleagues during the 1960s. No one debated the subject's importance. No one denied that if ways could be found to raise the level of a person's self-esteem, any number of positive consequences would follow. "But how do you raise an adult's self-esteem?" was a question I heard more than once, with a note of skepticism that it could be done. As was evident from their writings, the issue—and the challenge—were largely ignored.

Pioneering family therapist Virginia Satir talked of the importance of self-esteem, but she was not a theoretician of the subject and said little about its dynamics except in a limited family context. Carl Rogers, an-other great pioneer in psychotherapy, focused essentially on only one aspect of self-esteem—self-acceptance—and we shall see that while the two are intimately related, they are not identical in meaning.

Still, awareness of the importance of the topic was growing, and during the seventies and eighties, an increasing number of articles ap-peared in professional journals, aimed chiefly at establishing correlations between self-esteem and some aspect of behavior. However, there was no general theory of self-esteem nor even an agreed-on definition of the term. Different writers meant different things by "self-esteem." Conse-quently they often measured different phenomena. Sometimes one set of findings seemed to invalidate another. The field was a Tower of Babel. Today there is still no widely shared definition of self-esteem.

In the 1980s, the idea of self-esteem caught fire. After a quiet buildup over decades, more and more people began talking about its importance to human well-being. Educators in particular began thinking about the relevance of self-esteem to success or failure at school. We have a National Council for Self-Esteem, with chapters opening in more and more cities. Almost every week somewhere in the country we have conferences in which discussions of self-esteem figure prominently.

The interest in self-esteem is not confined to the United States. It is becoming worldwide. In the summer of 1990 I had the privilege of delivering, near Oslo, Norway, the opening keynote address at the First International Conference on Self-Esteem. Educators, psychologists, and psychotherapists from the United States, Great Britain, and various countries in Europe, including the Soviet Union, streamed into Norway to attend lectures, seminars, and workshops devoted to discussions of the applications of self-esteem psychology to personal development, school systems, social problems, and business organizations. Notwithstanding the differences among participants in background, culture, primary focus of interest, and understanding of what precisely "self-esteem" meant, the atmosphere was charged with excitement and the conviction that self-esteem was an idea whose historical moment had arrived. Growing out of the Oslo conference, we now have an International Council on Self-Esteem, with more and more countries being represented.

In the former Soviet Union a small but growing group of thinkers is keenly aware of the importance of self-esteem to the transitions their country is attempting to achieve. Commenting on the urgent need for education in self-esteem, a visiting Russian scholar remarked to me, "Not only are our people without any tradition of entrepreneurship, but our managers have absolutely no grasp of the idea of personal responsibility and accountability that the average American manager takes for granted. And you know what a gigantic problem passivity and envy is here. The psychological changes we need may be even more formidable than the political or economic changes."

Throughout the world there is an awakening to the fact that, just as a human being cannot hope to realize his or her potential without healthy self-esteem, neither can a society whose members do not respect themselves, do not value their persons, do not trust their minds.

But with all of these developments, what precisely self-esteem *is*—and what specifically its attainment depends on—*remain the great questions*.

At one conference, when I stated that the practice of living consciously was essential to healthy self-esteem, one woman demanded angrily, "Why are you trying to impose your white, middle-class values on the rest of the world?" (This left me wondering who the class of humanity was for whom living consciously was *not* important to psychological well-being.) When I spoke of personal integrity as vital to the protection of a positive self-concept, and the betrayal of integrity as psychologically harmful, no one volunteered agreement or wanted that idea recorded in our report. They preferred to focus only on how *others* might wound one's feelings of worth, not how one might inflict the wound oneself. This attitude is typical of those who believe one's self-esteem is primarily determined by other people. I will not deny that experiences such as these, and the feelings they ignite, have intensified my desire to write this book.

In working with self-esteem, we need to be aware of two dangers. One is that of oversimplifying what healthy self-esteem requires, and thereby of catering to people's hunger for quick fixes and effortless solutions. The other is that of surrendering to a kind of fatalism or determinism that assumes, in effect, that individuals "either have good self-esteem or they haven't," that everyone's destiny is set (forever?) by the first few years of life, and there's not much to be done about it (except perhaps years or decades of psychotherapy). Both views encourage passivity; both obstruct our vision of what is possible.

My experience is that most people underestimate their power to change and grow. They believe implicitly that yesterday's pattern must be tomorrow's. They do not see choices that—objectively—do exist. They rarely appreciate how much they can do on their own behalf if genuine growth and higher self-esteem are their goals and if they are willing to take responsibility for their own lives. The belief that they are powerless becomes a self-fulfilling prophecy.

This book, ultimately, is a call to action. It is, I now realize, an amplification in psychological terms of the battle cry of my youth: A self is to be actualized and celebrated—not aborted and renounced. This book is addressed to all men and women who wish to participate actively in the process of their evolution—as well as to psychologists, parents, teachers, and those responsible for the culture of organizations. It is a book about what is possible.

PART I

Self-Esteem:
Basic Principles

Self-Esteem:
The Immune System of
Consciousness

There are realities we cannot avoid. One of them is the importance of self-esteem.

Regardless of what we do or do not admit, we cannot be indifferent to our self-evaluation. However, we can run from this knowledge if it makes us uncomfortable. We can shrug it off, evade it, declare that we are only interested in "practical" matters, and escape into baseball or the evening news or the financial pages or a shopping spree or a sexual adventure or a drink.

Yet self-esteem is a fundamental human need. Its impact requires neither our understanding nor our consent. It works its way within us with or without our knowledge. We are free to seek to grasp the dynamics of self-esteem or to remain unconscious of them, but in the latter case we remain a mystery to ourselves and endure the consequences.

Let us look at the role of self-esteem in our lives.

A Preliminary Definition

By "self-esteem" I mean much more than that innate sense of self-worth that presumably is our human birthright—that spark that psychotherapists and teachers seek to fan in those they work with. That spark is only the anteroom to self-esteem.

Self-esteem, fully realized, is the experience that we are appropriate to life and to the requirements of life. More specifically, self-esteem is:

1. confidence in our ability to think, confidence in our ability to cope with the basic challenges of life; and
2. confidence in our right to be successful and happy, the feeling of being worthy, deserving, entitled to assert our needs and wants, achieve our values, and enjoy the fruits of our efforts.

Later I will refine and condense this definition.

I do not share the belief that self-esteem is a gift we have only to claim (by reciting affirmations, perhaps). On the contrary, its possession over time represents an achievement. The goal of this book is to examine the nature and roots of that achievement.

The Basic Pattern

To trust one's mind and to know that one is worthy of happiness is the essence of self-esteem.

The power of this conviction about oneself lies in the fact that it is more than a judgment or a feeling. It is a motivator. It inspires behavior.

In turn, it is directly affected by how we act. Causation flows in both directions. There is a continuous feedback loop between our actions in the world and our self-esteem. The level of our self-esteem influences how we act, and how we act influences the level of our self-esteem.

To trust one's mind and to know that one is worthy of happiness is the essence of self-esteem.

If I trust my mind and judgment, I am more likely to operate as a thinking being. Exercising my ability to think, bringing appropriate awareness to my activities, my life works better. This reinforces trust in my mind. If I distrust my mind, I am more likely to be mentally passive, to bring less awareness than I need to my activities, and less persistence in the face of difficulties. When my actions lead to disappointing or painful results, I feel justified in distrusting my mind.

With high self-esteem, I am more likely to persist in the face of difficulties. With low self-esteem, I am more likely to give up or go through the motions of trying without really giving my best. Research shows that high-self-esteem subjects will persist at a task significantly longer than low-self-esteem subjects.[1] If I persevere, the likelihood is that I will succeed more often than I fail. If I don't, the likelihood is that I will fail more often than I succeed. Either way, my view of myself will be reinforced.

If I respect myself and require that others deal with me respectfully, I send out signals and behave in ways that increase the likelihood that others will respond appropriately. When they do, I am reinforced and confirmed in my initial belief. If I lack self-respect and consequently accept discourtesy, abuse, or exploitation from others as natural, I unconsciously transmit this, and some people will treat me at my self-estimate. When this happens, and I submit to it, my self-respect deteriorates still more.

The value of self-esteem lies not merely in the fact that it allows us to *feel* better but that it allows us to *live* better—to respond to challenges and opportunities more resourcefully and more appropriately.

The Impact of Self-Esteem: General Observations

The level of our self-esteem has profound consequences for every aspect of our existence: how we operate in the workplace, how we deal with people, how high we are likely to rise, how much we are likely to achieve—and, in the personal realm, with whom we are likely to fall in love, how we interact with our spouse, children, and friends, what level of personal happiness we attain.

There are positive correlations between healthy self-esteem and a variety of other traits that bear directly on our capacity for achievement and for happiness. Healthy self-esteem correlates with rationality, realism, intuitiveness, creativity, independence, flexibility, ability to manage change, willingness to admit (and correct) mistakes, benevolence, and cooperativeness. Poor self-esteem correlates with irrationality, blindness to reality, rigidity, fear of the new and unfamiliar, inappropriate conformity or inappropriate rebelliousness, defensiveness, overcompliant or overcontrolling behavior, and fear of or hostility toward others. We shall see that there is a logic to these correlations. The implications for survival, adaptiveness, and personal fulfillment are obvious. Self-esteem is life supporting and life enhancing.

High self-esteem seeks the challenge and stimulation of worthwhile and demanding goals. Reaching such goals nurtures good self-esteem. Low self-esteem seeks the safety of the familiar and undemanding. Confining oneself to the familiar and undemanding serves to weaken self-esteem.

The more solid our self-esteem, the better equipped we are to cope with troubles that arise in our personal lives or in our careers; the quicker we are to pick ourselves up after a fall; the more energy we have to begin anew. (An extraordinarily high number of successful entrepreneurs have two or more bankruptcies in their past; failure did not stop them.)

The higher our self-esteem, the more ambitious we tend to be, not necessarily in a career or financial sense, but in terms of what we hope to experience in life—emotionally, intellectually, creatively, spiritually. The lower our self-esteem, the less we aspire to and the less we are likely to achieve. Either path tends to be self-reinforcing and self-perpetuating.

The higher our self-esteem, the stronger the drive to express ourselves, reflecting the sense of richness within. The lower our self-esteem, the more urgent the need to "prove" ourselves—or to forget ourselves by living mechanically and unconsciously.

The higher our self-esteem, the more open, honest, and appropriate our communications are likely to be, because we believe our thoughts have value and therefore we welcome rather than fear clarity. The lower our self-esteem, the more muddy, evasive, and inappropriate our communications are likely to be, because of uncertainty about our own thoughts and feelings and/or anxiety about the listener's response.

The higher our self-esteem, the more disposed we are to form nourishing rather than toxic relationships. The reason is that like is drawn to like, health is attracted to health. Vitality and expansiveness in others are naturally more appealing to persons of good self-esteem than are emptiness and dependency.

An important principle of human relationships is that we tend to feel most comfortable, most "at home," with persons whose self-esteem level resembles our own. Opposites may attract about some issues, but not about this one. High-self-esteem individuals tend to be drawn to high-self-esteem individuals. We do not see a passionate love affair, for example, between persons at opposite ends of the self-esteem continuum—just as we are not likely to see a passionate romance between intelligence and stupidity. (I am not saying we might never see a "one-night stand," but that is another matter. Note I am speaking of passionate love, not a brief infatuation or sexual episode, which can operate by a different set of dynamics.) Medium-self-esteem individuals are typically attracted to medium-self-esteem individuals. Low self-esteem seeks low self-esteem in others—not consciously, to be sure, but by the logic of that which leads us to feel we have encountered a "soul mate." The most disastrous relationships are those between persons who think poorly of themselves; the union of two abysses does not produce a height.

We tend to feel most comfortable, most
"at home," with persons whose self-esteem level
resembles our own.

The healthier our self-esteem, the more inclined we are to treat others with respect, benevolence, goodwill, and fairness—since we do not tend to perceive them as a threat, and since self-respect is the foundation of respect for others. With healthy self-esteem, we are not quick to interpret relationships in malevolent, adversarial terms. We do not approach encounters with automatic expectations of rejection, humiliation, treachery, or betrayal. Contrary to the belief that an individualistic orientation inclines one to antisocial behavior, research shows that a well-developed sense of personal value and autonomy correlates significantly with kindness, generosity, social cooperation, and a spirit of mutual aid, as is confirmed, for instance, in A. S. Waterman's comprehensive review of the research in *The Psychology of Individualism*.

And finally, research discloses that high self-esteem is one of the best predictors of personal happiness, as is discussed in D. G. Meyers' *The Pursuit of Happiness*. Logically enough, low self-esteem correlates with unhappiness.

Love

It is not difficult to see the importance of self-esteem to success in the arena of intimate relationships. There is no greater barrier to romantic happiness than the fear that I am undeserving of love and that my destiny is to be hurt. Such fears give birth to self-fulfilling prophecies.

If I enjoy a fundamental sense of efficacy and worth, and experience myself as lovable, then I have a foundation for appreciating and loving others. The relationship of love feels natural; benevolence and caring feel natural. I have something to give; I am not trapped in feelings of deficiency; I have a kind of emotional "surplus" that I can channel into loving. And happiness does not make me anxious. Confidence in my competence and worth, and in your ability to see and appreciate it, also gives birth to self-fulfilling prophecies.

There is no greater barrier to romantic happiness than the fear that I am undeserving of love and that my destiny is to be hurt.

But if I lack respect for and enjoyment of who I am, I have very little to give—except *my unfilled needs.* In my emotional impoverishment, I tend to see other people essentially as sources of approval or disapproval. I do not appreciate them for who they are in their own right. I see only what they can or cannot do for me. I am not looking for people whom I can admire and with whom I can share the excitement and adventure of life. I am looking for people who will not condemn me—and perhaps will be impressed by my persona, the face I present to the world. My ability to love remains undeveloped. This is one of the reasons why attempts at relationships so often fail—not because the vision of passionate or romantic love is intrinsically irrational, but because the self-esteem needed to support it is absent.

We have all heard the observation, "If you do not love yourself, you will be unable to love others." Less well understood is the other half of the story. If I do not feel lovable, it is very difficult to believe that anyone else loves me. If I do not accept myself, how can I accept your love for me? Your warmth and devotion are confusing: it confounds my self-concept, since I "know" I am not lovable. Your feeling for me cannot possibly be real, reliable, or lasting. If I do not feel lovable, your love for me becomes an effort to fill a sieve, and eventually the effort is likely to exhaust you.

Even if I consciously disown my feelings of being unlovable, even if I insist that I am "wonderful," the poor self-concept remains deep within to undermine my attempts at relationships. Unwittingly I become a saboteur of love.

I attempt love but the foundation of inner security is not there. Instead there is the secret fear that I am destined only for pain. So I pick someone who inevitably will reject or abandon me. (In the beginning I pretend I do not know this, so the drama can be played out.) Or, if I pick someone with whom happiness might be possible, I subvert the relationship by demanding excessive reassurances, by venting irrational possessiveness, by making catastrophes of small frictions, by seeking to control through subservience or domination, by finding ways to reject my partner before my partner can reject me.

A few vignettes will convey how poor self-esteem shows up in the area of the intimately personal:

"Why do I always fall for Mr. Wrong?" a woman in therapy asks me. Her father abandoned the family when she was seven, and on more than one occasion her mother had screamed at her, "If you weren't so much trouble, maybe your father wouldn't have left us!" As an adult, she "knows" that her fate is to be abandoned. She "knows" that she does not deserve love. Yet she longs for a relationship with a man. The conflict is resolved by selecting men—often married—who clearly do not care for her in a way that would sustain her for any length of time. She is proving that her tragic sense of life is justified.

When we "know" we are doomed, we behave in ways to make reality conform to our "knowledge." We are anxious when there is dissonance between our "knowledge" and the perceivable facts. Since our "knowledge" is not to be doubted or questioned, it is the facts that have to be altered: hence self-sabotage.

A man falls in love, the woman returns his feeling, and they marry. But nothing she can do is ever enough to make him feel loved for longer than a moment; he is insatiable. However, she is so committed to him that she perseveres. When at last she convinces him that she really loves him and he is no longer able to doubt it, he begins to wonder whether he set his standards too low. He wonders whether she is really good enough for him. Eventually he leaves her, falls in love with another woman, and the dance begins again.

Everyone knows the famous Groucho Marx joke that he would never join a club that would have him for a member. That is exactly the idea by which some low-self-esteem people operate their love life. If you love me, obviously you are not good enough for me. Only someone who will reject me is an acceptable object of my devotion.

> A woman feels compelled to tell her husband, who adores her, all the ways in which other women are superior to her. When he does not agree, she ridicules him. The more passionately he worships her, the more cruelly she demeans him. Finally she exhausts him, and he walks out of their marriage. She is hurt and astonished. How could she have so misjudged him? she wonders. Soon she tells herself, "I always knew no one could ever truly love me." She always felt she was unlovable and now she has proved it.

The tragedy of many people's lives is that, given a choice between being "right" and having an opportunity to be happy, they invariably choose being "right." That is the one ultimate satisfaction they allow themselves.

> A man "knows" that it is not his destiny to be happy. He feels he does not deserve to be. (And besides, his happiness might wound his parents, who have never known any happiness of their own.) But when he finds a woman he admires and who attracts him, and she responds, he is happy. For a while, he forgets that romantic fulfillment is not his "story," not his "life script." Surrendering to his joy, he temporarily forgets that it does violence to his self-concept and thus makes him feel out of alignment with "reality." Eventually, however, the joy triggers anxiety, as it would have to for one who feels misaligned with the way things *really* are. To reduce his anxiety, he must reduce his joy. So, guided unconsciously by the deepest logic of his self-concept, he begins to destroy the relationship.

Once again we observe the basic pattern of self-destruction: If I "know" my fate is to be unhappy, I must not allow reality to confuse me with happiness. It is not I who must adjust to reality, but reality that must adjust to me and to my "knowledge" of the way things are and are meant to be.

Note that it is not always necessary to destroy the relationship entirely, as in the vignettes above. It may be acceptable that the relationship continue, *providing I am not happy.* I may engage in a project called *struggling to be happy* or *working on our relationship.* I may read books on the subject, participate in seminars, attend lectures, or enter psycho-therapy with the announced aim of being happy *in the future*. But not now; not today. The possibility of happiness in the present is too terrifyingly immediate.

———

What is required for many of us, paradoxical though it may sound, is the courage to tolerate *happiness without self-sabotage.*

———

"Happiness anxiety" is very common. Happiness can activate internal voices saying I don't deserve this, or it will never last, or I'm riding for a fall, or I'm killing my mother or father by being happier than they ever were, or life is not like this, or people will be envious and hate me, or happiness is only an illusion, or nobody else is happy so why should I be?

What is required for many of us, paradoxical though it may sound, is the courage to *tolerate* happiness without self-sabotage until such time as we lose the fear of it and realize that it will not destroy us (and need not disappear). One day at a time, I will tell clients; see if you can get through today without doing anything to undermine or subvert your good feelings—and if you "fall off the wagon," don't despair, pull yourself back and recommit yourself to happiness. Such perseverance is self-esteem building.

Further, we need to confront those destructive voices, not run from them; engage them in inner dialogue; challenge them to give their reasons; patiently answer and refute their nonsense—dealing with them as one might deal with real people; and distinguish them from the voice of our adult self.

The Workplace

Next, consider workplace examples of behavior inspired by poor self-esteem:

A man receives a promotion in his company and is swallowed by panic at the thought of not possibly being able to master the new challenges and responsibilities. "I'm an impostor! I don't belong here!" he tells himself. Feeling in advance that he is doomed, he is not motivated to give his best. Unconsciously he begins a process of self-sabotage: coming to meetings underprepared, being harsh with staff one minute and placating and solicitous the next, clowning at inappropriate moments, ignoring signals of dissatisfaction from his boss. Predictably, he is fired. "I knew it was too good to be true," he tells himself.

If I die by my own hand, at least I am still in control; I spare myself the anxiety of waiting for destruction from some unknown source. The anxiety of feeling out of control is unbearable; I must end it any way I can.

A manager reads a superb idea proposed by a subordinate, feels a sinking sense of humiliation that the idea did not occur to her, imagines being overtaken and surpassed by the subordinate—and begins plotting to bury the proposal.

This kind of destructive envy is a product of an impoverished sense of self. Your achievement threatens to expose my emptiness; the world will see—worse still, *I* will see—how insignificant I am. Generosity toward the achievements of others is emblematic of self-esteem.

A man meets his new boss—and is dismayed and angered because the boss is a woman. He feels wounded and diminished in his masculinity. He fantasizes degrading her sexually—"putting her in her place." His feeling of being threatened shows up as sullen and subtly uncooperative behavior.

It would be hard to name a more certain sign of poor self-esteem than the need to perceive some other group as inferior. A man whose notion of "power" is stuck at the level of "sexual domination" is a man frightened of women, frightened of ability or self-assurance, frightened of *life*.

It would be hard to name a more certain sign of poor self-esteem than the need to perceive some other group as inferior.

The head of a research and development lab is informed that the firm has brought in a brilliant scientist from another company. He immediately translates this to mean that his superiors are dissatisfied with his work, in spite of much evidence to the contrary. He imagines his authority and status slipping away. He imagines the new man eventually being appointed head of the department. In a fit of blind rebelliousness, he allows his work to deteriorate. When his lapses are gently pointed out to him, he lashes out defensively—and quits.

When our illusion of self-esteem rests on the fragile support of never being challenged, when our insecurity finds evidence of rejection where no rejection exists, then it is only a matter of time until our inner bomb explodes. The form of the explosion is self-destructive behavior—and the fact that one may have an extraordinary intelligence is no protection. Brilliant people with low self-esteem act against their interests every day.

An auditor from an independent accounting firm meets with the CEO of the client organization. He knows he needs to tell this man some news he will not want to hear. Unconsciously he fantasizes being in the presence of his intimidating father—and stutters and stammers and does not communicate one third of what he had intended. His hunger for this CEO's approval, or the wish to avoid his disapproval, overwhelms his professional judgment. Later, after putting into his written report all the things he should have said to the CEO in person before the report was released, when remedial action might still have been possible, he sits in his office, trembling with anxiety, anticipating the CEO's reaction.

When we are moved primarily by fear, sooner or later we precipitate the very calamity we dread. If we fear condemnation, we behave in ways that ultimately elicit disapproval. If we fear anger, eventually we make people angry.

A woman who is new to the marketing department of her firm gets what she believes is a brilliant idea. She imagines putting it on paper, marshaling arguments to support it, working toward getting it to the person with authority to act. Then an inner voice whispers, "Who are you to have good ideas? Don't make yourself conspicuous. Do you want people to laugh at you?" She imagines the angry face of her mother, who had always been jealous of her intelligence; the wounded face of her father, who had been threatened by it. Within a few days she can barely remember what the idea was.

When we doubt our minds, we tend to discount its products. If we fear intellectual self-assertiveness, perhaps associating it with loss of love, we mute our intelligence. We dread being visible; so we make ourselves invisible, then suffer because no one sees us.

> He is a boss who always has to be right. He takes pleasure in emphasizing his superiority. In encounters with staff, he cannot hear a suggestion without the urge to "massage it into something better," something that "puts my stamp on it." "Why aren't my people more innovative?" he likes to say. "Why can't they be more creative?" But he also likes to say, "There's only one king of the jungle" or, in more restrained moments, "But someone has to lead the organization." With a pretense at regret he will sometimes declare, "I can't help it—I have a big ego." The truth is, he has a small one, but his energies are invested in never knowing that.

Once again we note that poor self-esteem can show up as lack of generosity toward the contributions of others or a tendency to fear their ability—and, in the case of a leader or manager, an inability to elicit their best from people.

The point of such stories is certainly not to condemn or ridicule those who suffer from poor self-esteem but to alert us to the power of self-esteem in influencing our responses. Problems such as I am describing can all be reversed. But the first step is to appreciate the dynamics involved.

Self-Fulfilling Prophecies

Self-esteem creates a set of implicit expectations about what is possible and appropriate to us. These expectations tend to generate the actions that turn them into realities. And the realities confirm and strengthen the original beliefs. Self-esteem—high or low—tends to be a generator of self-fulfilling prophecies.

Such expectations may exist in the mind as subconscious or semiconscious visions of our future. Educational psychologist E. Paul Torrance, commenting on the accumulating scientific evidence that our implicit assumptions about the future powerfully affect motivation, writes, "In fact, a person's image of the future may be a better predictor of future attainment than his past performances."[2] What we make an effort to learn and what we achieve is based, at least in part, on what we think is possible and appropriate to us.

======

Self-esteem—high or low—tends to be a generator
of self-fulfilling prophecies.

======

While an inadequate self-esteem can severely limit an individual's aspirations and accomplishments, the consequences of the problem need not be so obvious. Sometimes the consequences show up in more indirect ways. The time bomb of a poor self-concept may tick silently for years while an individual, driven by a passion for success and exercising genuine ability, may rise higher and higher in his profession. Then, without real necessity, he starts cutting corners, morally or legally, in his eagerness to provide more lavish demonstrations of his mastery. Then he commits more flagrant offenses still, telling himself that he is "beyond good and evil," as if challenging the Fates to bring him down. Only at the end, when his life and career explode in disgrace and ruin, can we see for how many years he has been moving relentlessly toward the final act of an unconscious life script he may have begun writing at the age of three. It is not difficult to think of well-publicized figures who might fit this description.

Self-concept is destiny. Or, more precisely, it tends to be. Our self-concept is who and what we consciously and subconsciously think we are—our physical and psychological traits, our assets and liabilities, possibilities and limitations, strengths and weaknesses. A self-concept contains or includes our level of self-esteem, but is more global. We cannot understand a person's behavior without understanding the self-concept behind it.

In less spectacular ways than in the story above, people sabotage themselves at the height of their success all the time. They do so when success clashes with their implicit beliefs about what is appropriate to them. It is frightening to be flung beyond the limits of one's idea of who one is. If a self-concept cannot accommodate a given level of success, and if the self-concept does not change, it is predictable that the person will find ways to self-sabotage.

Here are examples from my psychotherapy practice:

"I was on the verge of getting the biggest commission of my career," an architect says, "and my anxiety shot through the roof—because this project would have lifted me to a level of fame beyond anything I could have handled. I hadn't taken a drink in three years. So I told myself it was safe to have one drink—to celebrate. I ended up smashed, insulted the people who would have given me the assignment, lost it of course, and my partner was so enraged he quit on me. I was devastated, but I was back in 'safe territory' again, struggling to rise but not yet breaking through. I'm comfortable there."

"I was determined," says a woman who owns a small chain of boutiques, "not to be stopped by my husband or anyone else. I did not fault my husband because he earned less than I did, and I would not allow him to fault me for earning more than he did. But there was this voice inside saying I was not supposed to be this successful—no woman was. I didn't deserve it—no woman could. I became careless. Neglected important phone calls. Became irritable with staff—and customers. And kept getting angrier and angrier with my husband, without ever naming the real issue. After a particularly bad fight with him, I was having lunch with one of our buyers, and something she said set me off, and there was this great big blowup, right there in the restaurant. I lost the account. I began making inexcusable mistakes. . . . Now, three years and a lot of nightmares later, I'm trying to build the business back up again."

"I was in line for a promotion I had wanted for a long time," says an executive. "My life was in perfect order. A good marriage; healthy kids doing well in school. And it had been years since I'd fooled around with another woman. If there was a problem, it was only that I really wanted more money, and now I seemed all set to get it. It was anxiety that tipped me over. I woke up in the middle of the night, wondering if I were having a heart attack, but the doctor said it was just anxiety. Why it came, who knows? Sometimes I feel I'm just not meant to be too happy. It feels wrong. I don't think I've ever felt I deserved it. Whatever it was, the anxiety kept building, and one day, at an office party, I came on to the wife of one of my bosses—stupidly and clumsily. It's a miracle I wasn't fired; when she told her husband, I expected to be. I didn't get the promotion, and the anxiety died down."

What is the common element in these stories? Happiness anxiety; success anxiety. The dread and disorientation that persons with poor self-esteem experience when life goes well in ways that conflict with their deepest view of themselves and of what is appropriate to them.

Regardless of the context in which self-destructive behavior occurs, or the form it takes, the motor of such behavior is the same: poor self-esteem. *It is poor self-esteem that places us in an adversarial relationship to our well-being.*

Self-Esteem as a Basic Need

If the power of self-esteem derives from the fact that it is a profound need, what precisely is a *need*?

A need is that which is required for our effective functioning. We do not merely *want* food and water, we *need* them; without them, we die. However, we have other nutritional needs, such as for calcium, whose impact is less direct and dramatic. In some regions in Mexico the soil contains no calcium; the inhabitants of these regions do not perish outright, but their growth is stunted, they are generally debilitated, and they are prey to many diseases to which the lack of calcium makes them highly susceptible. *They are impaired in their ability to function.*

Self-esteem is a need analogous to calcium, rather than to food or water. Lacking it to a serious degree, we do not necessarily die, but we are impaired in our ability to function.

To say that self-esteem is a need is to say:

That it makes an essential contribution to the life process.

That it is indispensable to normal and healthy development.

That it has survival value.

We should note that sometimes lack of self-esteem does eventuate in death in fairly direct ways—for example, by a drug overdose, defiantly reckless driving of an automobile, remaining with a murderously abusive spouse, participating in gang wars, or suicide. However, for most of us the consequences of poor self-esteem are subtler, less direct, more circuitous. We may need a good deal of reflection and self-examination to appreciate how our deepest view of ourselves shows up in the ten thousand choices that add up to our destiny.

An inadequate self-esteem may reveal itself in a bad choice of mate, a marriage that brings only frustration, a career that never goes anywhere, aspirations that are somehow always sabotaged, promising ideas that die stillborn, a mysterious inability to enjoy successes, destructive eating and living habits, dreams that are never fulfilled, chronic anxiety or depression, persistently low resistance to illness, overdependence on drugs, an insatiable hunger for love and approval, children who learn nothing of self-respect or the joy of being. In brief, a life that feels like a long string of defeats, for which the only consolation, perhaps, is that sad mantra, "So who's happy?"

When self-esteem is low, our resilience in the face of life's adversities is diminished. We crumble before vicissitudes that a healthier sense of self could vanquish. We are far more likely to succumb to a tragic sense of our existence and to feelings of impotence. We tend to be more influenced by the desire to avoid pain than to experience joy. Negatives have more power over us than positives. If we do not believe in ourselves—neither in our efficacy nor in our goodness—the universe is a frightening place.

High-self-esteem people can surely be knocked down by an excess of troubles, but they are quicker to pick themselves up again.

For this reason I have come to think of positive self-esteem as, in effect, *the immune system of consciousness,* providing resistance, strength, and a capacity for regeneration. Just as a healthy immune system does not guarantee that one will never become ill, but makes one less vulnerable to disease and better equipped to overcome it, so a healthy self-esteem does not guarantee that one will never suffer anxiety or depression in the face of life's difficulties, but makes one less susceptible and better equipped to cope, rebound, and transcend. High-self-esteem people can surely be knocked down by an excess of troubles, but they are quicker to pick themselves up again.

That self-esteem has more to deal with resilience than with imperviousness to suffering needs be emphasized. I am reminded of an experience some years ago while writing *Honoring the Self.* For reasons that are irrelevant here, I had great difficulty in the writing of that book; while I am happy with the final result, it did not come easily. There was one week that was very bad; nothing my brain produced was right. One afternoon my publisher dropped by for a visit. I was feeling tired, depressed, and a bit irritable. Sitting opposite him in my living room, I remarked, "This is one of those days when I ask myself whatever made me imagine I know how to write a book. Whatever made me think I know anything about self-esteem? Whatever made me think I had anything to contribute to psychology?" Just what a publisher likes to hear from his author. As I had written six books by then and been lecturing on self-esteem for many years, he was understandably dismayed. "What?" he exclaimed. "*Nathaniel Branden* has such feelings?" The expression of disorientation and astonishment on his face was comical—so much so that I burst out laughing. "Well, of course," I answered. "The only distinction I'll claim is that I have a sense of humor about it. And that I know these feelings will pass. And that whatever I think, say, or feel this week, I know that in the end the book will be good."

Too Much Self-Esteem?

The question is sometimes asked, "Is it possible to have too much self-esteem?" No, it is not; no more than it is possible to have too much physical health or too powerful an immune system. Sometimes self-esteem is confused with boasting or bragging or arrogance; but such traits reflect not too much self-esteem, but too little; they reflect a lack of self-esteem. Persons of high self-esteem are not driven to make themselves superior to others; they do not seek to prove their value by measuring themselves against a comparative standard. Their joy is in being who they are, not in being better than someone else. I recall reflecting on this issue one day while watching my dog playing in the backyard. She was running about, sniffing flowers, chasing squirrels, leaping into the air, showing great joy in being alive (from my anthropomorphic perspective). She was not thinking (I am sure) that she was *more* glad to be alive than was the dog next door. She was simply delighting in her own existence. That image captures something essential of how I understand the experience of healthy self-esteem.

People with troubled self-esteem are often uncomfortable in the presence of those with higher self-esteem and may feel resentful and declare, "They have *too much* self-esteem." But what they are really making is a statement about themselves.

Insecure men, for instance, often feel more insecure in the presence of self-confident women. Low-self-esteem individuals often feel irritable in the presence of people who are enthusiastic about life. If one partner in a marriage whose self-esteem is deteriorating sees that the partner's self-esteem is growing, the response is sometimes anxiety and an attempt to sabotage the growth process.

The sad truth is, whoever is successful in this world runs the risk of being a target. People of low achievement often envy and resent people of high achievement. Those who are unhappy often envy and resent those who are happy.

And those of low self-esteem sometimes like to talk about the danger of having "too much self-esteem."

When Nothing Is "Enough"

As I observed above, a poor self-esteem does not mean that we will necessarily be incapable of achieving any real values. Some of us may have the talent, energy, and drive to achieve a great deal, in spite of feelings of inadequacy or unworthiness—like the highly productive workaholic who is driven to prove his worth to, say, a father who predicted he would always be a loser. But it does mean that we will be less effective and less creative than we have the power to be; and it means that we will be crippled in our ability to find joy in our achievements. Nothing we do will ever feel like "enough."

If my aim is to prove I am "enough," the project goes on to infinity—because the battle was already lost on the day I conceded the issue was debatable.

While poor self-esteem often undercuts the capacity for real accomplishment, even among the most talented, it does not necessarily do so. *What is far more certain is that it undercuts the capacity for satisfaction.* This is a painful reality well known to many high achievers. "Why," a brilliantly successful businessman said to me, "is the pain of my failures so much more intense and lasting than the pleasure of my successes, even though there have been so many more successes than failures? Why is happiness so fleeting and mortification so enduring?" A few minutes later he added, "In my mind I see the face of my father mocking me." The subconscious mission of his life, he came to realize, was not to express who he was but to show his father (now deceased for over a decade) that he could amount to something.

When we have unconflicted self-esteem, joy is our motor, not fear. It is happiness that we wish to experience, not suffering that we wish to avoid. Our purpose is self-expression, not self-avoidance or self-justification. Our motive is not to "prove" our worth but to live our possibilities.

If my aim is to prove I am "enough," the project goes on to infinity—because the battle was already lost on the day I conceded the issue was debatable. So it is always "one more" victory—one more promotion, one more sexual conquest, one more company, one more piece of jewelry, a larger house, a more expensive car, another award—yet the void within remains unfilled.

In today's culture some frustrated people who hit this impasse announce that they have decided to pursue a "spiritual" path and renounce their egos. This enterprise is doomed to failure. An ego, in the mature and healthy sense, is precisely what they have failed to attain. They dream of giving away what they do not possess. No one can successfully bypass the need for self-esteem.

A Word of Caution

If one error is to deny the importance of self-esteem, another is to claim too much for it. In their enthusiasm, some writers today seem to suggest that a healthy sense of self-value is all we need to assure happiness and success. The matter is more complex than that. Self-esteem is not an all-purpose panacea. Aside from the question of the external circumstances and opportunities that may exist for us, a number of internal factors clearly can have an impact—such as energy level, intelligence, and achievement drive. (Contrary to what we sometimes hear, this last is not correlated with self-esteem in any simple or direct way, in that such a drive can be powered by negative motivation as well as by positive, as, for example, when one is propelled by fear of losing love or status rather than by the joy of self-expression.) A well-developed sense of self is a necessary condition of our well-being but not a sufficient condition. Its presence does not guarantee fulfillment, but its lack guarantees some measure of anxiety, frustration, or despair.*

Self-esteem is not a substitute for a roof over one's head or food in

---

* One difficulty with much of the research concerning the impact of self-esteem, as I said in the Introduction, is that different researchers use different definitions of the term and are not necessarily measuring or reporting on the same phenomenon. Another difficulty is that self-esteem does not operate in a vacuum; it can be hard to track in isolation; it interacts with other forces in the personality.

one's stomach, but it increases the likelihood that one will find a way to meet such needs. Self-esteem is not a substitute for the knowledge and skills one needs to operate effectively in the world, but it increases the likelihood that one will acquire them.

In Abraham Maslow's famous "hierarchy of needs," he places self-esteem "above" (that is, as coming after) core survival needs such as for food and water, and there is one obvious sense in which this is valid. At the same time, it is a misleading oversimplification. People sometimes relinquish life itself in the name of issues crucial to their self-esteem. And surely his belief that being "accepted" is a more basic need than self-esteem must also be challenged.[3]

Self-esteem is not a substitute for a roof over one's head or food in one's stomach, but it increases the likelihood that one will find a way to meet such needs.

The basic fact remains that self-esteem is an urgent need. It proclaims itself as such by virtue of the fact that its (relative) absence impairs our ability to function. This is why we say it has survival value.

The Challenges of the Modern World

The survival value of self-esteem is especially evident today. We have reached a moment in history when self-esteem, which has always been a supremely important psychological need, has also become a supremely important economic need—the attribute imperative for adaptiveness to an increasingly complex, challenging, and competitive world.

In the past two or three decades, extraordinary developments have occurred in the American and global economies. The United States has shifted from a manufacturing society to an information society. We have witnessed the transition from physical labor to mind work as the dominant employee activity. We now live in a global economy characterized by rapid change, accelerating scientific and technological break-throughs, and an unprecedented level of competitiveness. These developments create demands for higher levels of education and training than were required of previous generations. Everyone acquainted with business culture knows this. What is not understood is that these developments also create new demands on our psychological resources. Specifically, these developments ask for a greater capacity for innovation, self-management, personal responsibility, and self-direction. This is not just asked at the top. It is asked at every level of a business enterprise, from senior management to first-line supervisors and even to entry-level personnel.

=====

We have reached a moment in history when self-esteem, which has always been a supremely important psychological need, has also become a supremely important economic need.

=====

As an example of how the world has changed, here is *Fortune* magazine's description of the position of manufacturing production operator at Motorola, *an entry-level job:* "Analyze computer reports and identify problems through experiments and statistical process control. Communicate manufacturing performance metrics to management, and understand the company's competitive position."[4]

A modern business can no longer be run by a few people who think and many people who do what they are told (the traditional military, command-and-control model). Today, organizations need not only an unprecedentedly higher level of knowledge and skill among all those who participate but also a higher level of independence, self-reliance, self-trust, and the capacity to exercise initiative—in a word, self-esteem. This means that persons with a decent level of self-esteem are now needed economically in large numbers. Historically, this is a new phenomenon.

The challenge extends further than the world of business. We are freer than any generation before us to choose our own religion, philosophy, or moral code; to adopt our own life-style; to select our own criteria for the good life. We no longer have unquestioning faith in "tradition." We no longer believe that government will lead us to salvation—nor church, nor labor unions, nor big organizations of any kind. No one is coming to rescue us, not in any aspect of life. We are thrown on our own resources.

We have more choices and options than ever before in every area. Frontiers of limitless possibilities now face us in whatever direction we look. To be adaptive in such an environment, to cope appropriately, we have a greater need for personal autonomy—because there is no widely accepted code of rules and rituals to spare us the challenge of individual decision making. We need to know who we are and to be centered within ourselves. We need to know what matters to us; otherwise it is easy to be swept up and swept along by alien values, pursuing goals that do not nourish who we really are. We must learn to think for ourselves, to cultivate our own resources, and to take responsibility for the choices, values, and actions that shape our lives. We need reality-based self-trust and self-reliance.

The greater the number of choices and decisions we need to make at a conscious level, the more urgent our need for self-esteem.

In response to the economic and cultural developments of the past few decades, we are witnessing a reawakening of the American self-help tradition, a great proliferation of mutual-aid groups of every kind, private networks to serve any number of different needs and purposes, a growing emphasis on "learning as a way of life," a new emphasis on self-reliance that expresses itself, for instance, in an attitude of greater personal responsibility for health care and an increasing tendency to question authority.

If we lack adequate self-esteem, the amount of choice offered to us today can be frightening.

The entrepreneurial spirit has been stimulated not only in business but also in our personal lives. Intellectually, we are all challenged to be "entrepreneurs"—to produce new meanings and values. We have been flung into what T. George Harris has called "the era of conscious choice."[5] The choice of this religion or that religion or none. The choice to marry or simply to live together. To have children or not to. To work for an organization or for oneself. To enter any one of a thousand new careers that did not even exist a few decades ago. To live in the city, the suburbs, or the country—or to move abroad. On a simpler level, there are unprecedented choices in clothing styles, foods, automobiles, new products of every kind—all demanding *that we make a decision.*

If we lack adequate self-esteem, the amount of choice offered to us today can be frightening, something like the anxiety of a Soviet citizen on first encountering an American supermarket. And just as some visitors elected to run back to the "security" of a dictatorship, some of us seek escape in the "security" of cults, or religious fundamentalism, or "correct" political, social, or cultural subgroups, or brain-destroying substances. Neither our upbringing nor our education may have adequately prepared us for a world with so many options and challenges. This is why the issue of self-esteem has become so urgent.

2

The Meaning of Self-Esteem

Self-esteem has two interrelated components. One is a sense of basic confidence in the face of life's challenges: *self-efficacy*. The other is a sense of being worthy of happiness: *self-respect*.

I do not mean to imply that a person of high or healthy self-esteem consciously *thinks* in terms of these components, but rather that if we look closely at the *experience* of self-esteem, we inescapably find them.

Self-efficacy means confidence in the functioning of my mind, in my ability to think, understand, learn, choose, and make decisions; confidence in my ability to understand the facts of reality that fall within the sphere of my interests and needs; self-trust; self-reliance.

Self-respect means assurance of my value; an affirmative attitude toward my right to live and to be happy; comfort in appropriately asserting my thoughts, wants, and needs; the feeling that joy and fulfillment are my natural birthright.

We will need to consider these two ideas in more detail, but for the moment consider the following: If an individual felt inadequate to face the challenges of life, if an individual lacked fundamental self-trust, confidence in his or her mind, we would recognize a self-esteem deficiency, no matter what other assets he or she possessed. Or, if an individual lacked a basic sense of self-respect, felt unworthy or undeserving of the love or respect of others, unentitled to happiness, fearful of asserting thoughts, wants, or needs—again we would recognize a self-esteem deficiency, no matter what other positive attributes he or she exhibited. Self-efficacy and self-respect are the dual pillars of healthy self-esteem; absent either one, self-esteem is impaired. They are the defining characteristics of the term because of their fundamentality. They represent not derivative or secondary meanings of self-esteem but its essence.

The experience of self-efficacy generates the sense of control over one's life that we associate with psychological well-being, the sense of being at the vital center of one's existence—as contrasted with being a passive spectator and a victim of events.

The experience of self-respect makes possible a benevolent, non-neurotic sense of community with other individuals, the fellowship of independence and mutual regard—as contrasted with either alienated estrangement from the human race, on the one hand, or mindless submergence into the tribe, on the other.

Within a given person, there will be inevitable fluctuations in self-esteem levels, much as there are fluctuations in all psychological states. We need to think in terms of a person's *average level of self-esteem*. While we sometimes speak of self-esteem as a conviction about oneself, it is more accurate to speak of a *disposition* to experience oneself a particular way. What way?

To sum up in a formal definition: *Self-esteem is the disposition to experience oneself as competent to cope with the basic challenges of life and as worthy of happiness.*

Note that this definition does not specify the childhood environmental influences that support healthy self-esteem (physical safety, nurturing, and so forth); nor the later internal generators (the practice of living consciously, self-acceptingly, self-responsibly, and so on); nor emotional or behavioral consequences (compassion, willingness to be accountable, openness to new experience, and the like). *It merely identifies what the self-evaluation concerns and consists of.*

In Part III, Chapter 17, we will examine the idea of self-esteem in the context of culture, but for the moment let me stress one point. The concept of "competence" as used in my definition is metaphysical, not "Western." That is, it pertains to the very nature of things—to our fundamental relationship to reality. It is not the product of a particular cultural "value bias." There is no society on earth, no society even conceivable, whose members do not face the challenges of fulfilling their needs—who do not face the challenges of appropriate adaptation to nature and to the world of human beings. The idea of efficacy in this fundamental sense is not, as I have heard suggested, a "Western artifact." I believe this will become still clearer when we explore in depth what self-efficacy and self-respect mean and entail.

It would be unwise to dismiss definitions as "mere semantics" or a concern with exactitude as pedantry. The value of a precise definition is that it allows us to distinguish a particular aspect of reality from all others so that we can think about it and work with it with clarity and focus. If we wish to know what self-esteem depends on, how to nurture it in our children, support it in schools, encourage it in organizations, strengthen it in psychotherapy, or develop it in ourselves, we need to know what precisely we are aiming at. *We are unlikely to hit a target we cannot see.* If our idea of self-esteem is vague, the means we adopt will reflect this vagueness. If our enthusiasm for self-esteem is not matched by appropriate intellectual rigor, we run the risk not only of failing to produce worthwhile results but also of discrediting the field.

===

To have high self-esteem is to feel confidently appropriate to life.

===

Am I suggesting that the definition of self-esteem I offer is written in stone and can never be improved on? Not at all. Definitions are contextual; they relate to a given level of knowledge; as knowledge grows, definitions tend to become more precise. I may find a better, clearer, more exact way to capture the essence of the concept during my lifetime. Or someone else may. But within the context of the knowledge we now possess, I can think of no alternative formulation that identifies with more precision the unique aspect of human experience we are exploring in this book.

To have high self-esteem, then, is to feel confidently appropriate to life, that is, competent and worthy in the sense I have indicated. To have low self-esteem is to feel inappropriate to life; wrong, not about this issue or that, but *wrong as a person.* To have average self-esteem is to fluctuate between feeling appropriate and inappropriate, right and wrong as a person; and to manifest these inconsistencies in behavior, sometimes acting wisely, sometimes acting foolishly—thereby reinforcing the uncertainty about who one is at one's core.

The Root of Our Need for Self-Esteem

We saw in the previous chapter that self-esteem is a basic need. But why is this so? We cannot fully understand the meaning of self-esteem apart from understanding what about us as a species gives rise to such a need. (I have the impression that this question has been almost entirely neglected.) This discussion, then, is intended to illuminate further what self-esteem ultimately means.

The question of the efficacy of their consciousness or the worthiness of their beings does not exist for lower animals. But human beings wonder: Can I trust my mind? Am I competent to think? Am I adequate? Am I enough? Am I a good person? Do I have integrity, that is, is there congruence between my ideals and my practice? Am I worthy of respect, love, success, happiness?

Our need for self-esteem is the result of two basic facts, both intrinsic to our species. The first is that we depend for our survival and our successful mastery of the environment on the appropriate use of our consciousness; our life and well-being depend on our ability to think. The second is that the right use of our consciousness is not automatic, is not "wired in" by nature. In the regulating of its activity, there is a crucial element of choice—therefore, of personal responsibility.

Like every other species capable of awareness, we depend for our survival and well-being on the guidance of our distinctive form of consciousness, the form uniquely human, our conceptual faculty—the faculty of abstraction, generalization, and integration: our *mind*.

The right use of our consciousness is not automatic, is not "wired in" by nature.

Our human essence is our ability to reason, which means to grasp relationships. It is on this ability—ultimately—that our life depends. Think of what it took to bring to your table the food you ate today; to produce the clothes you are wearing; to build the home that protects you from the elements; to build the industry in which you earn your living; to give you the experience of a great symphony in your living room; to develop the medicines that restore your health; to create the light by which you may now be reading. All that is the product of mind.

Mind is more than immediate explicit awareness. It is a complex architecture of structures and processes. It includes more than the verbal, linear, analytic processes popularly if misleadingly described sometimes as "left-brain" activity. It includes the totality of mental life, including the subconscious, the intuitive, the symbolic, all that which sometimes is associated with the "right brain." Mind is all that by means of which we reach out to and apprehend the world.

To learn to grow food, to construct a bridge, to harness electricity, to grasp the healing possibilities of some substance, to allocate resources so as to maximize productivity, to see wealth-producing possibilities where they had not been seen before, to conduct a scientific experiment, to create—all require a process of thought. To respond appropriately to the complaints of a child or a spouse, to recognize that there is a disparity between our behavior and our professed feelings, to discover how to deal with hurt and anger in ways that will heal rather than destroy—all require a process of thought. Even to know when to abandon conscious efforts at problem solving and turn the task over to the subconscious, to know when to allow conscious thinking to stop or when to attend more closely to feelings or intuition (subconscious perceptions or integrations) require a process of thought, a process of rational connection.

---

*We are the one species that can formulate
a vision of what values are worth pursuing—
and then pursue the opposite.*

The problem and the challenge is that, although thinking is a necessity of successful existence, we are not programmed to think automatically. We have a choice.

We are not responsible for controlling the activities of our heart, lungs, liver, or kidneys; they are all part of the body's self-regulating system (although we are beginning to learn that some measure of control of these activities may be possible). Nor are we obliged to supervise the homeostatic processes by which, for instance, a constant temperature is maintained. Nature has designed the organs and systems of our bodies to function automatically in the service of our life without our volitional intervention. But our minds operate differently.

Our minds do not pump knowledge as our hearts pump blood, when and as needed. Our minds do not automatically guide us to act on our best, most rational and informed understanding, even when such understanding would clearly be beneficial. We do not begin to think "instinctively" merely because nonthinking, in a given situation, would be dangerous to us. Consciousness does not "reflexively" expand in the face of the new and unfamiliar; sometimes we contract it instead. *Nature has given us an extraordinary responsibility: the option of turning the searchlight of consciousness brighter or dimmer.* This is the option of seeking awareness or not bothering to seek it or actively avoiding it. The option of thinking or not thinking. This is the root of our freedom and our responsibility.

We are the one species that can formulate a vision of what values are worth pursuing—and then pursue the opposite. We can decide that a given course of action is rational, moral, and wise—and then suspend consciousness and proceed to do something else. We are able to monitor our behavior and ask if it is consistent with our knowledge, convictions, and ideals—and we are also able to evade asking that question. The option of thinking or not thinking.

Our *free will* pertains to the choice we make about the operation of our consciousness in any given situation—to focus it with the aim of expanding awareness or unfocus it with the aim of avoiding awareness. The choices we make concerning the operations of our consciousness have enormous ramifications for our life in general and our self-esteem in particular.

Consider the impact on our life and on our sense of self entailed by the following options:

Focusing versus nonfocusing.

Thinking versus nonthinking.

Awareness versus unawareness.

Clarity versus obscurity or vagueness.

Respect for reality versus avoidance of reality.

Respect for facts versus indifference to facts.

Respect for truth versus rejection of truth.

Perseverance in the effort to understand versus abandonment of the effort.

Loyalty in action to our professed convictions versus disloyalty—the issue of integrity.

Honesty with self versus dishonesty.

Self-confrontation versus self-avoidance.

Receptivity to new knowledge versus closed-mindedness.

Willingness to see and correct errors versus perseverance in error.

Concern with congruence (consistency) versus disregard of contradictions.

Reason versus irrationalism; respect for logic, consistency, coherence, and evidence versus disregard or defiance of these.

Loyalty to the responsibility of consciousness versus betrayal of that responsibility.

If one wishes to understand what self-esteem depends on, this list is a good place to begin.

No one could seriously suggest that our sense of our competence to cope with the challenge of life or our sense of our goodness could remain unaffected over time by the pattern of our choices in regard to the above options.

A disservice is done to people if they are offered "feel good" notions of self-esteem that divorce it from questions of consciousness, responsibility, and moral choice.

The point is not that our self-esteem "should" be affected by the choices we make but rather that by our natures it *must* be affected. If we develop habit patterns that cripple or incapacitate us for effective functioning and that cause us to distrust ourselves, it would be irrational to suggest that we "should" go on feeling just as efficacious and worthy as we would feel if our choices had been better. This would imply that our actions have or should have nothing to do with how we feel about ourselves. It is one thing to caution against identifying oneself with a particular behavior; it is another to assert that there should be *no* connection between self-assessment and behavior. A disservice is done to people if they are offered "feel good" notions of self-esteem that divorce it from questions of consciousness, responsibility, and moral choice. There is great joy in self-esteem, and often joy in the process of building or strengthening it, but this should not obscure the fact that more is required than blowing oneself a kiss in the mirror (or numerous other strategies that have been proposed, of equal profundity).

The level of our self-esteem is not set once and for all in childhood. It can grow as we mature, or it can deteriorate. There are people whose self-esteem was higher at the age of ten than at the age of sixty, and the reverse is also true. Self-esteem can rise and fall and rise again over the course of a lifetime. Mine certainly has.

I can think back over my history and observe changes in the level of my self-esteem that reflect choices I made in the face of particular challenges. I can recall instances when I made choices I am proud of and others I bitterly regret—choices that strengthened my self-esteem and others that lowered it. We all can.

With regard to choices that lower self-esteem, I think of times when (never mind the "reasons") I was unwilling to see what I saw and know what I knew—times when I needed to raise awareness and instead I lowered it; when I needed to examine my feelings and instead I disowned them; when I needed to announce a truth and instead I clung to silence; when I needed to walk away from a relationship that was harming me and instead I struggled to preserve it; when I needed to stand up for my deepest feelings and assert my deepest needs and instead I waited for a miracle to deliver me.

Any time we have to act, to face a challenge, to make a moral decision, we affect our feelings about ourselves for good or bad—depending on the nature of our response and the mental processes behind it. And if we avoid action and decisions in spite of their obvious necessity, that, too, affects our sense of self.

Our need for self-esteem is the need to know we are functioning as our life and well-being require.

Competence

I have given the name *self-efficacy* to that experience of basic power or competence that we associate with healthy self-esteem, and *self-respect* to the experience of dignity and personal worth. While their meaning is clear in a general way, I want to examine them more closely.

First, self-efficacy.

To be efficacious (in the basic, dictionary sense) is to be capable of producing a desired result. Confidence in our basic efficacy is confidence in our ability to learn what we need to learn and do what we need to do in order to achieve our goals, *insofar as success depends on our own efforts.* Rationally we do not judge our competence, in the sense meant here, by factors outside our control. The experience of self-efficacy does not require omniscience or omnipotence.

Self-efficacy is not the conviction that we can never make an error. It is the conviction that we are able to think, to judge, to know—and to correct our errors. It is trust in our mental processes and abilities.

Self-efficacy is not the certainty that we will be able to master any and every challenge that life presents. It is the conviction that we are capable in principle of learning what we need to learn and that we are committed to doing our rational and conscientious best to master the tasks and challenges entailed by our values.

Self-efficacy is deeper than confidence in our specific knowledge and skills, based on past successes and accomplishments, although it is clearly nurtured by them. It is confidence in what made it possible for us to acquire knowledge and skills and to achieve successes. It is confidence in our ability to think, in our consciousness and how we choose to use it. Again, *trust in our processes*—and, as a consequence, *a disposition to expect success for our efforts.*

To be lacking in the experience of self-efficacy, to anticipate defeat rather than victory, is to be interrupted or undermined or paralyzed (to varying degrees) in our efforts to cope with the tasks and challenges life presents to us. "Who am I to think? Who am I to master challenges? Who am I to choose—decide—leave the comfort of the familiar—persevere in the face of obstacles—fight for my values?"

In a world in which the total of human knowledge is doubling about every ten years, our security can rest only on our ability to learn.

As far as our upbringing is concerned, one of the roots of self-efficacy is a home environment that is sufficiently sane, rational, and predictable as to allow us to believe understanding is *possible* and that thinking is not futile. As far as our own actions are concerned, one of its roots is *the will to efficacy itself*—a refusal to surrender to helplessness, persistence in the quest to understand even in the face of difficulties.

The distinction between trust in our processes and trust in some particular area of knowledge is of the highest importance in virtually every sphere of endeavor. In a world in which the total of human knowledge is doubling about every ten years, our security can rest only on our ability to learn. To clarify the distinction I am making, let us consider the following example.

Let us say that a businessman has acquired specific knowledge and a specific set of skills in the field in which he has worked for twenty years. Then he leaves that company and assumes leadership of an entirely different kind of enterprise with different requirements, rules, and problems. If he lacks a healthy sense of self-efficacy, the danger is that he will be overattached to what he already knows and inadequately adaptive to the new context. The consequence is that he will perform poorly and his feelings of inefficacy will be confirmed and reinforced. Alternatively, if he does experience healthy self-efficacy, his security lies less in what he knows than in his confidence in his ability to learn. The consequence is that he is likely to master the new context and perform well, and his feelings of self-efficacy will be confirmed and reinforced.

High-performing salespersons, accountants, engineers, and the like, are often promoted to the position of manager. But the skills needed to be a good manager are different from those needed to be competent in sales, accounting, or engineering. How well the person will do in his or her new job depends in part on the training for the new role provided by the company; but it also will be affected by the level of the individual's self-efficacy. Low self-efficacy tends to produce discomfort with the new and unfamiliar and overattachment to yesterday's skills. Higher self-efficacy makes it easier to move up from an earlier level of knowledge and development and to master new knowledge, skills, and challenges. Companies that understand this can build a self-esteem component into their training. They can inspire employees to value the virtues of consciousness, responsibility, curiosity, openness to change, above particular kinds of mastery that may no longer be relevant.

A woman who was promoted to manager consulted me because of feelings of panic about her ability to handle the new opportunity. Among the questions I invited her to explore were the following:

Why were you successful in your previous job?

What specifically did you do in the early months of that job that helped you to develop your skills so effectively?

What attitude of mind did you bring to the new things you had to learn?

As you progressed in the job, what other things did you do?

How did you adapt to changes in job requirements?

What allowed you to be so flexible?

From what you have learned about yourself and your success in your previous job, what insights do you have that you can use in this new position?

What is it in your inner attitudes and processes that could lead you to just as great a success in the future, even though the actual skills required will be different?

What can you do that will assure your success?

What is it about you—about the way your mind works—that will allow you to do it?

Such questions helped her isolate the basic inner sources of her past success as differentiated from particular skills. They focus on process rather than content. *They distinguish fundamental efficacy from any of its particular manifestations.*

I want to stress again that no one can expect to be equally competent in all areas—and no one needs to be. Our interests, values, and circumstances determine the areas in which we are likely to concentrate.

When I say that self-efficacy pertains to confidence in one's ability to cope with the basic challenges of life, what do I mean by "basic challenges"? For one, being able to support one's existence, that is, to earn a living; to take independent care of oneself in the world—*assuming the opportunity to do so exists.* (Wives and homemakers are not exempt. It does not serve a woman's interest to have developed no skills by which she can support herself and to be frightened of the marketplace.) For another, being able to function effectively in interactions with other human beings—being capable of giving and receiving benevolence, cooperation, trust, friendship, respect, love; being able to be responsibly self-assertive and to accept the self-assertiveness of others. For yet another, resilience in coping with misfortune and adversity—the opposite of passive surrender to pain; the ability to bounce back and regenerate oneself. Simple fundamentals that define our humanity.

In the examples above I focus on the workplace, but of course efficacy applies also to intimate relationships, as the preceding paragraph makes clear. No experience of efficacy can be complete if it does not include that of feeling competent in our human dealings. If I am unable to create personal and professional relationships that will be experienced as positive by both me and the other party (which is what "competence" in the human realm essentially means), then I am lacking at a very basic level; I am without efficacy in a vital sphere. And this reality is reflected in my self-esteem.

Sometimes people who feel fear in the human realm drop to a very low level of consciousness in their relationships and seek the safety and security of competence in the impersonal word of machines, mathematics, or abstract thought. No matter what heights they may attain professionally, their self-esteem remains flawed. We cannot with impunity run from so important an aspect of life.

Worthiness

Now the second component of self-esteem: self-respect.

Just as self-efficacy entails the expectation of success as natural, so self-respect entails the expectation of friendship, love, and happiness as natural, as a result of who we are and what we do. (We can isolate the two components conceptually, for the sake of analysis, but in the reality of our daily experience they constantly overlap and involve each other.)

Self-respect is the conviction of our own value. It is not the delusion that we are "perfect" or superior to everyone else. It is not comparative or competitive at all. It is the conviction that our life and well-being are worth acting to support, protect, and nurture; that we are good and worthwhile and deserving of the respect of others; and that our happiness and personal fulfillment are important enough to work for.

Self-respect entails the expectation of friendship, love, and happiness as natural, as a result of who we are and what we do.

As far as our upbringing is concerned, one of its roots is the experience of being treated with respect by parents and other family members. As far as our own actions are concerned, one of its roots is satisfaction with our moral choices—*which is a particular aspect of satisfaction with our mental processes.* (Indeed, a simple and informal self-esteem "test," though far from infallible, is to inquire of people whether they feel proud of and satisfied with their moral choices. To turn right or left at a street corner is not ordinarily a moral choice; to tell the truth or not to tell the truth, to honor one's promises and commitments or not, is.)

Not uncommonly we meet a person who is far more sure of his or her competence, at least in some areas, than of the right to be happy. Some aspect of self-respect is missing. Such an individual may achieve a great deal but lack the capacity to enjoy it. The feeling of personal worth that would support and sanction enjoyment is, if not entirely absent, then wounded and impaired.

We sometimes encounter this problem among successful businesspersons who are anxious away from their desks. For such persons, vacations are often more a source of stress than of pleasure. They are limited in their ability even to enjoy their families, much as they may feel they love them. They do not feel *entitled*. They feel they must continually prove and justify their worth through achievement. They are not devoid of self-esteem, but it is tragically flawed.

To appreciate why our need for self-respect is so urgent, consider the following: To live successfully, we need to pursue and achieve values. To act appropriately, we need to value the beneficiary of our actions. We need to consider ourselves *worthy of the rewards of our actions*. Absent this conviction, we will not know how to take care of ourselves, protect our legitimate interests, satisfy our needs, or enjoy our own achievements. (Thus, our experience of self-efficacy also will be impaired.)

Recently I counseled a brilliant lawyer who was self-effacing almost to the point of self-destruction. She continually allowed others to take credit for her achievements in the law firm where she worked. Her boss took billing credit for hours that were hers. Associates took credit for many of her ideas. She remained cheerful to everyone and insisted she did not mind, while inwardly she was burning with resentment. She wanted to be liked, and she believed that self-abasement was the way to assure it, avoiding thoughts about the cost to her self-respect. Her one act of assertion and rebellion had been to become a lawyer, against the skepticism of her family, who had always minimized her worth. To become highly successful was beyond her view of what was possible or appropriate to her. She had the knowledge and the skill; she did not have the self-esteem. The low level of her self-respect was like a gravitational pull forbidding her to rise. What she learned in therapy was that bringing more consciousness to her choices, taking more responsibility for her self-sabotaging behavior, and acting against that gravitational pull—standing up for herself, in spite of fear—was the way to build her self-respect.

Three basic observations: (1) If we respect ourselves, we tend to act in ways that confirm and reinforce this respect, such as requiring others to deal with us appropriately. (2) If we do not respect ourselves, we tend to act in ways that lower our sense of our own value even further, such as accepting or sanctioning inappropriate behavior toward us by others, thereby confirming and reinforcing our negativity. (3) If we wish to raise the level of our self-respect, we need to act in ways that will cause it to rise—and this begins with a commitment to the value of our own person, which is then expressed through congruent behavior.

The need to see ourselves as good is the need to experience self-respect. It emerges very early. As we develop from childhood, we progressively become aware of the power to choose our actions. We become aware of our responsibility for the choices we make. We acquire our sense of being a person. We experience a need to feel that we are right—*right as a person*—right in our characteristic way of functioning. This is the need to feel that we are *good*.

We learn the concept from adults, from whom we first hear the words "good," "bad," "right," "wrong," but the need is inherent in our nature. It is tied to the issue of survival: Am I appropriate to life? To be right as a person is to be fit for success and happiness; to be wrong is to be threatened by pain. When a client in therapy says, "I don't feel entitled to be happy or successful," the meaning is, "I don't feel worthy as a human being."

A concern with right and wrong is not merely the product of social conditioning. A concern with morality or ethics arises naturally in the early stages of our development.

The need for self-respect is basic and inescapable. Inherent in our existence and humanity are such questions as: What kind of being should I seek to become? By what principles should I guide my life? What values are worth pursuing? I say "inherent in our existence" because a concern with right and wrong is not merely the product of social conditioning. A concern with morality or ethics arises naturally in the early stages of our development, much as our other intellectual abilities develop, and progresses in step with the normal course of our maturation. When we assess our own activities, inevitably our moral attitudes are part of our implicit context.

It is impossible to escape the realm of values and value-judgments because they are demanded by the very nature of life. "Good for me" or "bad for me" ultimately translates to "for my life and well-being" or "against them." Further, and essential to an understanding of self-esteem, *we cannot exempt ourselves from the realm of values and value judgments*. We cannot be indifferent to the moral meaning of our actions, although we may try to be or pretend to be. At some level, their value significance irresistibly registers in the psyche, leaving positive feelings about the self in their wake or negative ones. Whether the values by which we explicitly or implicitly judge ourselves are conscious or subconscious, rational or irrational, life serving or life threatening, everyone judges himself or herself by *some* standard. To the extent that we fail to satisfy that standard, to the extent there is a split between ideals and practice, self-respect suffers. Thus, personal integrity is intimately related to the moral aspect of self-esteem. For the optimal realization of our possibilities, we need to trust ourselves and we need to admire ourselves, *and the trust and admiration need to be grounded in reality, not generated out of fantasy and self-delusion.*

Pride

I want to say a few words about pride, as distinguished from self-esteem. Pride is *a unique kind of pleasure.*

Pride is the emotional reward of achievement. It is not a vice to be overcome but a value to be attained.

If self-esteem pertains to the experience of our fundamental competence and value, *pride* pertains to the more explicitly conscious pleasure we take in ourselves because of our actions and achievements. Self-esteem contemplates what needs to be done and says "I can." Pride contemplates what has been accomplished and says "I did."

Authentic pride has nothing in common with bragging, boasting, or arrogance. It comes from an opposite root. Not emptiness but satisfaction is its wellspring. It is not out to "prove" but to enjoy.

Nor is pride the delusion that we are without flaws or shortcomings (as religionists sometimes suggest). We can take pride in what we have done or what we have made of ourselves while acknowledging our errors and imperfections. We can feel pride while owning and accepting what Jungians call our "Shadow." In short, pride in no way entails obliviousness to reality.

Pride is the emotional reward of achievement. It is not a vice to be overcome but a value to be attained. (In a philosophical or moral context, when pride is considered not as an emotion or experience but as a *virtue,* an *action commitment,* I define it differently—as *moral ambitiousness,* the dedication to achieving one's highest potential in one's character and in one's life. I discuss this idea in *The Psychology of Self-Esteem.*)

Does achievement always result in pride? Not necessarily, as the following story illustrates.

The head of a medium-sized company consulted me because, he said, although he had made a great success of his business, he was depressed and unhappy and could not understand why. We discovered that what he had always wanted to be was a research scientist but that he had abandoned that desire in deference to his parents, who pushed him toward a career in business. Not only was he unable to feel more than the most superficial kind of pride in his accomplishments but he was wounded in his self-esteem. The reason was not difficult to identify. In the most important issue of his life he had surrendered his mind and values to the wishes of others out of the wish to be "loved" and to "belong." Clearly a still earlier self-esteem problem motivated such a capitulation. His depression reflected a lifetime of performing brilliantly while ignoring his deepest needs. While he operated within that framework, pride and satisfaction were beyond his reach. Until he was willing to challenge that framework, and to face the fear of doing so, no solution was possible.

This is an important point to understand, because we sometimes hear people say, "I have accomplished so much. Why don't I feel more proud of myself?" Although there are several reasons why someone may not enjoy his or her achievements, it can be useful to ask, "Who *chose* your goals? You, or the voice of some 'significant other' inside you?" Neither pride nor self-esteem can be supported by the pursuit of secondhand values that do not reflect who we really are.

But does anything take more courage—is anything more challenging and sometimes frightening—than to live by our own mind, judgment, and values? Is not self-esteem a summons to the hero within us? These questions will shortly lead us to the six pillars of self-esteem.

3

The Face of Self-Esteem

What does self-esteem look like?

There are some fairly simple and direct ways in which self-esteem manifests itself in ourselves and others. None of these items taken in isolation is a guarantee, but when all are present together, self-esteem seems certain.

Self-esteem expresses it itself in a face, manner, and way of talking and moving that projects the pleasure one takes in being alive.

It expresses itself in an ease in talking of accomplishments or short-comings with directness and honesty, since one is in friendly relationship to facts.

It expresses itself in the comfort one experiences in giving and receiving compliments, expressions of affection, appreciation, and the like.

It expresses itself in an openness to criticism and a comfort about acknowledging mistakes, because one's self-esteem is not tied to an image of "being perfect."

It expresses itself when one's words and movements tend to have a quality of ease and spontaneity, reflecting the fact that one is not at war with oneself.

It expresses itself in the harmony between what one says and does and how one looks, sounds, and moves.

It expresses itself in an attitude of openness to and curiosity about new ideas, new experiences, new possibilities of life.

It expresses itself in the fact that feelings of anxiety or insecurity, if they appear, will be less likely to intimidate or overwhelm, since accepting them, managing them, and rising above them rarely feel impossibly difficult.

It expresses itself in an ability to enjoy the humorous aspects of life, in oneself and others.

It expresses itself in one's flexibility in responding to situations and challenges, since one trusts one's mind and does not see life as doom or defeat.

It expresses itself in one's comfort with assertive (not belligerent) behavior in oneself and others.

It expresses itself in an ability to preserve a quality of harmony and dignity under conditions of stress.

Then, on the purely physical level, we can observe characteristics such as these:

We see eyes that are alert, bright, and lively; a face that is relaxed and (barring illness) tends to exhibit natural color and good skin vibrancy; a chin that is held naturally and in alignment with one's body; and a relaxed jaw.

We see shoulders relaxed yet erect; hands that tend to be relaxed and graceful; arms that tend to hang in an easy, natural way; a posture that tends to be unstrained, erect, well-balanced; a walk that tends to be purposeful (without being aggressive and overbearing).

Relaxation implies that we are not hiding from
ourselves and are not at war with who we are.

We hear a voice that tends to be modulated with an intensity appropriate to the situation and with clear pronunciation.

Notice that the theme of relaxation occurs again and again. Relaxation implies that we are not hiding from ourselves and are not at war with who we are. Chronic tension conveys a message of some form of internal split, some form of self-avoidance or self-repudiation, some aspect of the self being disowned or held on a very tight leash.

Self-Esteem in Action

In the beginning of this book I said that healthy self-esteem is significantly correlated with rationality, realism, intuitiveness, creativity, independence, flexibility, ability to manage change, willingness to admit (and correct) mistakes, benevolence, and cooperativeness. If we understand what self-esteem actually means, the logic of these correlations becomes fairly obvious.

Rationality. This is the exercise of the integrative function of consciousness—the generation of principles from concrete facts (induction), the application of principles to concrete facts (deduction), and the relating of new knowledge and information to our existing context of knowledge. It is the pursuit of meaning and an understanding of relationships. Its guide is the law of noncontradiction—nothing can be true and not true (A and non-A) at the same time and in the same respect. Its base is respect for facts.

Rationality should not be confused, as it so often is, with compulsive rule following or unreflective obedience to what the people of a given time or place have proclaimed to be "reasonable." On the contrary, rationality often must challenge what some group calls "reasonable." (When a particular notion of the "reasonable" has been overthrown by new evidence, it is that notion *and not reason* that has been vanquished.) The quest of reason is for the noncontradictory integration of experience—which implies openness and availability to experience. It is the servant neither of tradition nor consensus.

High self-esteem is intrinsically reality oriented.

It is very far from that odd notion of rationality that identifies it with the unimaginative, narrowly analytic, accounting mentality, as we find, for instance, in Peters and Waterman's *In Search of Excellence,* where "rationality" is characterized in this way and then criticized. Rationality is *consciousness operating in its explicitly integrative mode.*

Thus understood, we see that a commitment to rationality and the practice of living consciously entail each other.

Realism. In this context the term simply means a respect for facts, a recognition that what is, is, and what is not, is not. No one can feel competent to cope with the challenges of life who does not treat seriously the distinction between the real and the unreal; obliviousness to that distinction is incapacitating. High self-esteem is intrinsically reality oriented. (Good reality orientation, in conjunction with effective self-discipline and self-management, is what psychologists mean by the concept of "ego strength.")

In tests, low-self-esteem individuals tend to underestimate or overestimate their abilities; high-self-esteem individuals tend to assess their abilities realistically.

Intuitiveness. Very often—especially, for example, in making complex decisions—the number of variables that need to be processed and integrated are far more than the conscious mind can handle. Complex, superrapid integrations can occur beneath conscious awareness and present themselves as "intuitions." The mind can then scan data for supporting or conflicting evidence. Men and women who have a context of being highly conscious and highly experienced sometimes find themselves relying on these subconscious integrations, since a record of success has taught them that in doing so they succeed more often than they fail. However, when and if that pattern of success shifts and they find themselves making mistakes, they go back to more explicit and conscious forms of rationality. Because the intuitive function often allows them to make unexpected leaps that ordinary thinking may be slower to arrive at, they experience intuition as central to their process; high-level business executives sometimes credit intuition for many of their achievements. A mind that has learned to trust itself is more likely to rely on this process (and manage it effectively with appropriate reality testing) than one that has not. This is equally true in business, athletics, the sciences, the arts—in most complex human activities. *Intuition is significant relative to self-esteem only insofar as it expresses high sensitivity to, and appropriate regard for, internal signals.* Early in this century Carl Jung stressed the importance of this respect for internal signals to creativity. More recently Carl Rogers linked it to self-acceptance, authenticity, and psychological health.

Creativity. Creative persons listen to and trust their inner signals more than the average. Their minds are less subservient to the belief systems of others, at least in the area of their creativity. They are more self-sufficient. They may learn from others and be inspired by others. But they value their own thoughts and insights more than the average person does.

Studies tell us that creative people are far more likely to record interesting ideas in a notebook; spend time nursing and cultivating them; put energy into exploring where they might lead. *They value the productions of their mind.*

Persons of low self-esteem tend to discount the productions of their mind. It is not that they never get worthwhile ideas. But they do not value them, do not treat them as potentially important, often do not even remember them very long—*rarely follow through with them.* In effect, their attitude is, "If the idea is mine, how good can it be?"

Independence. A practice of thinking for oneself is a natural corollary—both a cause and a consequence—of healthy self-esteem. So is the practice of taking full responsibility for one's own existence—for the attainment of one's goals and the achievement of one's happiness.

A mind that trusts itself is light on its feet.

Flexibility. To be flexible is to be able to respond to change without inappropriate attachments binding one to the past. A clinging to the past in the face of new and changing circumstances is itself a product of insecurity, a lack of self-trust. Rigidity is what animals sometimes manifest when they are frightened: they freeze. It is also what companies sometimes manifest when faced with superior competition. They do not ask, "What can we learn from our competitors?" They cling blindly to what they have always done, in defiance of evidence that it is no longer working. (This has been the response of too many business leaders and workers to the challenge of the Japanese since the 1970s.) Rigidity is often the response of a mind that does not trust itself to cope with the new or master the unfamiliar—or that has simply become complacent or even slovenly. Flexibility, in contrast, is the natural consequence of self-esteem. A mind that trusts itself is light on its feet, unemcumbered by irrelevant attachments, able to respond quickly to novelty *because it is open to seeing.*

Able to manage change. Self-esteem does not find change frightening, for the reasons stated in the preceding paragraph. Self-esteem flows with reality; self-doubt fights it. Self-esteem speeds up reaction time; self-doubt retards it. (For this reason alone, in a global economy as fast-moving as ours, the business community will need to examine how principles of self-esteem can be incorporated into training programs as well as into an organization's culture. And schools will need these same principles to prepare students for the world they will be entering and in which they will have to earn a living.) The ability to manage change is thus correlated with good reality orientation, mentioned above, and thus with ego strength.

Willingness to admit (and correct) mistakes. A basic characteristic of healthy self-esteem is a strong reality orientation. Facts are a higher priority than beliefs. Truth is a higher value than having been right. Consciousness is perceived as more desirable than self-protective unconsciousness. If self-trust is tied to respect for reality, then correcting an error is esteemed above pretending not to have made one.

Healthy self-esteem is not ashamed to say, when the occasion warrants it, "I was wrong." Denial and defensiveness are characteristics of insecurity, guilt, feelings of inadequacy, and shame. It is low self-esteem that experiences a simple admission of error as humiliation and even self-damnation.

Benevolence and cooperativeness. Students of child development know that a child who is treated with respect tends to internalize that respect and then treat others with respect—in contrast to a child who is abused, internalizes self-contempt, and grows up reacting to others out of fear and rage. If I feel centered within myself, secure with my own boundaries, confident in my right to say yes when I want to say yes and no when I want to say no, benevolence is the natural result. There is no need to fear others, no need to protect myself behind a fortress of hostility. If I am secure in my right to exist, confident that I belong to myself, unthreatened by certainty and self-confidence in others, then cooperation with them to achieve shared goals tends to develop spontaneously. Such a response clearly is to my self-interest, satisfies a variety of needs, and is not obstructed by fear and self-doubt.

Empathy and compassion, no less than benevolence and cooperativeness, are far more likely to be found among persons of high self-esteem than among low; my relationship to others tends to mirror and reflect my relationship to myself. Commenting on the admonition to love thy neighbor as thyself, longshoreman-philosopher Eric Hoffer remarks somewhere that the problem is that this is precisely what people do: Persons who hate themselves hate others. The killers of the world, literally and figuratively, are not known to be in intimate or loving relationship to their inner selves.

4

The Illusion of Self-Esteem

When self-esteem is low, we are often manipulated by fear. Fear of reality, to which we feel inadequate. Fear of facts about ourselves—or others—that we have denied, disowned, or repressed. Fear of the collapse of our pretenses. Fear of exposure. Fear of the humiliation of failure and, sometimes, the responsibilities of success. We live more to avoid pain than to experience joy.

If we feel that crucial aspects of reality with which we must deal are hopelessly closed to our understanding; if we face the key problems of life with a basic sense of helplessness; if we feel that we dare not pursue certain lines of thought because of the unworthy features of our own character that would be brought to light—if we feel, in any sense whatever, *that reality is the enemy of our self-esteem (or pretense at it)*—these fears tend to sabotage the efficacy of consciousness, thereby worsening the initial problem.

If we face the basic problems of life with an attitude of "Who am I to know? Who am I to judge? Who am I to decide?"—or "It is *dangerous* to be conscious"—or "It is *futile* to try to think or understand"—we are undercut at the outset. A mind does not struggle for that which it regards as impossible or undesirable.

Not that the level of our self-esteem *determines* our thinking. The causation is not that simple. What self-esteem affects is our *emotional incentives*. Our feelings tend to encourage or discourage thinking, to draw us toward facts, truth, and reality, or away from them—toward efficacy or away from it.

That is why the first steps of building self-esteem can be difficult: We are challenged to raise the level of our consciousness in the face of emotional resistance. We need to challenge the belief that our interests are best served by blindness. What makes the project often difficult is our feeling that it is only our unconsciousness that makes life bearable. Until we can dispute this idea, we cannot begin to grow in self-esteem.

The danger is that we will become the prisoners of our negative self-image. We allow it to dictate our actions. We define ourselves as mediocre or weak or cowardly or ineffectual and our performance reflects this definition.

While we are capable of challenging and acting contrary to our negative self-image—and many people do so, at least on some occasions—the factor that tends to stand in the way is our resignation to our own state. We submit to feelings of psychological determinism. We tell ourselves we are powerless. We are rewarded for doing so, in that we do not have to take risks or awaken from our passivity.

We are challenged to raise the level of our consciousness in the face of emotional resistance.

Poor self-esteem not only inhibits thought, it tends to distort it. If we have a bad reputation with ourselves, and attempt to identify the motivation of some behavior, we can react anxiously and defensively and twist our brains not to see what is obvious—or, out of a sense of guilt and generalized unworthiness, we can be drawn not to the most logical explanation of our behavior but to the most *damaging,* to that which puts us in the worst light morally. Only self-condemnation feels appropriate. Or, if we are confronted with unjust accusations from others, we may feel disarmed and incapable of confuting their claims; we may accept the charges as true, paralyzed and exhausted by a heavy feeling of "How can I decide?"

The base and motor of poor self-esteem is not confidence but fear. Not to live, but to escape the terror of life, is the fundamental goal. Not creativity, but safety, is the ruling desire. And what is sought from others is not the chance to experience real contact but an escape from moral values, a promise to be forgiven, to be accepted, on some level to be taken care of.

If low self-esteem dreads the unknown and unfamiliar, high self-esteem seeks new frontiers. If low self-esteem avoids challenges, high self-esteem desires and needs them. If low self-esteem looks for a chance to be absolved, high self-esteem looks for an opportunity to admire.

In these opposite principles of motivation we have a guide to the health of the mind or spirit. We can say that an individual is healthy to the extent that the basic principle of motivation is that of motivation by confidence (love of self, love of life); the degree of motivation by fear is the measure of underdeveloped self-esteem.

Pseudo Self-Esteem

Sometimes we see people who enjoy worldly success, are widely esteemed, or who have a public veneer of assurance and yet are deeply dissatisfied, anxious, or depressed. They may project the appearance of self-efficacy and self-respect—they may have the *persona* of self-esteem—but do not possess the reality. How might we understand them?

We have noted that to the extent we fail to develop authentic self-esteem, the consequence is varying degrees of anxiety, insecurity, and self-doubt. This is the sense of being, in effect, *inappropriate to existence* (though of course no one thinks of it in those terms; perhaps, instead, one thinks *something is wrong with me* or *I am lacking something essential*). This state tends to be painful. And because it is painful, we are often motivated to evade it, to deny our fears, rationalize our behavior, and create the appearance of a self-esteem we do not possess. We may develop what I have termed *pseudo self-esteem.*

―――――

*I can project an image of assurance and poise that
fools almost everyone and yet secretly tremble
with a sense of my inadequacy.*

―――――

Pseudo self-esteem is the illusion of self-efficacy and self-respect without the reality. It is a nonrational, self-protective device to diminish anxiety and to provide a spurious sense of security—to assuage our need for authentic self-esteem while allowing the real causes of its lack to remain unexamined.

It is based on values unrelated to that which genuine self-efficacy and self-respect require, although sometimes the values are not without merit in their own context. For example, a large house can certainly represent a legitimate value, but it is not an appropriate measure or proof of personal efficacy or virtue. On the other hand, acceptance into a gang of criminals is not normally a rational value; nor does it strengthen authentic self-esteem (which is not to say it may not provide a temporary illusion of security or sense of having a "home" or of "belonging").

Nothing is more common than to pursue self-esteem by means that will not and cannot work. Instead of seeking self-esteem through consciousness, responsibility, and integrity, we may seek it through popularity, material acquisitions, or sexual exploits. Instead of valuing personal authenticity, we may value belonging to the right clubs, or the right church, or the right political party. Instead of practicing appropriate self-assertion, we may practice uncritical compliance to our particular group. Instead of seeking self-respect through honesty, we may seek it through philanthropy—I must be a good person, I do "good works." Instead of striving for the power of competence (the ability to achieve genuine values), we may pursue the "power" of manipulating or controlling other people. The possibilities for self-deception are almost endless—all the blind alleys down which we can lose ourselves, not realizing that what we desire cannot be purchased with counterfeit currency.

Self-esteem is an intimate experience; it resides in the core of one's being. It is what *I* think and feel about myself, not what someone else thinks or feels about me. This simple fact can hardly be overemphasized. I can be loved by my family, my mate, and my friends, and yet not love myself. I can be admired by my associates and yet regard myself as worthless. I can project an image of assurance and poise that fools almost everyone and yet secretly tremble with a sense of my inadequacy. I can fulfill the expectations of others and yet fail my own; I can win every honor and yet feel I have accomplished nothing; I can be adored by millions and yet wake up each morning with a sickening sense of fraudulence and emptiness. To attain "success" without attaining positive self-esteem is to be condemned to feeling like an impostor anxiously awaiting exposure.

The acclaim of others does not create our self-esteem. Neither does erudition, material possessions, marriage, parenthood, philanthropic endeavors, sexual conquests, or face-lifts. These things can sometimes make us feel better about ourselves temporarily or more comfortable in particular situations. But comfort is not self-esteem.

The tragedy of many people's lives is that they look for self-esteem in every direction except within, and so they fail in their search. In this book we shall see that positive self-esteem is best understood as a spiritual attainment, that is, *as a victory in the evolution of consciousness.* When we begin to understand self-esteem in this way, we appreciate the foolishness of believing that if we can only manage to make a positive impression on others we will then enjoy good self-regard. We will stop telling ourselves: If only I get one more promotion—if only I become a wife and mother—if only I am perceived to be a good provider—if only I can afford a bigger car—if I can write one more book—acquire one more company—one more lover—one more award—one more acknowledgment of my "selflessness"—then I will *really* feel at peace with myself.

If self-esteem is the judgment that I am appropriate to life, the experience of competence and worth—if self-esteem is self-affirming consciousness, a mind that trusts itself—no one can generate and sustain this experience except myself.

Unfortunately, teachers of self-esteem are no less impervious to the worship of false gods than anyone else. I recall listening to a lecture by a man who offers self-esteem seminars to the general public and to corporations. He announced that one of the best ways to raise our self-esteem is to surround ourselves with people who think highly of us. I thought of the nightmare of low self-esteem in persons surrounded by praise and adulation—like rock stars who have no idea how they got where they are and who cannot survive a day without drugs. I thought of the futility of telling a person of low self-esteem, who feels lucky if he or she is accepted by *anyone,* that the way to raise self-esteem is to seek the company only of admirers.

The ultimate source of self-esteem is and can only be internal—in what we do, not what others do. When we seek it in externals, in the actions and responses of others, we invite tragedy.

Certainly it is wiser to seek companions who are the friends of our self-esteem rather than its enemies. Nurturing relationships are obviously preferable to toxic ones. But to look to others as a primary source of our self-value is dangerous: first, because it doesn't work; and second, because it exposes us to the danger of becoming approval addicts.

I do not wish to suggest that a psychologically healthy person is unaffected by the feedback he or she receives from others. We are social beings and certainly others contribute to our self-perceptions, as we will discuss. But there are immense differences among people in the relative importance to their self-esteem of the feedback they receive—persons for whom it is almost the *only* factor of importance and persons for whom the importance is a good deal less. This is merely another way of saying there are immense differences among people in the degree of their autonomy.

---

*Innovators and creators are persons who can to a
higher degree than average accept the
condition of aloneness.*

Having worked for many years with persons who are unhappily preoccupied with the opinions of others, I am persuaded that the most effective means of liberation is by raising the level of consciousness one brings to one's own experience: The more one turns up the volume on one's inner signals, the more external signals tend to recede into proper balance. As I wrote in *Honoring the Self,* this entails learning to listen to the body, learning to listen to the emotions, learning to think for oneself. In subsequent chapters we shall say more about how this can be done.

Independence

The alternative to excessive dependence on the feedback and validation of others is a well-developed system of internal support. Then, the source of certainty lies within. The attainment of this state is essential to what I understand as proper human maturity.

Innovators and creators are persons who can to a higher degree than average accept the condition of aloneness—that is, the absence of supportive feedback from their social environment. They are more willing to follow their vision, even when it takes them far from the mainland of the human community. Unexplored spaces do not frighten them—or not, at any rate, as much as they frighten those around them. This is one of the secrets of their power—the great artists, scientists, inventors, industrialists. Is not the hallmark of entrepreneurship (in art or science no less than in business) the ability to see a possibility that no one else sees—and to actualize it? Actualizing one's vision may of course require the collaboration of many people able to work together toward a common goal, and the innovator may need to be highly skillful at building bridges between one group and another. But this is a separate story and does not affect my basic point.

That which we call "genius" has a great deal to do with independence, courage, and daring—a great deal to do with *nerve*. This is one reason we admire it. In the literal sense, such "nerve" cannot be *taught*, but we can support the process by which it is *learned*. If human happiness, well-being, and progress are our goals, it is a trait we must strive to nurture—in our child-rearing practices, in our schools, in our organizations, *and first of all in ourselves*.

PART II

Internal Sources of Self-Esteem

5

The Focus on Action

We begin not with the environment but with the individual. We begin not with what others choose to do but with what the individual chooses to do.

This requires an explanation. It might appear more logical to start with how the family environment positively or negatively influences the slowly emerging self of the child. Possible biological factors aside, surely this is where the story begins, it would seem. But for our purposes—no.

We begin by asking, What must an individual *do* to generate and sustain self-esteem? What pattern of *actions* must be adopted? What is the responsibility of you and me as adults?

In answering this, we have a standard by which to answer the question, What must a child *learn* to do if he or she is to enjoy self-esteem? What is the desirable path of childhood development? And also, What practices should caring parents and teachers seek to evoke, stimulate, and support in children?

Until we know what practices an individual must master to sustain self-esteem, until we identify what psychologically healthy adulthood consists of, we lack criteria by which to assess what constitutes a favorable or unfavorable childhood influence or experience. For example, we know that, as a species, our mind is our basic tool of survival and of appropriate adaptation. A child's life begins in a condition of total dependency, but an adult's life and well-being, from the attainment of the simplest necessities to the most complex values depend on the ability to think. Consequently, we recognize that childhood experiences that encourage and nurture thinking, self-trust, and autonomy are to be valued. We recognize that families in which reality is often denied and consciousness often punished place devastating obstacles to self-esteem; they create a nightmare world in which the child may feel that thinking is not only futile but dangerous.

In approaching the roots of self-esteem, why do we put our focus on *practices*, that is, on (mental or physical) *actions*? The answer is that every value pertaining to life requires action to be achieved, sustained, or enjoyed. In Ayn Rand's definition, life is a process of self-generated and self-sustaining action. The organs and systems within our body support our existence by continuous action. We pursue and maintain our values in the world through action. As I discuss in some detail in *The Psychology of Self-Esteem*, it is in the very nature of a value that it is the object of an action. And this includes the value of self-esteem.

———

*What determines the level of self-esteem is
what the individual does.*

———

If a child grows up in an appropriately nurturing home environment, the likelihood is increased that he or she will learn the actions that support self-esteem (although there is no guarantee). If a child is exposed to the right kind of teachers, the likelihood is increased that self-esteem-supporting behaviors will be learned. If a person experiences successful psychotherapy, in which irrational fears are dissolved and blocks to effective functioning are removed, a consequence is that he or she will manifest more of the kind of actions that support self-esteem. But it is *a person's actions* that are decisive. What determines the level of self-esteem is what the individual *does*, within the context of his or her knowledge and values. And since action in the world is a reflection of action within the mind of the individual, it is the *internal processes* that are crucial.

We shall see that "the six pillars of self-esteem"—the practices indispensable to the health of the mind and the effective functioning of the person—*are all operations of consciousness*. All involve choices. They are choices that confront us every hour of our existence.

Note that "practice" has connotations that are relevant here. A "practice" implies a discipline of acting in a certain way over and over again—

consistently. It is not action by fits and starts, or even an appropriate response to a *crisis*. Rather it is a way of operating day by day, in big issues and small, a way of behaving that is also *a way of being*.

Volition and Its Limits

Free will does not mean omnipotence. Volition is a powerful force in our lives, but it is not the only force. Neither for a young person nor for an adult is our freedom absolute and unlimited. Many factors can make the appropriate exercise of consciousness easier or harder. Some of these factors may be genetic, biological. Focused thinking may come more easily to some individuals than to others because of factors that precede any life experiences. There is reason to suspect that we may come into this world with certain inherent differences that may make it easier or harder to attain healthy self-esteem—differences pertaining to energy, resilience, disposition to enjoy life, and the like. Furthermore, we may come into this world with significant differences in our predisposition to experience anxiety or depression, and these differences again may make it easier or harder to develop self-esteem.

Then there are developmental factors. The environment can support and encourage the healthy assertion of consciousness, or it can oppose and undermine it. Many individuals suffer so much damage in the early years, before the self is fully formed, that it is all but impossible for healthy self-esteem to emerge later without intense psychotherapy.

Parenting and Its Limits

Research suggests that one of the best ways to have good self-esteem is to have parents who have good self-esteem and who model it, as is made clear in Stanley Coopersmith's *The Antecedents of Self-Esteem*. In addition, if we have parents who raise us with love and respect; who allow us to experience consistent and benevolent acceptance; who give us the supporting structure of reasonable rules and appropriate expectations; who do not assail us with contradictions; who do not resort to ridicule, humiliation, or physical abuse as means of controlling us; who project that they believe in our competence and goodness—we have a decent chance of internalizing their attitudes and thereby of acquiring the foundation for healthy self-esteem. But no research study has ever found this result to be inevitable. Coopersmith's study, for one, clearly shows that it is not. There are people who appear to have been raised superbly by the standards indicated above and yet are insecure, self-doubting adults. And there are people who have emerged from appalling backgrounds, raised by adults who did everything wrong, and yet they do well in school, form stable and satisfying relationships, have a powerful sense of their value and dignity, and as adults satisfy any rational criterion of good self-esteem. As children, these individuals seem to know how to extract nourishment from an environment that others find hopelessly barren; they find water where others see only a desert. Baffled psychologists and psychiatrists sometimes describe this group as "the invulnerables."[1]

Nonetheless, it is safe enough to say that if one lives in a sane human environment in which reality is respected and people's behavior is congruent, it is far easier to persevere in efforts to be rational and productive than if the signals are always switching, nothing seems real, facts are denied, and consciousness is penalized. Families that create such destructive environments are described as dysfunctional. Just as there are dysfunctional families, there are dysfunctional schools and dysfunctional organizations. They are dysfunctional because they place obstacles in the path of the appropriate exercise of mind.

Inner Blocks

Within an individual's psyche itself, there may be obstructions to thinking. Subconscious defenses and blocks may make us oblivious even to the need to think about a particular issue. Consciousness is a continuum; it exists on many levels. An unresolved problem at one level may subvert operations at another. For example, if I block my feelings about my parents—if I cut off access to those feelings through denial, disowning, and repression—and then try to think about my relationship with my boss, I may have disconnected myself from so much pertinent material that I can easily become muddled and discouraged and give up. Or, if I block major negative feelings about some assignment my manager has given me and find that my interactions with my team are persistently and mysteriously abrasive, I may experience great difficulty in thinking how to resolve the abrasiveness as long as I remain unconscious of the deeper source of the disturbance. Even so, my self-esteem will be affected by whether I *try* to bring consciousness to my problem.

What We Do Know

While we may not know all the biological or developmental factors that influence self-esteem, we know a good deal about the specific (volitional) practices that can raise or lower it. We know that an honest commitment to understanding inspires self-trust and that an avoidance of the effort has the opposite effect. We know that people who live mindfully feel more competent than those who live mindlessly. We know that integrity engenders self-respect and that hypocrisy does not. We "know" all this implicitly, although it is astonishing how rarely such matters are discussed (by professionals or anyone else).

As adults, we cannot regrow ourselves, cannot relive our childhoods with different parents. We may, of course, need to consider psychotherapy. But that option aside, we can ask: What can I do today to raise the level of my self-esteem?

We will see that, whatever our histories, if we understand the nature of self-esteem and the practices it depends on, most of us can do a great deal. This knowledge is important for two reasons. First, if we wish to work on our own self-esteem, we need to know what specific practices have the power to raise it. Second, if we are working with others and wish to support their self-esteem, to inspire and bring out the best in them, we need to know what specific practices we aim to nurture or facilitate.

We must become what we wish to teach.

As an aside to parents, teachers, psychotherapists, and managers who may be reading this book to gain insight on how to support the self-esteem of others, I want to say that the place to begin is still with oneself. If one does not understand how the dynamics of self-esteem work internally—if one does not know by direct experience what lowers or raises one's own self-esteem—one will not have that intimate understanding of the subject necessary to make an optimal contribution to others. Also, the unresolved issues within oneself set the limits of one's effectiveness in helping others. It may be tempting, but it is self-deceiving to believe that what one says can communicate more powerfully than what one manifests in one's person. We must become what we wish to teach.

There is a story I like to tell psychotherapy students. In India, when a family encounters a problem, they are not likely to consult a psychotherapist (hardly any are available); they consult the local guru. In one village there was a wise man who had helped this family more than once. One day the father and mother came to him, bringing their nine-year-old son, and the father said, "Master, our son is a wonderful boy and we love him very much. But he has a terrible problem, a weakness for sweets that is ruining his teeth and health. We have reasoned with him, argued with him, pleaded with him, chastised him—nothing works. He goes on consuming ungodly quantities of sweets. Can you help us?" To the father's surprise, the guru answered, "Go away and come back in two weeks." One does not argue with a guru, so the family obeyed. Two weeks later they faced him again, and the guru said, "Good. Now we can proceed." The father asked, "Won't you tell us, please, why you sent us away for two weeks. You have never done that before." And the guru answered, "I needed the two weeks because I, too, have had a lifelong weakness for sweets. Until I had confronted and resolved that issue within myself, I was not ready to deal with your son."

Not all psychotherapists like this story.

Sentence-Completion Work

In the course of this book I give many examples of how sentence-completion exercises can be used to strengthen self-esteem. Sentence-completion work is a tool both of therapy and of research. Having begun working with it in 1970, I have found increasingly more extensive and illuminating ways to use it to facilitate self-understanding, melt repressive barriers, liberate self-expression, activate self-healing—and continually test and retest my own hypotheses. The essence of the method is that the client (or subject) is given a sentence stem, an incomplete sentence, and asked to repeat the stem over and over again, each time providing a different ending. Then another stem is given, and then another, allowing one to explore a particular area at deeper and deeper levels. This work may be done verbally or in writing.

Sentence-completion work plays a vital role in determining what things people do that raise or lower self-esteem. When certain patterns of endings show up again and again with different kinds of populations in different parts of the country and in different countries throughout the world, it is clear that fundamental realities are being illuminated.

In the chapters that follow I include many examples of the kind of sentence completions I use, for two reasons. One is to give readers an opportunity to carry the work further themselves if they wish to integrate the ideas of "the six practices" into their daily lives. The other is to provide a means by which psychologists and psychiatrists can test out the ideas of this book and see for themselves whether I have in fact identified the most important behaviors on which self-esteem depends.

The Six Practices

Since self-esteem is *a consequence*, a product of internally generated practices, we cannot work on self-esteem *directly*, neither our own nor anyone else's. We must address ourselves to the source. If we understand what these practices are, we can commit to *initiating* them within ourselves and to dealing with others in such a way as to *facilitate* or *encourage* them to do likewise. To encourage self-esteem in the schools or in the workplace, for instance, is to create a climate that supports and reinforces the practices that strengthen self-esteem.

What then, in briefest essence, does healthy self-esteem depend on? What are the practices of which I speak? I will name six that are demonstrably crucial. Working with people in psychotherapy to build self-efficacy and self-respect, I am persuaded for reasons I shall explain that these are the key issues. I have found no others of comparable fundamentality. That is why I call them "the six pillars of self-esteem." It will not be difficult to see why any improvements in these practices generate unmistakable benefits.

Once we understand these practices, we have the power to choose them, to work on integrating them into our way of life. The power to do so is the power to raise the level of our self-esteem, from whatever point we may be starting and however difficult the project may be in the early stages.

One does not have to attain "perfection" in these practices. One only needs to raise one's average level of performance to experience growth in self-efficacy and self-respect. I have often witnessed the most extraordinary changes in people's lives as a result of relatively small improvements in these practices. In fact, I encourage clients to think in terms of small steps rather than big ones because big ones can intimidate (and paralyze), while small ones seem more attainable, and one small step leads to another.

Here are the six pillars of self-esteem:

The practice of living consciously

The practice of self-acceptance

The practice of self-responsibility

The practice of self-assertiveness

The practice of living purposefully

The practice of personal integrity

In the next six chapters we shall examine each of them in turn.

6

The Practice of Living Consciously

In virtually all of the great spiritual and philosophical traditions of the world there appears some form of the idea that most human beings are sleepwalking through their own existence. Enlightenment is identified with waking up. Evolution and progress are identified with an expansion of consciousness.

We perceive consciousness as the highest manifestation of life. The higher the form of consciousness, the more advanced the form of life. Moving up the evolutionary ladder from the time consciousness first emerges on the planet, each life-form has a more advanced form of consciousness than that of the life-form on the rung below.

Among our own species, we carry this same principle further: We identify increasing maturity with wider vision, greater awareness, higher consciousness.

Why is consciousness so important? Because for all species that possess it, consciousness is the basic tool of survival—the ability to be aware of the environment in some form, at some level, and to guide action accordingly. I use *consciousness* here in its primary meaning: the state of being conscious or aware of some aspect of reality. We also may speak of consciousness as a *faculty*—the attribute of being able to be aware. To the distinctively *human* form of consciousness, with its capacity for concept formation and abstract thought, we give the name *mind*.

As we have discussed, we are beings for whom consciousness (at the conceptual level) is *volitional.* This means that the design of our nature contains an extraordinary option—that of seeking awareness or not bothering (or actively avoiding it), seeking truth or not bothering (or actively avoiding it), focusing our mind or not bothering (or choosing to drop to a lower level of consciousness). In other words, we have the option of exercising our powers or of subverting our means of survival and well-being. This capacity for self-management is our glory and, at times, our burden.

Our mind is our basic tool of survival.
Betray it and self-esteem suffers.

If we do not bring an appropriate level of consciousness to our activities, if we do not live mindfully, the inevitable penalty is a diminished sense of self-efficacy and self-respect. We cannot feel competent and worthy while conducting our lives in a mental fog. Our mind is our basic tool of survival. Betray it and self-esteem suffers. The simplest form of this betrayal is the evasion of discomfiting facts. For example:

"I know I am not giving my job my best, but I don't want to think about it."

"I know there are signs our business is falling into worse and worse trouble, but what we've done worked in the past, didn't it? Anyway the whole subject is upsetting, and maybe if I sit tight the situation will resolve itself—*somehow.*"

" 'Legitimate grievances?' What 'legitimate grievances?' My spouse has been influenced by those crazy women's libbers. That's why she's beating up on me."

"I know my children suffer from having so little of me, I know I am causing hurt and resentment, but one day—*somehow*—I'll change."

"What do you mean, I drink too much? I can stop anytime I want."

"I know the way I eat is wrecking my health, but—"

"I know I'm living beyond my means, but—"

"I know I'm phony and lie about my accomplishments, but—"

Through the thousands of choices we make between thinking and nonthinking, being responsible toward reality or evading it, we establish a sense of the kind of person we are. Consciously, we rarely remember these choices. But deep in our psyche they are added up, and the sum is that experience we call "self-esteem." *Self-esteem is the reputation we acquire with ourselves.*

We are not all equal in intelligence, but intelligence is not the issue. The *principle* of living consciously is unaffected by degrees of intelligence. *To live consciously means to seek to be aware of everything that bears on our actions, purposes, values, and goals—to the best of our ability, whatever that ability may be—and to behave in accordance with that which we see and know.*

The Betrayal of Consciousness

This last point bears emphasis. Consciousness that is not translated into appropriate action is a betrayal of consciousness; it is mind invalidating itself. Living consciously means more than seeing and knowing; it means acting on what one sees and knows. Thus, I can recognize that I have been unfair and hurtful to my child (or my spouse or my friend) and need to make amends. But I don't want to admit I made a mistake, so I procrastinate, claiming that I am still "thinking" about the situation. This is the opposite of living consciously. At a fundamental level, it is an avoidance of consciousness—avoidance of the meaning of what I am doing; avoidance of my motives; avoidance of my continuing cruelty.

Possible Misunderstandings

Let me anticipate and address possible misunderstandings about the application of the principle of living consciously.

1. It is in the nature of human learning that we automate new knowledge and skills, such as speaking a language or driving an automobile, so that they do not continue to require of us the level of explicit awareness that was necessary during the learning stage. As mastery is attained, they drop into the accumulated repertoire of the subconscious—thus freeing the conscious mind for the new and unfamiliar. Living consciously does not mean that we retain in explicit awareness everything we ever learned, which would be neither possible nor desirable.

2. To be operating consciously—to be in appropriate mental focus—does not mean that we must be engaged in some task of problem solving every moment of our waking existence. We may choose to meditate, for example, emptying our mind of all thought to make ourselves available to new possibilities of relaxation, rejuvenation, creativity, insight, or some form of transcendence. This can be an entirely appropriate mental activity—in fact, in some contexts, a highly desirable one. And, of course, there are still other alternatives to problem solving, such as creative daydreaming or abandonment to physical playfulness or erotic sensation. In matters of mental functioning, *context determines appropriateness.* To operate consciously does not mean always to be in the same mental state *but rather to be in the state appropriate to what I am doing.* If, for example, I am tumbling on the floor with a child, my mental state will obviously be very different from what it is when I am working on a book. But that I am operating consciously will show up in the fact that no matter how playfully silly I may become, part of my mind is monitoring the situation to see that the child remains physically safe. If, in contrast, I am oblivious to the fact that I am playing too hard and hurting the child, my level of consciousness is inadequate to the situation. The point is that the issue of the appropriateness of my state of consciousness can only be determined relative to my purposes. There is no "right" or "wrong" state in a vacuum.

3. Given the countless number of things in our world of which it is theoretically possible to be conscious, awareness clearly involves a process of selection. In choosing to attend here, I implicitly choose not to attend elsewhere—at least in this moment. Sitting at my computer and writing this book, I am relatively oblivious to the rest of my environment. If I shift my focus, I become aware of the sound of passing automobiles, the sound of a child shouting and a dog barking. In another instant all that will be lost to conscious awareness and my mind will be absorbed by the words on my computer screen and the words forming in my mind. My purpose and values dictate the standard of selection.

When I am writing, I am often in a state of such concentration as to be trancelike; a ruthless process of selection is at work, but within that context I would say I am operating at a high level of consciousness. However, if, without changing my state, still preoccupied with my thoughts and oblivious to my external environment, I were to drive my automobile, I could be charged with operating at a dangerously low level of consciousness because I had not adapted to the change of context and purpose. To say it once more: Only context can determine what mind-state is appropriate.

Being Responsible Toward Reality

Living consciously implies respect for the facts of reality. This means the facts of our inner world (needs, wants, emotions) as well as of the outer world. This contrasts with that disrespect for reality contained in an attitude that amounts to, "If I don't choose to see it or acknowledge it, it doesn't exist."

When we live consciously we do not imagine that our feelings are an infallible guide to truth.

Living consciously is living *responsibly toward reality.* We do not necessarily have to like what we see, but we recognize that that which is, is, and that which is not, is not. Wishes or fears or denials do not alter facts. If I desire a new outfit but need the money for rent, my desire does not transform reality and make the purchase rational. If I fear an operation my physician assures me is necessary to save my life, my fear does not mean I will live equally well without the operation. If a statement is true, my denying it will not make it false.

Thus, when we live consciously we do not confuse the subjective with the objective. We do not imagine that our feelings are an infallible guide to truth. We can learn from our feelings, to be sure, and they may even point us in the direction of important facts, but this will entail reflection and reality testing, and this entails the participation of reason.

This understood, let us look more closely at what the practice of living consciously includes.

The Specifics of Living Consciously

Living consciously entails:

A mind that is active rather than passive.

An intelligence that takes joy in its own function.

Being "in the moment," without losing the wider context.

Reaching out toward relevant facts rather than withdrawing from them.

Being concerned to distinguish among facts, interpretations, and emotions.

Noticing and confronting my impulses to avoid or deny painful or threatening realities.

Being concerned to know "where I am" relative to my various (personal and professional) goals and projects, and whether I am succeeding or failing.

Being concerned to know if my actions are in alignment with my purposes.

Searching for feedback from the environment so as to adjust or correct my course when necessary.

Persevering in the attempt to understand in spite of difficulties.

Being receptive to new knowledge and willing to reexamine old assumptions.

Being willing to see and correct mistakes.

Seeking always to expand awareness—*a commitment to learning*—therefore, a commitment to growth as a way of life.

A concern to understand the world around me.

A concern to know not only external reality but also internal reality, the reality of my needs, feelings, aspirations, and motives, so that I am not a stranger or a mystery to myself.

A concern to be aware of the values that move and guide me, as well as their roots, so that I am not ruled by values I have irrationally adopted or uncritically accepted from others.

Let us look at each of these items in turn.

A mind that is active rather than passive. Here we deal with the most fundamental act of self-assertion: the choice to think, to seek awareness, understanding, knowledge, clarity.

Implicit in this orientation is another self-esteem virtue, that of self-responsibility. Since I am responsible for my own existence and happiness, I choose to be conscious and to be guided by the clearest understanding of which I am capable. I do not indulge in the fantasy that someone else can spare me the necessity of thought or make my decisions for me.

An intelligence that takes joy in its own function. The natural inclination of a child is to take pleasure in the use of mind no less than of body. The child's primary business is learning. It is also the primary entertainment. To retain that orientation into adulthood, so that consciousness is not a burden but a joy, is the mark of a successfully developed human being.

Of course, as adults we cannot *choose* to feel pleasure in the assertion of consciousness if for one reason or another we associate it with fear, pain, or exhausting effort. But anyone who has persevered, overcome such barriers, and learned to live more consciously will say that such learning becomes an increasingly greater source of satisfaction.

Being "in the moment," without losing the wider context. Contained in the idea of living consciously is that of being *present* to what one is doing. If I am listening to the complaint of a customer, being *present* to the experience. If I am playing with my child, being *present* to the activity. If I am working with a psychotherapy client, being with the client and not somewhere else. *Doing what I am doing while I am doing it.*

This does not mean that my awareness is reduced only to immediate sensory experience, disconnected from the wider context of my knowledge. If I cannot remain related to that wider context, my consciousness is impoverished. I wish to be *in* the moment but not *trapped* in the moment. This is the balance that allows me to be in the most resourceful state.

Reaching out toward relevant facts rather than withdrawing from them. What determines "relevance" is my needs, wants, values, goals, and actions. Do I stay alert to and curious about any information that might cause me to modify my course or correct my assumptions, or do I proceed on the premise that there is nothing new for me to learn? Do I continually seek out new data actively that might be helpful, or do I close my eyes to it even when it is presented? We do not have to ask which option is the more empowering.

Being concerned to distinguish among facts, interpretations, and emotions. I *see* you frowning; I *interpret* this to mean you are angry with me; I *feel* hurt or defensive or wronged. In reality, I may be correct or incorrect in my interpretation. I may be appropriate or inappropriate in the feeling with which I respond. In any event, separate and distinct processes are involved. If I am not conscious of this, I tend to treat my feelings as the voice of reality, which can lead me to disaster.

Fear and pain should be treated as signals not to close our eyes but to open them wider.

Or again, I *hear* that physicists are struggling with a problem they find insurmountable (let us assume this is so); I *interpret* this to mean that reason and science have failed; I *feel* disheartened and disturbed, or elated and triumphant (depending on my other philosophical beliefs). In reality, all that is established is that physicists say they are stuck on a problem. The rest is what my mind makes of it, which may be rational or irrational, but which in either case says more about me than about external reality.

To live consciously, I need to be sensitive to these distinctions. What I perceive, what I interpret it to mean, and how I feel about it are three separate questions. If I do not distinguish among them, my grounding in reality becomes the first casualty. Which means my efficacy becomes the first casualty.

Noticing and confronting my impulses to avoid or deny painful or threatening realities. Nothing is more natural than to avoid what evokes fear or pain. Since this includes facts our self-interest requires us to face and consider, we may have to override avoidance impulses. But this requires that we be aware of such impulses. What we need then is an orientation of self-examination and self-awareness—of consciousness directed inward as well as outward. Part of living consciously is being on guard against the sometimes seductive pull of unconsciousness; this asks for the most ruthless honesty of which we are capable. Fear and pain should be treated as signals not to close our eyes but to open them wider, not to look away but to look more attentively. This is far from an easy or effortless task. It is unrealistic to imagine that we will always execute it perfectly. But there will be great differences among us with regard to the sincerity of our intention; and degrees matter. Self-esteem asks not for flawless success but for the earnest *intention* to be conscious.

Being concerned to know "where I am" relative to my various (per-

sonal and professional) goals and projects, and whether I am suc-ceeding or failing. If one of my goals is to have a successful and satis-fying marriage, what is the present state of my marriage? Do I know? Would my partner and I answer the same way? Are my partner and I happy with each other? Are there frustrations and unresolved issues? If so, what am I doing about them? Do I have an action plan, or am I merely hoping that "somehow" things will improve? If one of my aspirations is one day to have my own business, what am I doing about it? Am I closer to that goal than I was a month ago or a year ago? Am I on track or off? If one of my ambitions is to be a professional writer, where am I at present relative to the fulfillment of that ambition? What am I doing to actualize it? Will I be closer to fulfillment next year than this year? If so, why? Am I bringing as much consciousness to my projects as I need to?

Being concerned to know if my actions are in alignment with my purposes. This issue is closely related to the preceding one. Sometimes there was great lack of congruence between what we say our goals or purposes are and how we invest our time and energy. That which we profess to care about most may get least from us in attention—whereas that which we say matters much less receives far more from us. So living consciously entails monitoring my actions relative to my goals, looking for evidence of alignment or misalignment. If there is misalignment, either my actions or my goals need to be rethought.

Searching for feedback from the environment so as to adjust or correct my course when necessary. When a pilot flies from Los Angeles to New York, he or she is always slightly off course. This information, called feedback, is relayed back via instruments so that continuing ad-justments are made to keep the plane on the right path. In the conduct of our life and the pursuit of our goals, we cannot safely set our course once and remain blind thereafter. The potential always exists that new infor-mation will require an adjustment of our plans and intentions.

A business leader who operates at a high level of consciousness plans for tomorrow's market.

If we are operating a business, perhaps we need to revise our advertis-ing strategy. Perhaps the manager we counted on is proving unable to do the job. Perhaps the product that seemed like a brilliant idea when first conceived has been made obsolete by a competitor. Perhaps the sudden emergence of new competitors from other countries obliges us to rethink our global strategy. Perhaps recently reported changes in demographics has future implications for our business that we need to be examining now and relating to our present projections. How quick we will be to note such developments and respond appropriately has everything to do with the level of consciousness at which we operate.

A business leader who operates at a high level of consciousness plans for tomorrow's market; a leader operating at a more modest level thinks in terms of today's; a leader operating at a low level may not realize that he is still thinking in terms of yesterday's.

On a more personal level, suppose I would like certain new behaviors from my spouse. I take certain actions aimed at evoking these changes. Do I persist in these actions without noting whether they produce a desired result? Do my spouse and I have the identical conversation forty times? Or, if I see that what I am doing is not working, *do I try something else*? In other words, do I operate *mechanically* or *consciously*?

Persevering in the attempt to understand in spite of difficulties. In my pursuit of understanding and mastery I sometimes encounter difficulties. When this happens, I have a choice: to persevere or give up. Students face this alternative in their school studies. Scientists face it in struggling with research problems. Executives face it in the thousand challenges of everyday business. Everyone faces it in personal relationships.

If we persevere in the will to efficacy yet seem stopped by a barrier we cannot move through, we may take a rest or try a new approach, but we do not surrender to despair or resign ourselves to defeat. In contrast, if we give up, withdraw, fall into passivity, or go through the motions of trying without meaning it, we shrink the level of our consciousness—to escape the pain and frustration that accompanied our efforts. The world belongs to those who persevere. I am reminded of a story told about Winston Churchill. He was invited to address a graduating class at a school, and the students waited expectantly through the laudatory introduction he received, eager for what the great man would say. Finally, Churchill stood up, looked down at the class, and thundered, "Never-never-never-never-never-never-never give up!" Then he sat down.

Of course, sometimes we may rationally choose to discontinue our efforts to understand or master something because, in the context of our other values and concerns, a further expenditure of time, energy, and resources is unjustified. But that is a different issue and off our immediate point, except to note that the decision to discontinue should be *conscious.*

Being receptive to new knowledge and willing to reexamine old assumptions. We are not operating at a high level of consciousness if we are absorbed totally by what we believe we already know and are uninterested in, or closed to, new information that might bear on our ideas and convictions. Such an attitude excludes the possibility of growth.

The alternative is not to hold everything we think in doubt but rather to maintain an openness to new experience and knowledge—because even when we are not mistaken to begin with, even when our starting premises are valid, new clarifications, amendments, and improvements in our understanding are always possible. And sometimes our premises *are* mistaken and need to be revised. Which leads to the next point

Being willing to see and correct mistakes. When we accept certain ideas or premises as true, it is almost inevitable that over time we become attached to them. The danger then becomes that we may not wish to recognize evidence that we are mistaken.

It is said of Charles Darwin that any time he encountered some fact that seemed to militate against his theory of evolution, he wrote it down immediately because he did not trust his memory to retain it.

Living consciously implies that my first loyalty is to truth, not to making myself right. All of us are wrong some of the time, all of us make mistakes, but if we have tied our self-esteem (or our pseudo self-esteem) to being above error, or if we have become overattached to our own positions, we are obliged to shrink consciousness in misguided self-protection. To find it humiliating to admit an error is a certain sign of flawed self-esteem.

Seeking always to expand awareness—a commitment to learning—therefore, a commitment to growth as a way of life. In the second half of the nineteenth century the head of the U.S. Patent Office announced, "Everything of importance that can be invented has been invented." This was the prevailing viewpoint throughout almost all human history. Until very recently, for the hundreds of thousands of years that Homo sapiens has existed on this planet, people saw existence as essentially unchanging. They believed that the knowledge possible to humans was already known. The idea of human life as a process of advancing from knowledge to new knowledge, from discovery to discovery—let alone of one scientific and technological breakthrough following another with exhilarating and disorienting speed—is only a couple of seconds old, measured in evolutionary time. In contrast to all the centuries behind us, we are living in an age when the total of human knowledge *doubles about every ten years.*

Only a commitment to lifelong learning can allow us to remain adaptive to our world. Those who believe they have "thought enough" and "learned enough" are on a downward trajectory of increasing unconsciousness. The resistance of many people to becoming computer literate is a simple example. I recall a vice-president in a brokerage firm saying to me, "Having to struggle with learning a computer was devastating to my self-esteem. I didn't *want* to learn. Yet I had no choice—it was necessary. But what a battle!"

To find it humiliating to admit an error is a certain sign of flawed self-esteem.

A concern to understand the world around me. All of us are affected, in more ways than we can know, perhaps, by the world in which we live—physically, culturally, socially, economically, politically. The physical environment has consequences for our health. The cultural environment affects our attitudes, values, and the pleasure we take (or don't take) in what we see, hear, and read. The social environment may have an impact on the serenity or turbulence of our existence. Economic factors affect our standard of living. Political factors affect the measure of our freedom and the extent of our control over our lives. Some would add to this list of the significant constituents of our context the cosmic or religious or spiritual dimension, however one interprets those words. In any event, this list is clearly an oversimplification and is offered only to point in a direction.

To be oblivious to such forces, to imagine that we operate in a vacuum, is truly to live as a sleepwalker. Living consciously entails a desire to understand our full context.

Obviously a person of high intelligence with a philosophical disposition may carry this concern farther than a person of more limited intellect. But even among persons of modest powers we can discern differences in interest level with regard to these matters—differences in curiosity, thoughtfulness, awareness that there is something about which to think. And again, since we are neither omniscient nor infallible, it is our intention and its expression in action that is of primary importance.

A concern to know not only external reality but also internal reality, the reality of my needs, feelings, aspirations, and motives, so that I am not a stranger or a mystery to myself. In the course of my work as a psychotherapist I have met many people who are proud of their knowledge of the universe, from physics to political philosophy to aesthetics to the most recent information about Saturn to the teachings of Zen Buddhism—and yet who are blind to the operations of the private universe within. The wreckage of their personal life is a monument to the magnitude of their unconsciousness concerning the internal world of the self. They deny and disown their needs, rationalize their emotions, intellectualize (or "spiritualize") their behavior—while moving from one unsatisfactory relationship to another or remaining for a lifetime in the same one without doing anything practical to improve it. I am not living consciously if my consciousness is used for everything but self-understanding.

Sometimes our efforts at self-examination hit an impasse for which we require the assistance of a guide, teacher, or psychotherapist. My focus here, again, is on an underlying intention, an orientation: a concern to know the inner world of needs, feelings, motives, mental processes. As contrasted with what? That condition of self-estrangement and self-alienation that to varying degrees is the state of most people (and about which I wrote in *The Disowned Self*).

This intention or concern shows up in such simple questions as: Do I know what I am feeling at any particular moment? Do I recognize the impulses from which my actions spring? Do I notice if my feelings and actions are congruent? Do I know what needs or desires I may be trying to satisfy? Do I know what I actually want in a particular encounter with another person (not what I think I "should" want)? Do I know what my life is about? Is the "program" I am living one I accepted uncritically from others, or is it genuinely of my own choosing? Do I know what I am doing when I particularly like myself and what I am doing when I don't? These are the kind of questions that intelligent self-examination entails.

―――――

Do I know what I am doing when I particularly like myself and what I am doing when I don't?

―――――

Note that this is entirely different from a morbid self-absorption that consists of taking one's emotional temperature every ten minutes. I am not recommending obsessive self-preoccupation. I do not even like to talk about "introspection" in this context because it suggests something far more technical and remote from the average person's experience. I prefer to talk about "the art of noticing." Noticing the feelings in my body. Noticing my emotions during an encounter with someone. Noticing patterns in my behavior that may not be serving me. Noticing what excites me and what drains me. Noticing whether the voice inside my head is truly my own or belongs to someone else—perhaps my mother. To notice, I have to be interested. I have to think the practice worthwhile. I have to believe there is value in knowing myself. I may have to be willing to look at troublesome facts. I have to be convinced that, long-term, I have more to gain from consciousness than unconsciousness.

Why do we need to notice bodily feelings? Well, to offer only one of many possibilities, this would be very useful to a driven individual who would prefer to avoid a heart attack and who would thus benefit from advance warnings of stress. Why do we need to notice our emotions during an encounter with someone? To better understand our actions and reactions. Why do we need to notice our patterns of behavior? To know which actions are producing desired results and which aren't, and to discover what patterns need to be challenged. Why do we need to notice what is exciting and what is draining? To do more of the first and less of the second (a correction that by no means happens automatically or "instinctively"). Why might it be worth our efforts to identify the different voices speaking within? To recognize alien influences with alien agendas (the voice of a parent or a religious authority, for example), to learn how to distinguish one's own true voice from all others, to operate one's life as an autonomous human being.

A concern to be aware of the values that move and guide me, as well as their roots, so that I am not ruled by values I have irrationally adopted or uncritically accepted from others. This point is closely related to the foregoing. One of the forms that living unconsciously takes is obliviousness to the values guiding one's actions and even indifference to the question. All of us sometimes draw mistaken or irrational conclusions from our experience on the basis of which we may form values harmful to our well-being. All of us absorb values from the world around us—from family, peers, and culture—and these values are not necessarily rational or supportive of our true interests; often, in fact, they are not.

A young person may see many examples of dishonesty and hypocrisy while growing up, may conclude, in effect, "This is the way the world works, and I must adapt to it," and may as a consequence disvalue honesty and integrity.

A man may be socialized to identify personal worth with income; a woman may be socialized to identify personal worth with the status of the man she marries.

Such values subvert healthy self-esteem, and almost inevitably lead to self-alienation and to tragic life decisions. Living consciously, therefore, entails reflecting on and weighing in the light of reason and personal experience the values that set our goals and purposes.

A Note on Addictions

The avoidance of consciousness is clearly evident in problems of addiction. When we become addicted to alcohol or drugs or destructive relationships, the implicit intention is invariably to ameliorate anxiety and pain to escape awareness of one's core feelings of powerlessness and suffering. What we become addicted to are tranquilizers and anodynes. Anxiety and pain are not extinguished, they are merely rendered less conscious. Since they inevitably resurface with still greater intensity, larger and larger doses of poison are needed to keep consciousness at bay.

Self-destruction is an act best performed in the dark.

When we become addicted to stimulants, we are avoiding the exhaustion or depression they are intended to mask. Whatever else may be involved in a particular case, what is always involved is the avoidance of consciousness. Sometimes what is avoided are the implications of a lifestyle that requires stimulants to be sustained.

To the addict, consciousness is the enemy. If I have reason to know that alcohol is dangerous to me and I nonetheless take a drink, I must first turn down the light of awareness. If I know that cocaine has cost me my last three jobs and I nonetheless choose to take a snort, I must first blank out my knowledge, must refuse to see what I see and know what I know. If I recognize that I am in a relationship that is destructive to my dignity, ruinous for my self-esteem, and dangerous to my physical well-being, and if I nonetheless choose to remain in it, I must first drown out the voice of reason, fog my brain, and make myself functionally stupid. Self-destruction is an act best performed in the dark.

A Personal Example

All of us can look back over our life and think of times when we did not bring to some concern as much consciousness as was needed. We tell ourselves, "If only I had thought more!" "If only I hadn't been so impulsive!" "If only I had checked the facts more carefully!" "If only I had looked ahead a bit!"

I think of my first marriage, when I was twenty-two years old. I think of all the signs (apart from our youth) that we were making a mistake: the numerous conflicts between us, the incompatibilities in some of our values, the ways in which at the core we were not each other's "type." Why, then, did I proceed? Because of our shared commitment to certain ideas and ideals. Because of sexual attraction. Because I desperately wanted to have a woman in my life. Because she was the first person from whom I did not feel alienated—and I lacked the confidence that another would come along. Because I naively imagined that marriage could solve all the problems between us. There were "reasons," to be sure.

Still, if someone had said to me (or if I had somehow thought to say to myself), "If you were to bring a higher level of consciousness to your relationship with Barbara, and to do so steadily, day after day, what do you suppose might happen?" I have to wonder what I might have been led to face and come to grips with. To a mind that is receptive, so simple yet provocative a question can have astonishing potency.

The fact was, I examined neither the feelings driving me toward marriage nor the feelings signaling danger. I did not confront the logical and obvious questions: Why marry *now?* Why not wait until more is resolved between you? And because of what I did not do, my self-esteem suffered a subtle wound—some part of me knew I was avoiding awareness—although it would be years before I fully understood this.

There is an exercise that I give to therapy clients today that I wish I had known about then. The course of my life over the next decade or so might have been different. I will discuss this exercise and others like it below, but for the moment let me say this. If for two weeks I had sat at my desk each morning and wrote the following incomplete sentence in my notebook: "If I bring a higher level of consciousness to my relationship with Barbara—" and then wrote six to ten endings as rapidly as I could, without rehearsing, censoring, planning, or "thinking," I would have found myself making more and more conscious, explicit, and inescapable all the deep reservations I had about this relationship as well as my process of avoidance and denial.

I have given this exercise to clients who are confused or conflicted about some relationship, and the result almost invariably is major clarification. Sometimes the relationship radically improves; sometimes it ends.

Had I known to use this technique, I would have had to face the fact that loneliness was driving me more than admiration. If Barbara had done a similar exercise, she would have realized that she was no more rational than I in what we were preparing to do. Whether we would have had the courage and wisdom to stay at this higher level of awareness is something I can only speculate about now. That one wakes up for a time is no guarantee that one will remain awake. Still, judging from the experience of my clients, it would have been extraordinarily difficult for us to persist blindly on our course because we would no longer have been blind, and opening one door clears the way to opening another and then another.

Consciousness and the Body

It was the achievement of Wilhelm Reich to bring the body into psychotherapy—in other words, to make clinicians aware that when feelings and emotions are blocked and repressed, the process of implementation is physical: Breathing is restricted and muscles are contracted. When this happens repeatedly, the blocks become part of the body structure—"the body armor," in Reich's phrase—and what began as the psychological becomes somaticized. Breathing may be so habitually shallow and muscles so little contracted that the flow of feeling is obstructed and consciousness is diminished accordingly. When body therapists work to release the breathing and open areas of tight muscular contraction, the person *feels* more *and is more aware*. Body work can liberate blocked consciousness.

This is true in all the schools of body work that have gone beyond Reich to a more advanced understanding of the interactions between psyche and soma. Freeing the body contributes to freeing the mind.

In the early 1970s I went through a program of "rolfing" (named after founder Ida Rolf), more formally called "structural integration." This process involves deep massage and manipulation of the muscle fascia to realign the body in more appropriate relation to gravity, to correct imbalances caused by entrenched muscular contractions, and to open areas of blocked feeling and energy.

I was fascinated by the response of my clients. Many said they saw changes, week by week: I became more sensitive and more perceptive in my work. As my own body seemed to open to me and somehow to become more "available," I found that I could more expertly "read" the bodies of others. I saw how a client was sitting, standing, or moving, and I instantly knew volumes about his or her inner life. Spontaneously I had shifted to a much higher level of consciousness in my work through a process that began as increased consciousness of my own body.

When I reported this enthusiastically to the man who was rolfing me, he said that not everyone had that experience and that it was the result not of the rolfing alone but also of the high level of awareness with which I participated in the process. "It's like psychotherapy," he explained. "Clients who bring a lot of consciousness to the work do better than clients who are more passive, who just show up and expect the therapist to do everything."

The point I am making is that if one's goal is to operate at a high level of consciousness, a body armored against feeling is a serious impediment.

Sentence Completions to Facilitate the Art of Living Consciously

Sentence-completion work is a deceptively simple yet uniquely powerful tool for raising self-understanding, self-esteem, and personal effectiveness. It rests on the premise that all of us have more knowledge than we normally are aware of—more wisdom than we use, more potentials than typically show up in our behavior. Sentence completion is a tool for accessing and activating these "hidden resources."

Sentence completion can be used in many ways. Here I will describe a way I find particularly effective.

The essence of this procedure is to write an incomplete sentence, a sentence stem, and to keep adding different endings—the sole requirement being that each ending be a grammatical completion of the sentence. We want a minimum of six endings.

We should work as rapidly as possible—no pauses to "think," inventing if we get stuck, without worrying if any particular ending is true, reasonable, or significant. *Any* ending is fine, *just keep going*.

When doing sentence completion this way, we work with a notebook, typewriter, or computer. (An acceptable alternative is to do the sentence completions into a tape recorder, in which case you keep repeating the stem into a recorder, each time completing it with a difference ending. You play the work back later to reflect on it.)

Sentence-completion work can be used for many different purposes. Some of them will be examined in the course of this book. Right now, how might we use the technique to facilitate the process of learning to live more consciously?

First thing in the morning, before proceeding to the day's business, sit down and write the following stem:

Living consciously to me means—

Then, as rapidly as possible, without pausing for reflection, write as many endings for that sentence as you can in two or three minutes (never fewer than six, but ten is enough). Do not worry if your endings are literally true, make sense, or are "profound." Write *anything*, but write *something*.

Then, go on to the next stem:

If I bring 5 percent more awareness to my activities today—

(Why only 5 percent? Let us proceed in small, nonintimidating, "bite-size chews." Besides, most of the time 5 percent is plenty!)

Then:

If I pay more attention to how I deal with people today—

Then:

If I bring 5 percent more awareness to my most important relationships—

Then:

If I bring 5 percent more awareness to (fill in a particular problem you are concerned about—for example, your relationship with someone, or a barrier you've hit at work, or your feelings of anxiety or depression)—

When you are finished, proceed with your day's business.

At the end of the day, as your last task before dinner, do six to ten endings each for the following stems:

When I reflect on how I would feel if I lived more consciously—

When I reflect what happens when I bring 5 percent more awareness to my activities—

When I reflect on what happens when I bring 5 percent more
awareness to my most important relationships—

When I reflect on what happens when I bring 5 percent more
awareness to (whatever you've filled in)—

Do this exercise every day, Monday through Friday for the first week.
Do not read what you wrote the day before. Naturally there will be
many repetitions. But also, new endings will inevitably occur. You are
energizing all of your psyche to work for you.

Sometime each weekend, reread what you have written for the week,
and then write a minimum of six endings for this stem:

If any of what I wrote this week is true, it would be helpful if I—

In doing this work, the ideal is to empty your mind of any expectations
concerning what will happen or what is "supposed" to happen. Do not
impose any demands on the situation. Try to empty your mind of expectations. Do the exercise, go about your day's activities, and merely notice
any differences in how you feel or how you operate. You will discover
that you have set in motion forces that make it virtually impossible for
you to avoid operating more consciously.

An average session should not take longer than ten minutes. If it takes
much longer, you are "thinking" (rehearsing, calculating) too much.

Notice that the second set of stems of the day relate to the morning's
work. I call this the "bookend" approach to sentence completion. The
knowledge that those stems are waiting to be completed later in the day
energizes the motivation to be more conscious throughout the day.

The technique can be thought of as a procedure for learning to manage our attention—more broadly, to manage the mind's "spontaneous"
activities. There is a discipline to maintaining good self-esteem. And the
foundation is the discipline of consciousness itself. This is what the
technique aims to assist and support.

After you have worked with the above stems for, say, two weeks, you
acquire a sense of how the procedure works. Then you can begin to use
other stems to help raise your awareness with regard to particular issues
of concern. For example:

**If I bring 5 percent more awareness to when I am mentally active and
when I am mentally passive, I might see that—**

(Evening stem: When I notice what happens when I . . . etc.)
If I bring 5 percent more awareness to my relationship with (fill in a name)—
If I bring 5 percent more awareness to my insecurities—
If I bring 5 percent more awareness to my depression—
If I bring 5 percent more awareness to my concern about (fill it in)—
If I bring 5 percent more awareness to my impulses to avoid unpleasant facts—
If I bring 5 percent more awareness to my needs and wants—
If I bring 5 percent more awareness to my deepest values and goals—
If I bring 5 percent more awareness to my emotions—
If I bring 5 percent more awareness to my priorities—
If I bring 5 percent more awareness to how I sometimes stand in my own way—
If I bring 5 percent more awareness to the outcomes of my actions—
If I bring 5 percent more awareness to how I sometimes make it difficult for people to give me what I want—

A few career-oriented stems:
If I bring 5 percent more awareness to what my job requires of me—
If I bring 5 percent more awareness to what I know about being an effective manager—
If I bring 5 percent more awareness to what I know about making sales—
If I bring 5 percent more awareness to what I know about appropriate delegating—

A few stems to explore "resistance":
If I imagine bringing more consciousness into my life—
The scary thing about being more conscious might be—
If I bring 5 percent more awareness to my fear of operating more consciously—

I trust this is sufficient to make clear that the possibilities are almost inexhaustible. In each of the above examples, the corresponding evening stem is obvious.

In addition to my psychotherapy practice, I conduct weekly ongoing self-esteem groups where many of my self-esteem-building strategies are continually tested. Homework assignments using exercises such as the above have proven to be powerful in quietly and gently generating change. No one has ever done this particular "consciousness exercise" for a month or two without reporting (and showing signs of) operating at a higher level of awareness in the conduct of daily life. The exercise is adrenaline shot into the psyche.

A Challenge

Living consciously is both a practice and a mind-set, an orientation toward life. Clearly it exists on a continuum. No one lives entirely unconsciously. No one is incapable of expanding his or her consciousness.

If we reflect on this issue, we will notice that we tend to be more conscious in some areas of our life than in others. I have worked with athletes and dancers who are exquisitely aware of the slightest nuances within their body, as far as nerves, muscles, and blood flow are concerned—and yet who are quite unaware of the meaning of many of their emotions. We all know people who are brilliantly conscious in the area of work and are catastrophes of unconsciousness in their personal relationships.

———

We tend to be more conscious in some areas
of our life than in others.

———

The ways we know what area of our life needs more awareness are usually fairly obvious. We look at the area where our life is working least satisfactorily. We notice where the pains and frustrations are. We observe where we feel least effective. If we are willing to be honest, this is not a difficult task. Some of us may need to bring more awareness to the territory of our basic material needs. Others need more focus on relationships. Others need more focus on intellectual development. Others need to examine unexplored possibilities of creativity and achievement. Others need more concern with spiritual growth. Which need requires priority is a function of where we are in our overall evolution, and also of our objective circumstances. Context determines appropriateness.

Let us suppose that, meditating on the material in this chapter, you identify the areas in your life where you are at your most conscious and also the areas where you are at your least conscious. The next step is to reflect on what seems to be difficult about staying in high-level mental focus in the troublesome areas. Sentence-completion work can help. For example:

The hard thing about staying fully conscious here is—

Write six to ten endings as quickly as you can. Then try:

The good thing about not being fully conscious here is—

Then try:

If I were to stay more conscious here—

Then:

If I were to experiment with raising my consciousness 5 percent in this area—

(Remember the principle of "bite-size chews.")

Right now, before checking what sentence-completion work can accomplish, you might find it stimulating to consider the following questions:

If you choose to be more conscious at work, what might you do differently?

If you choose to be more conscious in your most important relationships, what might you do differently?

If you choose to pay more attention to how you deal with people— associates, employees, customers, spouse, children, or friends—what might you do differently?

If you feel fear or reluctance to expand consciousness in any of these areas, what are the imagined negatives you are avoiding?

If, without self-reproach, you bring more consciousness to your fears or reluctance, what might you notice?

If you wanted to feel more powerful and effective in the areas where your consciousness has been less than it needs to be, *what are you willing to do?*

The practice of living consciously is the first pillar of self-esteem.

7

The Practice of Self-Acceptance

Without self-acceptance, self-esteem is impossible.

In fact, it is so intimately bound up with self-esteem that one sometimes sees the two ideas confused. Yet they are different in meaning, and each needs to be understood in its own right.

Whereas self-esteem is something we *experience*, self-acceptance is something we *do*.

Stated in the negative, *self-acceptance is my refusal to be in an adversarial relationship to myself.*

The concept has three levels of meaning, and we will consider each of them in turn.

The First Level

To be self-accepting is to be on my own side—to be *for* myself. In the most fundamental sense, self-acceptance refers to an orientation of self-value and self-commitment that derives from the fact that I am alive and conscious. As such, it is more primitive than self-esteem. It is a pre-rational, premoral act of self-affirmation—a kind of natural egoism that is the birthright of every human being and yet that we have the power to act against and nullify.

Some people are self-rejecting at so deep a level that no growth work can even begin until and unless this problem is addressed. If it is not, no treatment will hold, no new learning will be properly integrated, no

significant advances can be made. Psychotherapists who do not understand this problem or do not detect its presence will be baffled as to
why certain clients, even after years of therapy, show no important
improvement.

---

*Self-acceptance is my refusal to be in an
adversarial relationship to myself.*

An attitude of basic self-acceptance is what an effective psychotherapist strives to awaken in a person of even the lowest self-esteem. This
attitude can inspire an individual to face whatever he or she most needs
to encounter within without collapsing into self-hatred, repudiating the
value of his or her person, or relinquishing the will to live. It entails the
declaration: "I choose to value myself, to treat myself with respect, to
stand up for my right to exist." This primary act of self-affirmation is the
base on which self-esteem develops.

It can lie sleeping and then suddenly awake. It can fight for our life,
even when we are filled with despair. When we are on the brink of
suicide, it can make us pick up the telephone and call for help. From the
depths of anxiety or depression, it can lead us to the office of a psychotherapist. After we have endured years of abuse and humiliation, it can
fling us finally into shouting "No!" When all we want to do is lie down
and die, it can impel us to keep moving. It is the voice of the life force. It is
"selfishness," in the noblest meaning of that word. If it goes silent, self-
esteem is the first casualty.

The Second Level

Self-acceptance entails our willingness to experience—that is, to make
real to ourselves, without denial or evasion—that we think what we
think, feel what we feel, desire what we desire, have done what we have
done, and are what we are. It is the refusal to regard any part of
ourselves—our bodies, our emotions, our thoughts, our actions, our
dreams—as alien, as "not me." It is our willingness to experience rather
than to disown whatever may be the facts of our being at a particular
moment—to think our thoughts, own our feelings, be present to the
reality of our behavior.

The willingness to experience and accept our feelings carries no implication that emotions are to have the last word on what we do. I may not be in the mood to work today; I can acknowledge my feelings, experience them, accept them—and then go to work. I will work with a clearer mind because I have not begun the day with self-deception.

Often, when we fully experience and accept negative feelings, we are able to let go of them; they have been allowed to have their say and they relinquish center stage.

Self-acceptance is the willingness to say of any emotion or behavior, "This is an expression of me, not necessarily an expression I like or admire, but an expression of me nonetheless, at least at the time it occurred." It is the virtue of realism, that is, of respect for reality, applied to the self.

If I am thinking these disturbing thoughts, I am thinking them; I accept the full reality of my experience. If I am feeling pain or anger or fear or inconvenient lust, I am feeling it—what is true, is true—I do not rationalize, deny, or attempt to explain away. I am feeling what I am feeling and I accept the reality of my experience. If I have taken actions of which I am later ashamed, the fact remains that I have taken them— that is reality—and I do not twist my brain to make facts disappear. I am willing to stand still in the presence of what I know to be true. What is, is.

To "accept" is more than simply to "acknowledge" or "admit." It is to experience, stand in the presence of, contemplate the reality of, absorb into my consciousness. I need to open myself to and fully experience unwanted emotions, not just perfunctorily recognize them. For example, suppose my wife asks me, "How are you feeling?" and I answer in a tense, distracted manner, "Rotten." Then she says sympathetically, "I see that you are really feeling depressed today." Then I sigh, the tension begins to flow out of my body, and in an altogether different tone of voice—the voice of someone who is now real to himself—I say, "Yes, I am feeling miserable, really miserable," and then I begin to talk about what is bothering me. When, with my body tensed to resist the experience of my feelings, I had answered "Rotten," I was denying my emotion at the same time that I was acknowledging it. My wife's sympathetic response helped me to experience it, which cleared the way for me to begin to deal with it. Experiencing our feelings has direct healing power.

I can acknowledge some fact and move on with such speed that I only imagine I am practicing self-acceptance; I am really practicing denial and self-deception. Suppose my supervisor is trying to explain why something I have done on the job was a mistake. She speaks benevolently and without recriminations, and yet I am irritable, impatient, and wish she would stop talking and go away. While she is talking, I am obliged to stay with the reality of having made an error. When she is gone I can banish the reality from my consciousness—*I admitted my mistake, isn't that enough?*—which increases the likelihood that I will make the error, or one like it, again.

Self-acceptance is the precondition of change and growth. Thus, if I am confronted with a mistake I have made, in accepting that it is mine I am free to learn from it and to do better in the future. I cannot learn from a mistake I cannot accept having made.

===

I cannot forgive myself for an action I will not acknowledge having taken.

===

If I refuse to accept that often I live unconsciously, how will I learn to live more consciously? If I refuse to accept that often I live irresponsibly, how will I learn to live more responsibly? If I refuse to accept that often I live passively, how will I learn to live more actively?

I cannot overcome a fear whose reality I deny. I cannot correct a problem in the way I deal with my associates if I will not admit it exists. I cannot change traits I insist I do not have. I cannot forgive myself for an action I will not acknowledge having taken.

A client once became angry with me when I attempted to explain these ideas to her. "How do you expect me to accept my abysmally low level of self-esteem?" she demanded indignantly. "If you do not accept the reality of where you are now," I answered, "how do you imagine you can begin to change?" To understand this point, we must remind ourselves that "accepting" does not necessarily mean "liking," "enjoying," or "condoning." I can accept what is—and be determined to evolve from there. It is not acceptance but denial that leaves me stuck.

I cannot be truly for myself, cannot build self-esteem, if I cannot accept myself.

The Third Level

Self-acceptance entails the idea of compassion, of being a friend to myself.

Suppose I have done something that I regret, or of which I am ashamed, and for which I reproach myself. Self-acceptance does not deny reality, does not argue that what is wrong is really all right, but it inquires into the context in which the action was taken. It wants to understand the why. It wants to know why something that is wrong or inappropriate felt desirable or appropriate or even necessary at the time.

Accepting, compassionate interest does not encourage undesired behavior but reduces the likelihood of it recurring.

We do not understand another human being when we know only that what he or she did is wrong, unkind, destructive, or whatever. We need to know the internal considerations that prompted the behavior. There is always some context in which the most offensive actions can have their own kind of sense. This does not mean they are justified, only that they can be understandable.

I can condemn some action I have taken and still have compassionate interest in the motives that prompted it. I can still be a friend to myself. This has nothing to do with alibiing, rationalizing, or avoiding responsibility. *After* I take responsibility for what I have done, I can go deeper—into the context. A good friend might say to me, "This was unworthy of you. Now tell me, What made it feel like a good idea, or at least a defensible one?" This is what I can say to myself.

I have found, with my clients and with myself, that this kind of accepting, compassionate interest does not encourage undesired behavior but reduces the likelihood of it recurring.

Just as when we need to reproach or correct others, we should wish to do so in ways that do not damage self-esteem—since future behavior will be shaped by self-concept—so we should bring this same benevolence to ourselves. This is the virtue of self-acceptance.

An Exercise

By way of introducing clients to the idea of self-acceptance, I often like to begin with a simple exercise. It can offer a profound learning experience.

Stand in front of a full-length mirror and look at your face and body. Notice your feelings as you do so. I am asking you to focus not on your clothes or your makeup but on *you*. Notice if this is difficult or makes you uncomfortable. It is good to do this exercise naked.

You will probably like some parts of what you see more than others. If you are like most people, you will find some parts difficult to look at for long because they agitate or displease you. In your eyes there may be a pain you do not want to confront. Perhaps you are too fat or too thin. Perhaps there is some aspect of your body you so dislike that you can hardly bear to keep looking at it. Perhaps you see signs of age and cannot bear to stay connected with the thoughts and emotions these signs evoke. So the impulse is to escape, to flee from awareness, to reject, deny, disown aspects of your self.

Still, as an experiment, I ask you to stay focused on your image in the mirror a few moments longer, and say to yourself, "Whatever my defects or imperfections, I accept myself unreservedly and completely." Stay focused, breathe deeply, and say this over and over again for a minute or two without rushing the process. Allow yourself to experience fully the meaning of your words.

You may find yourself protesting, "But I don't *like* certain things about my body, so how can I accept them unreservedly and completely?" But remember: "Accepting" does not necessarily mean "liking." "Accepting" does not mean we cannot imagine or wish for changes or improvements. It means experiencing, without denial or avoidance, that a fact is a fact. In this case, it means accepting that the face and body in the mirror are *your* face and body and that they are what they are.

If you persist, if you surrender to the reality of what is, if you surrender to awareness (which is what "accepting" ultimately means), you may notice that you have begun to relax a bit and perhaps feel more comfortable with yourself, and more real.

Even though you may not like or enjoy everything you see when you look in the mirror, you are still able to say, "Right now, that's me. And I don't deny the fact. I accept it." That is respect for reality.

When clients commit to do this exercise for two minutes every morning and again every night for two weeks, they soon begin to experience the relationship between self-acceptance and self-esteem: a mind that honors sight honors itself. But more than that: How can self-esteem not suffer if we are in a rejecting relationship to our own physical being? Is it realistic to imagine we can love ourselves while despising what we see in the mirror?

They make another important discovery. Not only do they enter a more harmonious relationship with themselves, not only do they begin to grow in self-efficacy and self-respect, but if aspects of the self they do not like are within their power to change, they are more motivated to make the changes once they have accepted the facts as they are now.

We are not moved to change those things whose reality we deny.

And for those things we cannot change, when we accept them we grow stronger and more centered; when we curse and protest them, we disempower ourselves.

Listening to Feelings

Both accepting and disowning are implemented through a combination of mental and physical processes.

The act of experiencing and accepting our emotions is implemented through (1) focusing on the feeling or emotion, (2) breathing gently and deeply, allowing muscles to relax, allowing the feeling to be felt, and (3) making real that this is *my* feeling (which we call *owning* it).

In contrast, we deny and disown our emotions when we (1) avoid awareness of their reality, (2) constrict our breathing and tighten our muscles to cut off or numb feeling, and (3) disassociate ourselves from our own experience (in which state we are often unable to recognize our feelings).

When we allow ourselves to experience our emotions and accept them, sometimes this allows us to move to a deeper level of awareness where important information presents itself.

One day a client began reproaching herself for feeling anger at her husband over the fact that he was leaving on a two-week business trip. She called herself irrational, she called herself stupid, she told herself it was ridiculous to feel that way, but the anger persisted. No one has ever talked herself (or anyone else) out of an unwanted emotion by hurling insults or delivering a moral lecture.

I asked her to describe her feeling of anger, to describe where in her body she experienced it and how exactly it felt to her. My goal was to have her enter the feeling more deeply. Annoyed and irritated by my request, she demanded, "What good would that do? I don't want to feel the anger, I want to get rid of it!" I persisted, and gradually she began to describe feelings of tension in her chest and a tight knot in her stomach. Then she exclaimed, "I feel indignant, I feel outraged, I feel: How can he do this to me?" Then, to her astonishment, the anger began to dissolve and another emotion emerged in its place—anxiety. I asked her to enter the anxiety and describe it, and again her first response was to protest and ask what good it would do. I guided her to experience the anxiety, to immerse herself in it, while being a witness to it, describing everything she could notice, and to discover if, perhaps, it would speak to her. "My God!" she cried. "I'm afraid of being left alone!" Again she began to rebuke herself. "What am I, a child? Can't I be on my own for two weeks?" I asked her to go more deeply into the fear of being alone. She said suddenly, "I'm afraid of what I might do when he's gone. You know—other men. I might get involved with another man. I don't trust myself."

By now, the anger was gone, the anxiety had dissolved, the fear of loneliness had faded away. To be sure, a problem remained that had to be dealt with, but now, since it was admitted into conscious awareness, it was *capable* of being dealt with.

A Personal Example

As a teenager, I understood very little about the art of handling unwanted emotions except by "conquering" them. Often I identified the ability to deny and disown with "strength."

I recall my sometimes acutely painful feelings of loneliness and of longing for someone with whom I could share thoughts, interests, and feelings. By sixteen I had accepted the idea that loneliness was a weakness and longing for human intimacy represented a failure of independence. I did not hold this view consistently, but I held it some of the time, and when I did, I had no answer to the pain except to tense my body against it, contract my breathing, reproach myself, and look for a distraction. I tried to convince myself I did not care. In effect, I clung to alienation as a virtue.

I did not give people much of a chance. I felt different from everyone and I saw the difference as an abyss between us. I told myself that I had my thoughts and my books and that that was enough—or should be, if I were properly self-reliant.

If I had accepted the naturalness of my desire for human contact, I would have looked for bridges of understanding between myself and other people. If I had allowed myself to feel fully the pain of my isolation, without self-reproach, I would have made friends with both sexes; I would have seen the interest and benevolence that was often extended to me. If I had given myself the freedom to pass through the normal stages of adolescent development and come out of the prison of my remoteness, I would not have set myself up for an unfortunate marriage. I would not have been so vulnerable to the first girl who seemed genuinely to share my interests.

My chief point here, however, is the effect of my disowning on my self-esteem. That there were "reasons" for my areas of non-self-acceptance is no doubt true, but that is not the focus now. What I felt was what I felt, whether I accepted it or not. Somewhere in my brain was the knowledge that I was condemning and repudiating a part of myself—the part that longed for human companionship. I was in an adversarial relationship to part of who I was. No matter what other areas of confidence and happiness I might enjoy, I was inflicting a wound on my self-esteem.

By the same logic, when I later learned to embrace the disowned parts of myself, I grew in self-esteem.

As a psychotherapist I see that nothing does as much for an individual's self-esteem as becoming aware of and accepting disowned parts of the self. The first steps of healing and growth are awareness and acceptance—consciousness and integration. They are the fountainhead of personal development.

An Experiment

I often find it useful to invite clients to do the following exercise, by way of deepening their understanding of self-acceptance.

Take a few minutes to contemplate some feeling or emotion of yours that is not easy for you to face—insecurity, pain, envy, rage, sorrow, humiliation, fear.

When you isolate the feeling, see if you can bring it into clearer focus, perhaps by thinking of or imagining whatever typically evokes it. Then breathe into the feeling, which means focus on the feeling while imagining you are directing the flow of air to it and then from it. Imagine what it would feel like not to resist this feeling but to accept it fully. Explore that experience. Take your time.

Practice saying to yourself, "I am now feeling such and such (whatever the feeling is) and I accept it fully." At first, this may be difficult; you may find that you tense your body in protest. But persevere; concentrate on your breathing; think of giving your muscles permission to let go of their tension; remind yourself, "A fact is a fact; that which is, is; if the feeling exists, it exists." Keep contemplating the feeling. Think of *allowing* the feeling to be there (rather than trying to wish or will it out of existence). You may find it useful, as I have, to tell yourself, "I am now exploring the world of fear or pain or envy or confusion (or whatever)."

Welcome to the practice of self-acceptance.

When Self-Acceptance Feels Impossible

Now let us consider the question: Suppose our negative reaction to some experience is so overwhelming that we feel we *cannot* practice self-acceptance with regard to it?

In this case, let us say, the feeling, thought, or memory is so distressing and agitating that acceptance feels out of the question. We feel powerless not to block and contract. The solution is not to try to resist our resistance. It is not useful to try to block a block. Instead, we need to do something more artful. If we cannot accept a feeling (or a thought or a memory), we should *accept our resistance*. In other words, start by accepting where we are. Be present to the now and experience it fully. If we stay with the resistance at a conscious level, *it will usually begin to dissolve.*

When we fight a block it grows stronger. When we acknowledge, experience, and accept it, it begins to melt.

If we can accept the fact that right now, at this moment, we *refuse* to accept that we feel envy, or anger, or pain, or longing, for example—or that we *refuse* to accept that we once did or believed such and such—if we acknowledge, experience, and accept our resistance—we discover a supremely important paradox: The resistance begins to collapse. When we fight a block it grows stronger. When we acknowledge, experience, and accept it, it begins to melt *because its continued existence requires opposition.*

Sometimes in therapy, when a person has difficulty accepting a feeling, I will ask if he or she is willing to accept the fact of *refusing* to accept the feeling. I asked this once of a client who was a clergyman and who had great difficulty in owning or experiencing his anger; just the same, he was a very angry man. My request disoriented him. "Will I accept that I won't accept my anger?" he asked me. When I answered, "That's right," he thundered, "I *refuse* to accept my anger and I *refuse* to accept my refusal!" I asked, "Will you accept your refusal to accept your refusal? We've got to begin somewhere. Let's begin there."

I asked him to face the group and say "I'm angry" over and over again. Soon he was saying it very angrily indeed.

Then I had him say "I *refuse* to accept my anger," which he shouted with escalating vigor.

Then I had him say "I *refuse* to accept my refusal to accept my anger," which he plunged into ferociously.

Then I had him say "But I am willing to accept my refusal to accept my refusal," and he kept repeating it until he broke down and joined in the laughter of the group.

"If you can't accept the experience, accept the resistance," he said, and I answered, "Right. And if you can't accept the resistance, accept your resistance to accepting the resistance. Eventually you'll arrive at a point you can accept. Then you can move forward from there. . . . So, are you angry?"

"I'm filled with anger."

"Can you accept that fact?"

"I don't like it."

"Can you accept it?"

"I can accept it."

"Good. Now we can begin to find out what you're angry about."

Two Fallacies

We typically encounter two fallacious assumptions when people have difficulty with the idea of self-acceptance. One is the belief that if we accept who and what we are, we must approve of everything about us. The other is the belief that if we accept who and what we are, we are indifferent to change or improvement. "I don't want to accept myself! I want to learn to be different!"

But of course the question is: If we cannot accept what is, where will we find the motivation to improve? If I deny and disown what is, how will I be inspired to grow?

There is a paradox here (a paradox, not a contradiction): Acceptance of what *is*, is the precondition of change. And denial of what is leaves me stuck in it.

Sentence Completions to Facilitate Self-Acceptance

What follows is a five-week sentence-completion program designed to facilitate self-acceptance. It is more detailed than the exercises offered for the other pillars because, having taught these ideas for many years, I find that people often have more difficulty fully grasping self-acceptance than any other practice I recommend.

Notice that I include stems dealing with issues I have not explicitly discussed, such as accepting conflicts or accepting excitement. For example, if I can accept my conflicts, I can deal with them and move toward resolving them; and if not, not. If I can accept my excitement, I can live it, I can look for appropriate outlets; if I am afraid of my excitement and try to extinguish it, I may kill the best part of myself. Fairly complex ideas are embedded in these stems. They bear studying and thinking about, and they entail many more implications than I can explore here.

WEEK 1. MORNINGS:
Self-acceptance to me means—
If I am more accepting of my body—
When I deny and disown my body—
If I am more accepting of my conflicts—

EVENINGS:
When I deny or disown my conflicts—
If I am more accepting of my feelings—
When I deny and disown my feelings—
If I am more accepting of my thoughts—
When I deny and disown my thoughts—

On the weekends, read over you have written and then write six to ten endings for **If any of what I have written is true, it would be helpful if I—**. Do this each weekend throughout the program.

WEEK 2. MORNINGS:
If I am more accepting of my actions—
When I deny or disown my actions—
I am becoming aware—

EVENINGS:
If I am willing to be realistic about my assets and shortcomings—
If I am more accepting of my fears—
When I deny and disown my fears—

WEEK 3. MORNINGS:
If I am more accepting of my pain—
When I deny and disown my pain—
If I am more accepting of my anger—
When I deny and disown my anger—

EVENINGS:
If I am more accepting of my sexuality—
When I deny and disown my sexuality—
If I am more accepting of my excitement—
When I deny and disown my excitement—

WEEK 4. MORNINGS:
If I am more accepting of my joy—
When I deny and disown my joy—
If I am willing to see what I see and know what I know—

EVENINGS:
If I bring a high level of consciousness to my fears—
If I bring a high level of consciousness to my pain—

WEEK 5. MORNINGS:
If I bring a high level of consciousness to my anger—
If I bring a high level of consciousness to my sexuality—
If I bring a high level of consciousness to my excitement—
If I bring a high level of consciousness to my joy—

EVENINGS:
When I think of the consequences of not accepting myself—
If I accept the fact that what is, is, regardless of whether I admit it—
I am beginning to see that—

Other useful sentence stems to explore this territory can be found in *How to Raise Your Self-Esteem* and *The Art of Self-Discovery.*

The Ultimate Crime Against Ourselves: The Disowning of Positives

Anything we have the possibility of experiencing, we have the possibility of disowning, either immediately or later, in memory. As the philosopher Nietzsche wrote: " 'I did it,' says memory. 'I couldn't have,' says pride, and remains relentless. Eventually memory yields."

I can rebel against my memories, thoughts, emotions, actions. I can reject rather than accept virtually any aspect of my experience and any act of self-expression. I can declare, "Not me. Not mine."

==

We can be as frightened of our assets
as of our shortcomings.

==

I can refuse to accept my sensuality; I can refuse to accept my spirituality. I can disown my sorrow; I can disown my joy. I can repress the memory of actions of which I am ashamed; I can repress the memory of actions of which I am proud. I can deny my ignorance; I can deny my intelligence. I can refuse to accept my limitations; I can refuse to accept my potentials. I can conceal my weaknesses; I can conceal my strengths. I can deny my feelings of self-hatred; I can deny my feelings of self-love. I can pretend that I am more than I am; I can pretend that I am less than I am. I can disown my body; I can disown my mind.

We can be as frightened of our assets as of our shortcomings—as frightened of our genius, ambition, excitement, or beauty as of emptiness, passivity, depression, or unattractiveness. If our liabilities pose the problem of inadequacy, our assets pose the challenge of responsibility.

We can run not only from our dark side but also from our bright side—from anything that threatens to make us stand out or stand alone, or that calls for the awakening of the hero within us, or that asks that we break through to a higher level of consciousness and reach a higher ground of integrity. The greatest crime we commit against ourselves is not that we may deny and disown our shortcomings but that we deny and disown our greatness—because it frightens us. If a fully realized self-acceptance does not evade the worst within us, neither does it evade the best.

The practice of self-acceptance is the second pillar of self-esteem.

8

The Practice of Self-Responsibility

To feel competent to live and worthy of happiness, I need to experience a sense of control over my existence. This requires that I be willing to take responsibility for my actions and the attainment of my goals. This means that I take responsibility for my life and well-being.

Self-responsibility is essential to self-esteem, and it is also a reflection or manifestation of self-esteem. The relationship between self-esteem and its pillars is always reciprocal. The practices that generate self-esteem are also natural expressions and consequences of self-esteem, as we shall discuss in a later chapter.

The practice of self-responsibility entails these realizations:

I am responsible for the achievement of my desires.

I am responsible for my choices and actions.

I am responsible for the level of consciousness I bring to my work.

I am responsible for the level of consciousness I bring to my relationships.

I am responsible for my behavior with other people—coworkers, associates, customers, spouse, children, friends.

I am responsible for how I prioritize my time.

I am responsible for the quality of my communications.

I am responsible for my personal happiness.

I am responsible for accepting or choosing the values by which I live.

I am responsible for raising my self-esteem.

What does each of these items imply in terms of behavior?

The Action Implications of Self-Responsibility

I am responsible for the achievement of my desires. No one owes me the fulfillment of my wishes. I do not hold a mortgage on anyone else's life or energy. If I have desires, it is up to me to discover how to satisfy them. I need to take responsibility for developing and implementing an action plan.

If my goals require the participation of other people, I must be responsible for knowing what they require of me if they are to cooperate and for providing whatever is my rational obligation to provide. I respect their self-interest and know that if I wish their cooperation or assistance, I must be conscious of it and speak to it.

No one owes me the fulfillment of my wishes.

If I am unwilling to take responsibility for the attainment of my desires, they are not really desires—they are merely daydreams. For any professed desire to be taken seriously, I must be prepared to answer, in realistic terms: *What am I willing to do to get what I want?*

I am responsible for my choices and actions. To be "responsible" in this context means responsible not as the recipient of moral blame or guilt, but responsible as the chief causal agent in my life and behavior. If my choices and actions are *mine*, then I am their source. I need to own this fact. I need to stay connected with it when I choose and act. What difference would that make? If you would like to discover the answer for yourself, write six endings, as fast as you can, for the stem **If I take full responsibility for my choices and actions—**.

I am responsible for the level of consciousness I bring to my work. This is an example of the point I just made about choice. No one else can possibly be accountable for the level of awareness I bring to my daily activities. I can give my work the best I have to give, or I can seek to get away with as little consciousness as possible, or anywhere in between. If I stay connected with my responsibility in this area, I am more likely to operate at a high level of consciousness.

I am responsible for the level of consciousness I bring to my relationships. The principle just discussed applies equally to my interactions with others—to my choice of companions and to the awareness I bring or fail to bring to any encounter. Am I fully present in my encounters with others? Am I present to what is being said? Do I think about the implications of my statements? Do I notice how others are affected by what I say and do?

I am responsible for my behavior with other people—coworkers, associates, customers, spouse, children, friends. I am responsible for how I speak and how I listen. I am responsible for the promises I keep or fail to keep. I am responsible for the rationality or irrationality of my dealings. We evade responsibility when we try to blame others for our actions, as in "She's driving me crazy," "He pushes my buttons," "I would act reasonably if only she would . . ."

I am responsible for how I prioritize my time. Whether the choices I make about the disposition of my time and energy reflect my professed values or are incongruous with them is my responsibility. If I insist that I love my family more than anyone yet am rarely alone with them and spend most of my leisure time playing cards or golf, always surrounded by friends, I need to confront my contradiction and think about its implications. If I declare that my most important task at work is finding new clients for the firm but spend 90 percent of my time bogged down in office trivia that produces very little income—I need to reexamine how I am investing my energy.

In my consulting work, when I give executives the stem **If I take responsibility for how I prioritize my time—** I get endings such as "I would learn to say no more often"; "I would eliminate about 30 percent of my current activities"; "I'd be much more productive"; "I'd enjoy work more"; "I'd be appalled how out of control I've been"; "I'd actualize more of my potential."

I am responsible for the quality of my communications. I am responsible for being as clear as I know how to be; for checking to see if the listener has understood me; for speaking loudly and distinctly enough to be heard; for the respect or disrespect with which I convey my thoughts.

I am responsible for my personal happiness. One of the characteristics of immaturity is the belief that it is someone else's job to make me happy—much as it was once my parents' job to keep me alive. If only someone would love me, then I would love myself. If only someone would take care of me, then I would be contented. If only someone would spare me the necessity of making decisions, then I would be carefree. If only someone would make me happy.

Here's a simple but powerful stem to wake one up to reality: **If I take full responsibility for my personal happiness—**.

Taking responsibility for my happiness is empowering. It places my life back in my own hands. Ahead of taking this responsibility, I may imagine it will be a burden. What I discover is that it sets me free.

Taking responsibility for my happiness is empowering. It places my life back in my own hands.

I am responsible for accepting or choosing the values by which I live. If I live by values I have accepted or adopted passively and unthinkingly, it is easy to imagine that they are just "my nature," just "who I am," and to avoid recognizing that choice is involved. If I am willing to recognize that choices and decisions are crucial when values are adopted, then I can take a fresh look at my values, question them, and if necessary revise them. Again, it is taking responsibility that sets me free.

I am responsible for raising my self-esteem. Self-esteem is not a gift I can receive from someone else. It is generated from within. To wait passively for something to happen that will raise my self-esteem is to sentence myself to a life of frustration.

Once when I was lecturing to a group of psychotherapists on the six pillars of self-esteem, one of them asked me, "Why do you put your emphasis on what the individual must do to grow in self-esteem? Isn't the source of self-esteem the fact that we are children of God?" I have encountered this question a number of times.

Whether one believes in a God, and whether one believes we are God's children, is irrelevant to the issue of what self-esteem requires. Let us imagine that there is a God and that we are his/her/its children. In this respect, then, we are all equal. Does it follow that everyone is or should be equal in self-esteem, regardless of whether anyone lives consciously or unconsciously, responsibly or irresponsibly, honestly or dishonestly? Earlier in this book we saw that this is impossible. There is no way for our mind to avoid registering the choices we make in the way we operate and no way for our sense of self to remain unaffected. If we are children of God, the questions remain: *What are we going to do about it? What are we going to make of it? Will we honor our gifts or betray them?* If we betray ourselves and our powers, if we live mindlessly, purposelessly, and without integrity, can we buy our way out, can we acquire self-esteem, by claiming to be God's relatives? Do we imagine we can thus relieve ourselves of personal responsibility?

When people lack healthy self-esteem, they often identify self-esteem with being "loved." If they did not feel loved by their families, sometimes they comfort themselves with the thought that God loves them, and they try to tie their self-esteem to this idea. With the best will in the world, how can we understand this strategy except as a manifestation of passivity?

I do not believe we are intended to remain dependent children. I believe we are intended to grow into adults, which means to become responsible for ourselves—to become self-supporting psychologically as well as financially. Whatever role a belief in God may play in our lives, surely it is not to justify a default on consciousness, responsibility, and integrity.

A Clarification

In stressing that we need to take responsibility for our life and happiness, I am not suggesting that a person never suffers through accident or through the fault of others, or that a person is responsible for everything that may happen to him or her.

I do not support the grandiose notion that "I am responsible for every aspect of my existence and everything that befalls me." Some things we have control over; others we do not. If I hold myself responsible for matters beyond my control, I put my self-esteem in jeopardy, since inevitably I will fail my expectations. If I deny responsibility for matters that are within my control, again I jeopardize my self-esteem. I need to know the difference between that which is up to me and that which is not. The only consciousness over which I have volitional control is my own.

Examples

It is easy enough in work situations to observe the difference between those who practice self-responsibility and those who do not. Self-responsibility shows up as an *active* orientation to work (and life) rather than a *passive* one.

If there is a problem, men and women who are self-responsible ask, "What can I do about it? What avenues of action are possible to me?" If something goes wrong, they ask, "What did I overlook? Where did I miscalculate? How can I correct the situation?" They do not protest, "But no one told me what to do!" or "But it's not my job!" They indulge neither in alibis nor in blaming. They are typically *solution oriented.*

In every organization we encounter both types: those who wait for someone else to provide a solution and those who take responsibility for finding it. It is only by grace of the second type that organizations are able to operate effectively.

Here are examples from the personal realm, where sentence completion is used to illuminate:

"If I were to give up blaming my parents for my unhappiness," said a "child" of forty-six, "I'd have to take responsibility for my actions; I'd have to face the fact that I've always felt sorry for myself, and enjoyed it; I'd have to recognize that I still dream of being rescued by my father; I'd admit I like seeing myself as a victim; I'd have to act in new ways; I'd get out of my apartment and look for a job; I couldn't just suffer."

"If I were to accept that I am responsible for my happiness," said an older man who drank too much, "I'd stop complaining that my wife drives me to drink; I'd keep out of bars; I wouldn't spend hours in front of the TV, blaming 'the system'; I'd go to the gym and start getting in shape; I'd give my boss more for his money; I'd probably have to stop feeling sorry for myself; I don't think I could go on abusing my body as I do now; I'd be a different person; I'd respect myself more; I could get my life moving again."

"If I take responsibility for my emotions," said a woman who exhausted her family and friends with her complaining, "I wouldn't be so depressed; I'd see how I often make myself miserable; I'd see how much rage I'm denying; I'd admit how much of my unhappiness is spite; I'd focus more often on the good things in my life; I'd realize I'm trying to make people feel sorry for me; I'd see I can be happy more often."

A Personal Example

In the overall conduct of my life, I would say that I have always operated at a fairly high level of self-responsibility. I did not look to others to provide for my needs or wants. But I can think of a time when I failed my own principles rather badly, with painful results.

In my twenties I formed an intense relationship with novelist-philosopher Ayn Rand. Over the course of eighteen years, our relationship passed through almost every form imaginable: from student and teacher to friends and colleagues to lovers and partners—and, ultimately, to adversaries. The story of this relationship is the dramatic centerpiece of *Judgment Day*. In the beginning and for some years, the relationship was nurturing, inspiring, valuable in many ways; I learned and grew enormously. But eventually it became constricting, toxic, destructive—a barrier to my further intellectual and psychological development.

I did not take the initiative and propose that our relationship be redefined and reconstituted on a different basis. I told myself I did not want to cause pain. I waited for her to see what I saw. I looked to her rationality and wisdom to reach the decision that would be right for both of us. In effect, I was relating to an abstraction, the author of *The Fountainhead* and *Atlas Shrugged*, rather than to the concrete woman in front of me. I did not confront the fact that her agenda was very different from mine and that she was totally absorbed in her own needs. I delayed facing the fact that nothing would change unless I made it change. And because I delayed, I caused suffering and humiliation to us both. I avoided a responsibility that was mine to take. No matter what explanations I gave myself, there was no way for my self-esteem to remain unaffected. Only when I began to take the initiative did I begin the process of regaining what I had lost.

We often see this pattern in marriages. One partner sees before the other that the relationship is finished. But he or she does not want to be "the bad guy," the one to end things. So instead manipulation begins, to lead the other to make the first move. It is cruel, degrading, lacking in dignity, and hurtful to both people. It is self-demeaning and self-diminishing.

To the extent that I evade responsibility, I inflict wounds on my self-esteem. In accepting responsibility, I build self-esteem.

Productiveness

No one can be said to be living self-responsibly who has no productive purposes. Through work we support our existence. Through the exercise of our intelligence toward some useful ends, we become more fully human. Without productive goals and productive effort, we remain forever children.

True, we are limited by the opportunities that exist for us at a given place and time. But in any given context, the mark of independence and self-responsibility is the orientation that asks, "What actions are possible to me?" "What needs to be done?" "How can I improve my condition?" "How can I move beyond this impasse?" "What will be the best use of my energies in this situation?"

Self-responsibility is expressed through an *active* orientation to life. It is expressed through the understanding that no one is here on earth to spare us the necessity of independence, and through the understanding that without work, independence is impossible.

Thinking for Oneself

Living actively entails independent thinking in contrast to passive conformity to the beliefs of others.

Independent thinking is a corollary both of living consciously and of self-responsibility. To live consciously is to live by the exercise of one's own mind. To practice self-responsibility is to think for oneself.

A person cannot think through the mind of another. We learn from one another, to be sure, but knowledge implies understanding, not mere imitation or repetition. We can either exercise our own mind or else pass on to others the responsibility of knowledge and evaluation and accept their verdicts more or less uncritically. The choice we make is crucial for the way we experience ourselves as well as for the kind of life we create.

Often what people call "thinking" is merely recycling the opinions of others.

That we are sometimes influenced by others in ways we do not recognize does not alter the fact that there is a distinction between the psychology of those who try to understand things, think for themselves, and judge for themselves, and those to whom such a possibility rarely occurs. What's important here is intention, the nature of an individual's goal.

To speak of "thinking independently" is useful because the redundancy has value in terms of emphasis. Often what people call "thinking" is merely recycling the opinions of others. So we can say that thinking independently—about our work, our relationships, the values that guide our life, the goals we set for ourselves—strengthens self-esteem. And healthy self-esteem results in a natural inclination to think independently.

The Moral Principle

Embracing self-responsibility not merely as a personal preference but as a philosophical principle entails one's acceptance of a profoundly important moral idea. In taking responsibility for our own existence we implicitly recognize that other human beings are not our servants and do not exist for the satisfaction of our needs. We are not morally entitled to treat other human beings as means to our ends, just as we are not a means to theirs. As I have suggested above, a consistent application of the principle of self-responsibility implies the following rule of human relationships: *Never ask a person to act against his or her self-interest as he or she understands it.* If we wish people to take some action or provide some value, we are obliged to offer reasons that are meaningful and persuasive in terms of their interests and goals. This policy is the moral foundation of mutual respect, goodwill, and benevolence among human beings. It rejects the notion that some people may be treated as sacrificial fodder for the goals of others, which is the premise underlying all dictatorships and, for that matter, most political systems.

Sentence Completions to Facilitate Self-Responsibility

In my therapy practice and my self-esteem groups, I work with a great number of sentence stems that allow clients to explore the psychology of self-responsibility. I offer a representative sampling below. The homework assignment would be broken up into weekly installments, as follows:

WEEK 1

Self-responsibility to me means—
At the thought of being responsible for my own existence—
If I accepted responsibility for my own existence, that would mean—
When I avoid responsibility for my own existence—

WEEK 2

If I accept 5 percent more responsibility for the attainment of my own goals—
When I avoid responsibility for the attainment of my goals—
If I took more responsibility for the success of my relationships—
Sometimes I keep myself passive by—

WEEK 3

If I take responsibility for what I do about the messages I received from my mother—
If I take responsibility for what I do about the messages I received from my father—
If I take responsibility for the ideas I accept or reject—
If I bring greater awareness to the ideas that motivate me—

WEEK 4

If I accept 5 percent more responsibility for my personal happiness—
If I avoid responsibility for my personal happiness—
If I accept 5 percent more responsibility for my choice of companions—
When I avoid responsibility for my choice of companions—

WEEK 5

If I accept 5 percent more responsibility for the words that come out of my mouth—
When I avoid responsibility for the words that come out of my mouth—
If I bring greater awareness to the things I tell myself—
If I take responsibility for the things I tell myself—

WEEK 6

I make myself helpless when I—
I make myself depressed when I—

I make myself anxious when I—
If I take responsibility for making myself helpless—

WEEK 7
If I take responsibility for making myself depressed—
If I take responsibility for making myself anxious—
When I am ready to understand what I have been writing—
It is not easy for me to admit that—
If I take responsibility for my present standard of living—

WEEK 8
I feel most self-responsible when I—
I feel least self-responsible when I—
If I am not here on earth to live up to anyone else's expectations—
If my life belongs to me—

WEEK 9
If I give up the lie of being unable to change—
If I take responsibility for what I make of my life from this point on—
If no one is coming to rescue me—
I am becoming aware—

The power of the method is that it generates shifts in the consciousness and orientation of the individual without lengthy "discussions" or "analyses." The solution is largely generated from within.

If you keep a journal and over time write six to ten endings for each of these incomplete sentences, not only will you learn a great deal but it will be almost impossible not to grow in the practice of self-responsibility. The best way of working is to do the week's stems Monday through Friday, then do the weekend stem **If any of what I have been writing is true, it might be helpful if I—** and then move on to the next week's stem on Monday.

No One Is Coming

Having worked with people for so many years with the aim of building self-esteem, I have always been on the lookout for decisive moments in psychotherapy, instances when a "click" seems to occur in the client's mind and new forward motion begins.

One of the most important of such moments is when the client grasps that *no one is coming.* No one is coming to save me; no one is coming to make life right for me; no one is coming to solve my problems. If I don't do something, *nothing is going to get better.*

The dream of a rescuer who will deliver us may offer a kind of comfort, but it leaves us passive and powerless. We may feel *If only I suffer long enough, if only I yearn desperately enough, somehow a miracle will happen,* but this is the kind of self-deception one pays for with one's life as it drains away into the abyss of unredeemable possibilities and irretrievable days, months, decades.

Some years ago, in my group therapy room, we hung on the wall a number of sayings that I often found useful in the course of my work. A client made me a gift of several of these sayings done in needlepoint, each with its own frame. One of these was "It isn't what they think; it's what you know." Another was "No one is coming."

One day a group member with a sense of humor challenged me about "No one is coming."

"Nathaniel, it's not true," he said. "*You* came."

"Correct," I admitted, "but I came to say that no one is coming."

The practice of self-responsibility is the third pillar of self-esteem.

9

The Practice of Self-Assertiveness

Some years ago I was addressing a graduate class in psychology and I wanted them to understand at what subtle level the fear of self-assertion can show up.

I asked if anyone present believed he or she had a right to exist. Everyone's hand went up. Then I asked for a volunteer to assist me with a demonstration. A young man came to the front of the room, and I said to him, "Would you please just stand facing the class, and say aloud, several times, 'I have a right to exist.' Say it slowly and notice how you feel saying it. And while you are doing this, I want everyone in the class to consider: Do you believe him? Do you think he really feels what he is saying?"

The young man put his hands on his hips and belligerently declared, "I have a right to exist." He said it as if preparing for battle. With each repetition he sounded more pugnacious.

"No one is arguing with you," I pointed out. "No one is challenging you. Can you say it without defiance or defensiveness?"

He could not. The anticipation of an attack was always in his voice. No one believed in his conviction about what he was saying.

A young woman came up and said in a pleading voice and a smile begging to be forgiven, "I have a right to exist." No one believed her, either.

Someone else came up. He sounded arrogant, supercilious, affected, an actor playing a part with embarrassing ineptitude.

A student protested, "But this isn't a fair test. They're shy, not used to speaking in front of people, so they sound strained." I asked him to come to the front and say, simply, "Two and two make four." He did so with complete ease and conviction. Then I asked him to say, "I have a right to exist." He sounded tense, flippant, unconvincing.

The class laughed. They understood. Standing in front of the class and saying two and two make four was not difficult. Asserting the right to exist was.

"What does the statement 'I have a right to exist' mean to you?" I asked. "Obviously in this context we're not taking it primarily as a political statement, as in the Declaration of Independence. Here, we mean something more psychological. But what?" "It means my life belongs to me," said one student. "It means I can do my own thing," said another. "It means I don't have to fulfill my parents' expectations for me, I can fulfill my own," said another. "It means I can say no when I want to," said another. "It means I have a right to respect my self-interest." "It means what I want matters." "It means I can say and do what I think is right." "It means I can follow my own destiny." "It means my father can't tell me what to do with my life." "It means I don't have to build my whole life around not upsetting Mother."

These were some of the private meanings of the statement "I have a right to exist." And this is what they were unable to assert with serenity and confidence to a roomful of their peers. The point made, I began to talk with them about self-assertiveness and self-esteem.

What Is Self-Assertiveness?

Self-assertiveness means honoring my wants, needs, and values and seeking appropriate forms of their expression in reality.

Its opposite is that surrender to timidity that consists of consigning myself to a perpetual underground where everything that I am lies hidden or stillborn—to avoid confrontation with someone whose values differ from mine, or to please, placate, or manipulate someone, or simply to "belong."

Self-assertion does not mean belligerence or inappropriate aggressiveness; it does not mean pushing to the front of the line or knocking other people over; it does not mean upholding my own rights while being blind or indifferent to everyone else's. It simply means the willingness to stand up for myself, to be who I am openly, to treat myself with respect in all human encounters. It means the refusal to fake my person to be liked.

Self-assertiveness means the willingness to stand up for myself, to be who I am openly, to treat myself with respect in all human encounters.

To practice self-assertiveness is to live authentically, to speak and act from my innermost convictions and feelings—as a way of life, as a rule (allowing for the obvious fact that there may be particular circumstances in which I may justifiably choose not to do so—for example, when confronted by a holdup man).

Appropriate self-assertiveness pays attention to context. The forms of self-expression appropriate when playing on the floor with a child are obviously different from those appropriate at a staff meeting. To respect the difference is not to "sacrifice one's authenticity" but merely to stay reality focused. In every context there will be appropriate and inappropriate forms of self-expression. Sometimes self-assertiveness is manifested through volunteering an idea or paying a compliment; sometimes through a polite silence that signals nonagreement; sometimes by refusing to smile at a tasteless joke. In work situations one cannot necessarily voice all one's thoughts, and it is not necessary to do so. What is necessary is to know what one thinks—and to remain *real.*

While what is appropriate self-expression varies with the context, in every situation there is a choice between being authentic or inauthentic, real or unreal. If we do not want to face this, of course we will deny that we have such a choice. We will assert that we are helpless. But the choice is always there.

What Self-Assertiveness Is and Is Not

1. In a class society, when we see a superior talking to an inferior, it is the inferior's eyes that are lowered. It is the slave who looks down, not the master. In the South there was a time when a black man could be beaten for the offense of daring to look directly at a white woman. *Seeing* is an act of self-assertion and has always been understood as such.

The first and basic act of self-assertion is the assertion of consciousness. This entails the choice to see, to think, to be aware, to send the light of consciousness outward toward the world and inward toward our own being. To ask questions is an act of self-assertion. To challenge authority is an act of self-assertion. To think for oneself—and to stand by what one thinks—is the root of self-assertion. To default on this responsibility is to default on the self at the most basic level.

Note that self-assertiveness should not be confused with mindless rebelliousness. "Self-assertiveness" without consciousness is not self-assertiveness; it is drunk-driving.

Sometimes people who are essentially dependent and fearful choose a form of assertiveness that is self-destructive. It consists of reflexively saying "No!" when their interests would be better served by saying "Yes." Their only form of self-assertiveness is protest—whether it makes sense or not. We often see this response among teenagers—and among adults who have never matured beyond this teenage level of consciousness. The intent is to protect their boundaries, which is not wrong intrinsically; but the means they adopt leaves them stuck at an arrested stage of development.

While healthy self-assertiveness requires the ability to say no, it is ultimately tested not by what we are against but by what we are for. A life that consists only of a string of negations is a waste and a tragedy. Self-assertiveness asks that we not only oppose what we deplore but that we live and express our values. In this respect, it is intimately tied to the issue of integrity.

Self-assertiveness begins with the act of thinking but must not end there. Self-assertiveness entails bringing ourselves into the world. To aspire is not yet self-assertion, or just barely; but to bring our aspirations into reality is. To hold values is not yet self-assertion, or just barely; to pursue them and stand by them in the world is. One of the great self-delusions is to think of oneself as "a valuer" or "an idealist" while not pursuing one's values in reality. To dream one's life away is not self-assertion; to be able to say, at the end, "While my life was happening, *I was there, I lived it*," is.

2. To practice self-assertiveness logically and consistently is to be committed to my right to exist, which proceeds from the knowledge that my life does not belong to others and that I am not here on earth to live up to someone else's expectations. To many people, this is a terrifying responsibility. It means their life is in their own hands. It means that Mother and Father and other authority figures cannot be counted on as protectors. It means they are responsible for their own existence—and

for generating their own sense of security. Not fear of this responsibility but *surrender to the fear* is a chief contributor to the subversion of self-esteem. If I will not stand up for my right to exist—my right to belong to myself—how can I experience a sense of personal dignity? How can I experience a decent level of self-esteem?

My life does not belong to others and I am not here on earth to live up to someone else's expectations.

To practice self-assertiveness consistently I need the conviction that my ideas and wants are important. Unfortunately, this conviction is often lacking. When we were young, many of us received signals conveying that what we thought and felt or wanted was *not* important. We were taught, in effect, "What you want isn't important; what's important is what *others* want." Perhaps we were intimidated by accusations of "selfishness" when we attempted to stand up for ourselves.

It often takes courage to honor what we want and to fight for it. For many people, self-surrender and self-sacrifice are far easier. They do not require the integrity and responsibility that intelligent selfishness requires.

A man of forty-eight who has worked hard for many years to support his wife and three children dreams of quitting his demanding and stressful job when he turns fifty and taking a job that will earn less money but that will afford him some of the leisure he has never permitted himself. He has always wanted more time to read, travel, and think, without the pressure of feeling he was neglecting some urgent matter at work. When he announces his intention at a family dinner, everyone becomes agitated and has only a single concern: How will each one's standard of living be affected if he takes a job that pays less money. No one shows interest in his context, needs, or feelings. "How can I stand against my family?" he asks himself. "Isn't a man's first duty to be a good provider?" He wants his family to think he is a good man, and if the price is to relinquish his own yearnings, he is willing to pay it. He does not even have to reflect about it. The habit of duty has been ingrained across a lifetime. In the space of one dinner conversation, he steps across a threshold into the beginning of old age. As a sop to the pain he cannot entirely bury, he tells himself, "At least I'm not selfish. Selfishness is evil—isn't it?"

The sad irony is that when people cease to honor or even attend to their deepest needs and wants, they sometimes become selfish not in the noble but in the petty sense, grasping at trivia after they have surrendered their deeper yearnings, rarely even knowing what they have betrayed and given up.

3. Within an organization, self-assertiveness is required not merely to have a good idea but to develop it, fight for it, work to win supporters for it, do everything within one's power to see that it gets translated into reality. It is the lack of this practice that causes so many potential contributions to die before they are born.

As a consultant, when I am asked to work with a team that has difficulty functioning effectively on some project, I often find that one source of the dysfunction is one or more people who do not really participate, do not really put themselves into the undertaking, because of some feeling that they do not have the power to make a difference, do not believe that their contribution can matter. In their passivity they became saboteurs. A project manager remarked to me, "I'd rather worry about handling some egomaniac who thinks he's the whole project than struggle with some self-doubting but talented individual whose insecurities stop him from kicking in what he's got to offer."

Without appropriate self-assertiveness, we are spectators, not participants. Healthy self-esteem asks that we leap into the arena—that we be willing to get our hands dirty.

4. Finally, self-assertion entails the willingness to confront rather than evade the challenges of life and to strive for mastery. When we expand the boundaries of our ability to cope, we expand self-efficacy and self-respect. When we commit ourselves to new areas of learning, when we take on tasks that stretch us, we raise personal power. We thrust ourselves further into the universe. We assert our existence.

When we are attempting to understand something and we hit a wall, it is an act of self-assertiveness to persevere. When we undertake to acquire new skills, absorb new knowledge, extend the reach of our mind across unfamiliar spaces—when we commit ourselves to moving to a higher level of competence—we are practicing self-assertiveness.

Healthy self-esteem asks that we leap into the arena—that we be willing to get our hands dirty.

When we learn how to be in an intimate relationship without abandoning our sense of self, when we learn how to be kind without being self-sacrificing, when we learn how to cooperate with others without betraying our standards and convictions, we are practicing self-assertiveness.

Fear of Self-Assertiveness

The American tradition is one of individualism, and some expressions of self-assertiveness are relatively more acceptable in the United States than in some other cultures. Not all cultures attach the value to the individual that we do. Not all cultures see equal merit in self-expression. Even in the United States, many forms of self-assertiveness are more acceptable for men than for women. Women are still often penalized when they practice the natural self-assertiveness that is their birthright as human beings.

In our society or any other, if one believes that it is more desirable to fit in than to stand out, one will not embrace the virtue of self-assertiveness. If one's primary source of safety and security is through affiliation with the tribe, the family, the group, the community, the company, the collective, then even self-esteem can be perceived as threatening and frightening—because it signifies individuation (self-realization, the unfolding of personal identity), therefore separateness.

Individuation raises the specter of isolation to those who have not achieved it and do not understand that far from being the enemy of community, it is its necessary precondition. A healthy society is a union of self-respecting individuals. It is not a coral bush.

A well-realized man or woman is one who has moved successfully along two lines of development that serve and complement each other: the track of individuation and the track of relationship. Autonomy, on the one hand; the capacity for intimacy and human connectedness, on the other.

Persons with an underdeveloped sense of identity often tell themselves, if I express myself, I may evoke disapproval. If I love and affirm myself, I may evoke resentment. If I am too happy with myself, I may evoke jealousy. If I stand out, I may be compelled to stand alone. They remain frozen in the face of such possibilities—and pay a terrible price in loss of self-esteem.

In this country psychologists understand such fears, which are very common, but we (some of us) tend to see them as evidence of immaturity. We say: Have the courage to be who you are. This sometimes brings us into conflict with spokespersons for other cultural perspectives. When I wrote about the challenges of individuation in *Honoring the Self*, a Hawaiian psychologist objected, saying, in effect, "How American!" He argued that his culture places a higher value on "social harmony."

While the term "individuation" is modern, the idea it expresses is at least as old as Aristotle. We think of the striving of the human being toward wholeness, toward completion, an internal thrust toward self-realization or self-actualization reminiscent of Aristotle's concept of entelechy. The thrust toward self-realization is intimately associated with our highest expressions of artistic and scientific genius. In the modern world, it is also associated with political freedom, with the liberation of humankind from centuries of servitude to one kind of tribe or another.

Examples

Some people stand and move as if they have no right to the space they occupy. Some speak as if their intention is that you not be able to hear them, either because they mumble or speak faintly or both. Some signal at the most crudely obvious level that they do not feel they have a right to exist. They embody lack of self-assertiveness in its most extreme form. Their poor self-esteem is obvious. In therapy, when such men and women learn to move and speak with more assurance, they invariably report (after some initial anxiety) a rise in self-esteem.

Not all manifestations of non-self-assertiveness are obvious. The average life is marked by thousands of unremembered silences, surrenders, capitulations, and misrepresentations of feelings and beliefs that corrode dignity and self-respect. When we do not express ourselves, do not assert our being, do not stand up for our values in contexts where it is appropriate to do so, we inflict wounds on our sense of self. The world does not do it to us—we do it to ourselves.

A young man sits alone in the darkness of a movie theater, deeply inspired by the drama unfolding before him. The story touches him so deeply that tears come to his eyes. He knows that in a week or so he will want to come back and see this film again. In the lobby he spots a friend who was at the same screening, and they greet each other. He searches his friend's face for clues to his feelings about the movie; but the face is blank. The friend inquires, "How'd you like the picture?" The young man feels an instant stab of fear; he does not want to appear "uncool." He does not want to say the truth—"I loved it. It touched me very deeply." So instead he shrugs indifferently and says, "Not bad." He does not know that he has just slapped his own face; or rather, he does not know it consciously. His diminished self-esteem knows it.

Some people stand and move as if they have no right to the space they occupy.

A woman is at a cocktail party where she hears someone make an ugly racial slur that causes her inwardly to cringe. She wants to say, "I found that offensive." She knows that evil gathers momentum by being un-contested. But she is afraid of evoking disapproval. In embarrassment she looks away and says nothing. Later, to appease her sense of uneasiness, she tells herself, "What difference does it make? The man was a fool." But her self-esteem knows what difference it makes.

A college student goes to a lecture given by a writer whose work the student greatly admires. Afterward, he joins the group who surround the writer with questions. He wants to say how much this woman's books mean to him, how much he has benefited from them, what a difference they have made in his life. But he remains silent, telling himself, "Of what importance would my reaction be to a famous writer?" She looks at him expectantly, but he remains awkwardly silent. He senses that if he spoke . . . who knows what might happen? Perhaps she would care. But fear wins, and he tells himself, "I don't want to be pushy."

A married woman hears her husband putting forth some view she regards as both misguided and objectionable. She struggles with an impulse to challenge him, to express her own idea. But she is afraid to "rock the boat" of their marriage, afraid her husband may withdraw approval if she disagrees with him. "A good wife," her mother had taught her, "supports her husband—right or wrong." She had once heard her minister declare in his Sunday sermon, "A woman's relationship to her husband should be as man's relationship to God." The memory of these voices still resonates in her mind. She remains silent, as she has remained silent on such occasions in the past, and does not realize that the root of her vague sense of guilt is the knowledge of her self-betrayal.

A Personal Example

I have already mentioned the relationship that I began with Ayn Rand a month before my twentieth birthday and that came to an explosive parting of the ways eighteen years later. Among the many benefits that I received from her in the early years, one was an experience of profound visibility. I felt understood and appreciated by her to an extent that was without precedent. What made her response so important was the high esteem in which I held her; I admired her enormously.

Only gradually did I realize that she did not tolerate disagreement well. Not among intimates. She did not require full agreement among acquaintances, but with anyone who wanted to be truly close, enormous enthusiasm was expected for every deed and utterance. I did not notice the steps by which I learned to censor negative reactions to some of her behavior—when, for example, I found her self-congratulatory remarks excessive or her lack of empathy disquieting or her pontificating unworthy of her. I did not give her the kind of corrective feedback everyone needs from time to time; in its absence we can become too insulated from reality, as she did.

In later years, after the break, I often reflected on why I did not speak up more often—I who was (at least relatively) freer with her than anyone else in our circle. The simple truth was, I valued her esteem too much to place it in jeopardy. I had, in effect, become addicted to it. It seems to me in retrospect that she had a genius for inspiring just such addictions by the subtlety, artistry, and astonishing insightfulness with which she could make people feel better understood and appreciated than they had ever felt before. I do not deny personal responsibility; no one can be seduced without consent. In exchange for the intoxicating gratification of being treated as a demigod by the person I valued above all others and whose good opinion I treasured above all others, I leashed my self-assertiveness in ways that over time were damaging to my self-regard.

The temptation to self-betrayal can sometimes be worst with those about whom we care the most.

In the end, I learned an invaluable lesson. I learned that surrenders of this kind do not work; they merely postpone confrontations that are inevitable and necessary. I learned that the temptation to self-betrayal can sometimes be worst with those about whom we care the most. I learned that no amount of admiration for another human being can justify sacrificing one's judgment.

Sentence Completions to Facilitate Self-Assertiveness

Here are sentence stems that can facilitate reaching a deeper understanding of self-assertiveness, as well as energizing its practice.

WEEK 1
Self-assertiveness to me means—
If I lived 5 percent more self-assertively today—
If someone had told me my wants were important—
If I had the courage to treat my wants as important—

WEEK 2
If I brought more awareness to my deepest needs and wants—
When I ignore my deepest yearnings—
If I were willing to say yes when I want to say yes and no when I want to say no—
If I were willing to voice my thoughts and opinions more often—

WEEK 3
When I suppress my thoughts and opinions—
If I am willing to ask for what I want—
When I remain silent about what I want—
If I am willing to let people hear the music inside me—

WEEK 4

If I am willing to let myself hear the music inside me—
If I am to express 5 percent more of myself today—
When I hide who I really am—
If I want to live more completely—

And on the weekend, after rereading the week's stems, write six to ten endings for **If any of what I have been writing is true, it might be helpful if I—**.

Of course there are other ways to work with these stems. In my self-esteem groups, for instance, we might work with all the stems on this list in one three-hour session, speaking our endings aloud, then discussing our endings and their action-implications.

Courage

Once again we can appreciate that the actions that support healthy self-esteem are also expressions of healthy self-esteem. Self-assertiveness both supports self-esteem and is a manifestation of it.

It is a mistake to look at someone who is self-assured and say, "It's easy for her to be self-assertive, she has good self-esteem." One of the ways we build self-esteem is by being self-assertive when it is not easy to do so. There are always times when self-assertiveness calls on our courage.

The practice of self-assertiveness is the fourth pillar of self-esteem.

10
The Practice of Living Purposefully

I have a friend in his late sixties who is one of the most brilliant and sought-after business speakers in the country. A few years ago he reconnected with a woman he had known and loved many years earlier, with whom he had been out of touch for three decades. She, too, was now in her sixties. They fell passionately in love.

Telling me about it one evening at dinner, my friend had never looked happier. It was wonderful to be with him and to see the look of rapture on his face. Thinking, perhaps, of the two divorces in his past, he said, wistfully and urgently, "God, I hope I handle things right this time. I want this relationship to succeed so much. I wish, I mean I want—I hope— you know, that I don't screw up." I was silent and he asked, "Got any advice?"

"Well, yes, I do," I answered. "If you want it to work, you must make it your *conscious purpose* that it work." He leaned forward intently, and I went on. "I can just imagine what your reaction would be if you were at IBM and some executive said, 'Gee, I *hope* we handle the marketing of this new product properly. I really want us to succeed with this, and I wish—' You'd be all over him in a minute saying, 'What is this *hope* stuff? What do you mean, you *wish?*' My advice is, apply what you know about the importance of purpose—and action plans—to your personal life. And leave 'hoping' and 'wishing' for children."

His elated smile said eloquently that he understood.

This leads me to the subject of living purposefully.

To live without purpose is to live at the mercy of chance—the chance event, the chance phone call, the chance encounter—because we have no standard by which to judge what is or is not worth doing. Outside forces bounce us along, like a cork floating on water, with no initiative of our own to set a specific course. Our orientation to life is reactive rather than proactive. We are drifters.

To live purposefully is to use our powers for the attainment of goals we have selected: the goal of studying, of raising a family, of earning a living, of starting a new business, of bringing a new product into the mar- ketplace, of solving a scientific problem, of building a vacation home, of sustaining a happy romantic relationship. It is our goals that lead us forward, that call on the exercise of our faculties, that energize our existence.

Productivity and Purpose

To live purposefully is, among other things, to live productively, which is a necessity of making ourselves competent to life. Productivity is the act of supporting our existence by translating our thoughts into reality, of setting our goals and working for their achievement, of bringing knowl- edge, goods, or services into existence.

Self-responsible men and women do not pass to others the burden of supporting their existence. It is not the degree of a person's productive ability that matters here but the person's choice to exercise such ability as he or she possesses. Nor is it the kind of work selected that is important, provided the work is not intrinsically antilife, but whether a person seeks work that offers an outlet for his or her intelligence, if the opportunity to do so exists.

Purposeful men and women set productive goals commensurate with their abilities, or try to. One of the ways their self-concept reveals itself is in the kind of purposes they set. Granted some deciphering may be necessary because of the complexities of private contexts, if we know the kind of goals people choose, we can know a good deal about their vision of themselves and about what they think is possible and appropriate to them.

Efficacy and Purpose

If self-esteem entails a basic experience of competence (or efficacy), what is the relationship of that competence to narrower, more localized areas of competence in particular areas?

We build our sense of fundamental efficacy through the mastery of particular forms of efficacy related to the attainment of particular tasks.

Fundamental efficacy cannot be generated in a vacuum; it must be created and expressed through some specific tasks successfully mastered. It is not that achievements "prove" our worth but rather that the process of achieving is the means by which we develop our effectiveness, our competence at living. I cannot be efficacious in the abstract without being efficacious about anything in particular. So, productive work has the potential of being a powerful self-esteem-building activity.

It is easier for people to understand these ideas as applied to work than to personal relationships. That may be why more people make a success of their work life than of their marriages.

The purposes that move us need to be specific if they are to be realized. I cannot organize my behavior optimally if my goal is merely "to do my best." The assignment is too vague. My goal needs to be: to exercise on the treadmill for thirty minutes four times a week; to complete my (precisely defined) task within ten days; to communicate to my team at our next meeting exactly what the project requires; to earn a specific sum of money in commissions by the end of the year; to achieve a specific market niche by a specific means by a specific target date. With such specificity, I am able to monitor my progress, compare intentions with results, modify my strategy or my tactics in response to new information, and be accountable for the results I produce.

To live purposefully is to be concerned with these questions: What am I trying to achieve? How am I trying to achieve it? Why do I think these means are appropriate? Does the feedback from the environment convey that I am succeeding or failing? Is there new information that I need to consider? Do I need to make adjustments in my course, or in my strategy, or in my practices? Do my goals and purposes need to be rethought? Thus, to live purposefully means to live at a high level of consciousness.

It is easier for people to understand these ideas as applied to work than to personal relationships. That may be why more people make a success of their work life than of their marriages. Everyone knows it is not enough to say "I love my work." One must show up at the office and do something. Otherwise, the business moves toward non-existence.

In intimate relationships, however, it is easy to imagine that "love" is enough, that happiness will just come, and if it doesn't, this means we are wrong for each other. People rarely ask themselves, "If my goal is to have a successful relationship, what must I do? What actions are needed to create and sustain trust, intimacy, continuing self-disclosure, excitement, growth?"

When a couple is newly married and very happy, it is useful to ask, "What is your action plan to sustain these feelings?"

If a couple is in conflict and professes a desire for resolution, it is useful to ask, "If restored harmony is your purpose, what actions are you prepared to take to bring it about? What actions do you desire from your partner? What do you see each of you doing to make things better?"

Purposes unrelated to a plan of action do not get realized. They exist only as frustrated yearnings.

Daydreams do not produce the experience of efficacy.

Self-Discipline

To live purposefully and productively requires that we cultivate within ourselves a capacity for self-discipline. Self-discipline is the ability to organize our behavior over time in the service of specific tasks. No one can feel competent to cope with the challenges of life who is without the capacity for self-discipline. Self-discipline requires the ability to defer immediate gratification in the service of a remote goal. This is the ability to project consequences into the future—to think, plan, and live long-range. Neither an individual nor a business can function effectively, let alone flourish, in the absence of this practice.

Like all virtues or practices that support self-esteem, self-discipline is a survival virtue—meaning that for human beings it is a requirement of the successful life process. One of the challenges of effective parenthood or effective teaching is to communicate a respect for the present that does not disregard the future, and a respect for the future that does not disregard the present. To master this balance is a challenge to all of us. It is essential if we are to enjoy the sense of being in control of our existence.

Perhaps I should mention that a purposeful, self-disciplined life does not mean a life without time or space for rest, relaxation, recreation, random or even frivolous activity. It merely means that such activities are chosen consciously, with the knowledge that it is safe and appropriate to engage in them. And in any event, the temporary abandonment of purpose also serves a purpose, whether consciously intended or not: that of regeneration.

What Living Purposefully Entails

As a way of operating in the world, the practice of living purposefully entails the following core issues.

Taking responsibility for formulating one's goals and purposes consciously.

Being concerned to identify the actions necessary to achieve one's goals.

Monitoring behavior to check that it is in alignment with one's goals.

Paying attention to the outcomes of one's actions, to know whether they are leading where one wants to go.

Taking responsibility for formulating one's goals and purposes consciously. If we are to be in control of our own life, we need to know what we want and where we wish to go. We need to be concerned with such questions as: What do I want for myself in five, ten, twenty years? What do I want my life to add up to? What do I want to accomplish professionally? What do I want in the area of personal relationships? If I wish to marry, why? What is my purpose? Within the context of a particular relationship, what are my goals? In relating to my children, what are my goals? If I have intellectual or spiritual aspirations, what are they? Are my goals clearly in focus or are they vague and indefinable?

Being concerned to identify the actions necessary to achieve one's goals. If our purposes are to be purposes and not daydreams, we need to ask: How do I get there from here? What actions are necessary? What subpurposes must be accomplished on the way to my ultimate purpose? If new knowledge is required, how will I obtain it? If new resources are needed, how will I acquire them? If our goals are long-range ones, action plans will almost certainly entail subaction plans—that is, plans for the attainment of subpurposes.

Do we take responsibility for thinking these steps out?

Success in life belongs to those who do.

Monitoring behavior to check that it is in alignment with one's goals. We can have clearly defined purposes and a reasonable action plan but drift off course by distractions, the emergence of unanticipated problems, the pull of other values, an unconscious reordering of priorities, lack of adequate mental focus, or resistance to doing what one has committed oneself to do. A conscious policy of monitoring actions relative to stated purposes helps us to manage problems of this kind. Sometimes the solution will be to rededicate ourselves to our original intentions. Sometimes we will need to rethink what our most important goals actually are and perhaps reformulate our purposes.

Paying attention to the outcomes of one's actions, to know whether they are leading where one wants to go. Our goals may be clear and our actions congruent, but our initial calculations about the right steps to take may prove incorrect. Perhaps there were facts we failed to consider. Perhaps developments have changed the context. So we need to keep asking: Are my strategy and tactics working? Am I getting where I want to go? Are my actions producing the results I anticipated?

We often see people in business failing this principle by blindly reciting, "But what we are doing always worked in the past." In a dynamic economy, yesterday's strategy and tactics are not necessarily adaptive today.

An example: Decades before the problems at General Motors became apparent to everyone, when the company was still at the height of its success, management consultant Peter Drucker warned that the policies that had worked well in the past would not be adaptive in the years to come and that General Motors was moving toward a crisis if it did not rethink its policies. He was met with ridicule and hostility by GM executives. Yet reality vindicated his analysis.

Our actions may fail to produce the consequences we intend, and they also may produce other consequences we did not foresee and do not want. They may work at one level and yet be undesirable at another. For example, incessant nagging and shouting may achieve short-term acquiescence while evoking long-term resentment and rebelliousness. A company may win quick profits by selling shoddy goods and destroy the business within a year as customers drift away. If we pay attention to outcomes, we are able to know not only whether we are achieving our goals but also what we might be achieving that we never intended and may not like.

Again, living purposefully entails living consciously.

Thinking Clearly About Purposeful Living

1. As an example of the confusions that can surround the issue of living purposefully, consider the extraordinary statement made by psychiatrist Irvin D. Yalom in his *Existential Psychotherapy*. He writes, "The belief that life is incomplete without goal fulfillment is not so much a tragic existential fact of life as it is a Western myth, a cultural artifact."

If there is anything we know it is that life is *impossible* without "goal fulfillment"—impossible on every level of evolution, from the amoeba to the human being. It is neither "a tragic existential fact" nor a "Western myth" but rather the simple nature of life—and often exhilarating.

The root of our self-esteem is not our achievements but those internally generated practices that, among other things, make it possible for us to achieve.

As a life orientation, the alternative to "goal fulfillment" is passivity and aimlessness. Is it a tragedy that such a state does not yield a joy equal to the joys of achievement?

Incidentally, let us remember that "goal fulfillment" is not confined to "worldly" goals. A life of study or meditation has its own kind of purposefulness—or it can have. But a life without purpose can hardly be said to be human.

2. To observe that the practice of living purposefully is essential to fully realized self-esteem should not be understood to mean that the measure of an individual's worth is his or her external achievements. We admire achievements—in others and in ourselves—and it is natural and appropriate for us to do so. But this is not the same thing as saying that our achievements are the measure or grounds of our self-esteem. The root of our self-esteem is not our achievements but those internally generated practices that, among other things, *make it possible for us to achieve*—all the self-esteem virtues we are discussing here.

Steel industrialist Andrew Carnegie once stated, "You can take away our factories, take away our trade, our avenues of transportation and our money—leave us with nothing but our organization—and in four years we could reestablish ourselves." His point was that power lies in the source of wealth, not in the wealth; in the cause, not the effect. The same principle applies to the relationship between self-esteem and external achievements.

3. Productive achievement may be an expression of high self-esteem, but it is not its primary cause. A person who is brilliantly talented and successful at work but irrational and irresponsible in his or her private life may *want* to believe that the sole criterion of virtue is productive performance and that no other sphere of action has moral or self-esteem significance. Such a person may hide behind work in order to evade feelings of shame and guilt stemming from other areas of life (or from painful childhood experiences), so that productive work becomes not so much a healthy passion as an avoidance strategy, a refuge from realities one feels frightened to face.

In addition, if a person makes the error of identifying self with his work (rather than with the internal virtues that make the work possible), if self-esteem is tied primarily to accomplishments, success, income, or being a good family provider, the danger is that economic circumstances beyond the individual's control may lead to the failure of the business or the loss of a job, flinging him into depression or acute demoralization. When a large airplane company closed a plant in one town, the suicide hot lines went crazy. (This problem is primarily one for males, who have been socialized to identify worth—and masculinity—with being a family's provider. Women are less prone to identify personal worth—let alone femininity—with earning ability.)

Some years ago, lecturing on this subject in Detroit, with members of the automotive industry in the audience, I made the following obser-vation: "Right now Washington is trying to decide whether to bail out Chrysler by guaranteeing a large loan. Never mind for the moment whether you think that's an appropriate government function; I don't think it is, but that's irrelevant. The point is, if you work for Chrysler and tie your self-esteem to being a high achiever in that company or to earning a good income this year, then what that means practically is that you are willing for some persons in Washington literally to hold your soul in their hands, to have total control over your sense of worth. Does that idea offend you? I hope so. It offends me."

It is bad enough, during economic hard times, to have to worry about money and our family's welfare and future, but it is still worse if we al-low our self-esteem to become undermined in the process—by telling ourselves, in effect, that our efficacy and worth are a function of our earnings.

On occasion I have counseled older men and women who found themselves unemployed, passed over in favor of people a good deal younger who were in no way better equipped, or even as well equipped, for the particular job. I have also worked with highly talented young people who suffered from a reverse form of the same prejudice, a discrimination against youth in favor of age—where, again, objective competence and ability were not the standard. In such circumstances, often those involved suffer a feeling of loss of personal effectiveness. Such a feeling is only a hairline away from a sense of diminished self-esteem—and often turns into it. It takes an unusual kind of person to avoid falling into the trap of this error. It takes a person who is already well centered and who understands that some of the forces operating are beyond personal control and, strictly speaking, do not have (or should not have) significance for self-esteem. It is not that they may not suffer or feel anxiety for the future; it is that they do not interpret the problem in terms of personal worth.

When a question of self-esteem is involved, the question to ask is: Is this matter within my direct, volitional control? Or is it at least linked by a direct line of causality to matters within my direct, volitional control? If it isn't, it is irrelevant to self-esteem and should be perceived to be, however painful or even devastating the problem may be on other grounds.

One day the teaching of this principle will be included in parents' understanding of proper child-rearing. One day it will be taught in the schools.

4. I asked a friend of mine, a businessman approaching sixty, what goals he had for the rest of his life. He answered, "I don't have any goals. All my life I've lived for the future, at the sacrifice of the present. I rarely stopped to enjoy my family or physical nature or any of the beautiful things the world has to offer. Now I don't think or plan ahead. I still manage my money, of course, and do occasional deals. But my primary goal is to enjoy life each day—to appreciate fully everything I can. In that sense I suppose you could say I'm still living purposefully."

It sounded, I told him, as if he had never learned how to balance projecting goals into the future with appreciating and living in the present. "That's always been a problem for me," he agreed.

As we have seen, this is not what living purposefully means or entails. It is appropriate to be blind neither to the future nor the present, but to integrate both into our experience and perceptions.

To the extent that our goal is to "prove" ourselves or to ward off the fear of failure, this balance is difficult to achieve. We are too driven. Not joy but anxiety is our motor.

But if our aim is self-expression rather than self-justification, the balance tends to come more naturally. We will still need to think about its daily implementation, but the anxiety of wounded self-esteem will not make the task nearly impossible.

Examples

All his life Jack dreamed of being a writer. He pictured himself at his typewriter, he visualized a growing stack of completed chapters, he saw his picture on the cover of *Time*. However, he was vague on what he wanted to write about. He could not have said what he wished to express. This did not disturb his pleasant reveries. He never thought about how to go about learning to write. In fact, he did not write. He merely daydreamed about writing. He drifted from one low-income job to another, telling himself he did not wish to be tied down or distracted, since his "real" profession was writing. The years went by and life seemed emptier and emptier. His fear of beginning to write escalated because now, by forty, he felt surely he should have begun. "Someday," he said. "When I'm ready." Looking at people around him, he told himself how mundane their lives were compared to his own. "They have no great visions," he thought. "No great dreams. My aspirations are so much higher than theirs."

Mary was an executive in an advertising agency. Her primary responsibilities were in marketing—developing new accounts. But she was a compassionate person, and she greatly enjoyed being helpful to those around her. She encouraged associates to drop into her office and talk about their problems; not only office problems but also personal ones. She enjoyed jokes to the effect that she was the "office shrink." She did not notice that a large amount of her time was drained in activities for which she had not been hired. She became agitated when her performance appraisal reflected dissatisfaction with her work. Yet she found it difficult to change her pattern; the ego-gratification of "helping others" had become addictive. Consequently, there was a poor match between her conscious work goals and her behavior—between her professed purposes and the allocation of her time. A goal she had not chosen consciously took precedence over one she had chosen consciously. Since she did not practice the discipline of monitoring her actions for just such a possibility, the full reality of her lapse did not penetrate her awareness—until she was fired.

Mark wanted to be an effective father. He wanted to teach his son self-respect and self-responsibility. He thought that a good way to achieve this was by lecturing to his son. He did not notice that the more he lectured the more intimidated and uncertain his son became. When the boy showed any kind of fear, the father said, "Don't be afraid!" When his son began to hide his feelings to avoid reproaches, the father said, "Speak up! If you've got something to say, say it!" As the son kept more and more to himself, the father said, "A real man participates in life!" The father wondered, "What's the matter with that boy? Why won't he ever listen to me?" In business, if the father tried something and it didn't work, he tried something else. He did not blame his customers or the universe; he looked for what he might do that would be more effective. He paid attention to the outcomes of his actions. At home, however, when neither lectures nor reproaches nor shouting worked, he did them more often and intensely. In this context he did not think of tracking the outcomes of his actions. What he knew in the professional realm he had forgotten in the personal: Doing more of what doesn't work doesn't work.

Personal Examples

When I think of what living purposefully means in my life, I think first of taking responsibility for generating the actions necessary to achieve my goals. Living purposefully overlaps significantly with self-responsibility.

I think of a time when I wanted something I could not afford that represented a significant improvement in my way of living. A fairly large expenditure of money was involved. For several years I remained uncharacteristically passive about finding a solution. Then one day I had a thought that certainly was not new to me and yet somehow had fresh impact: If I don't do something, nothing is going to change. This jolted me out of my procrastination, of which I had been dimly aware for a long time but had not confronted.

I proceeded to conceive and implement a project that was stimulating, challenging, profoundly satisfying and worthwhile—and that produced the additional income I needed.

In principle, I could have done it several years earlier. Only when I became bored and irritated with my own procrastination; only when I decided, "I commit myself to finding a solution over the next few weeks"; only when I applied what I know about living purposefully to my own situation—only then did I launch myself into action and toward a solution.

When I did, I noticed that not only was I happier but also that my self-esteem rose.

If I don't do something, nothing is going to change.

When I told this story in one of my self-esteem groups, I was challenged by someone who said, "That's okay for you. But not everyone is in a position to develop new projects. What are we to do?" I invited him to talk about his own procrastination and about the unfulfilled desire involved. "If you made it your *conscious purpose* to achieve that desire," I asked, "what might you do?" After a bit of good-natured prompting, he began to tell me.

Here is another personal example that involves self-discipline.

My wife, Devers, is exceptional in the degree of her benevolence, generosity, and kindness to other human beings and, above all, to me. Her consciousness—and consistency—in this aspect of life is very high. While my intentions have generally been good, I have never had her discipline in this area. My generosity has been more impulsive. This means that at times I could be unkind and uncompassionate without intention and without realizing it, simply from preoccupation.

One day, Devers said something that impressed me profoundly. "You are very kind, generous, and caring—when you stop long enough in what you are doing for it to occur to you. What you have never learned is *the discipline of kindness.* This means kindness that is not a matter of mood or convenience. It means kindness as a basic way of functioning. It is in you as a potential, but it doesn't happen without consciousness and discipline, which perhaps you've never thought about."

We had versions of this discussion more than once. An important step of my growth was when I integrated those discussions to the principle of living purposefully—*so that kindness became not merely an inclination but a conscious goal.*

For self-esteem, consistent kindness by intention is a very different experience from kindness by impulse.

Sentence-Completions to Facilitate Living Purposefully

Here are some stems that my clients find helpful in deepening their understanding of the ideas we have been discussing.

Living purposefully to me means—

If I bring 5 percent more purposefulness to my life today—

If I operate with 5 percent more purposefulness at work—

If I am 5 percent more purposeful in my communications—

If I bring 5 percent more purposefulness to my relationships at work—

If I operate 5 percent more purposefully in my marriage—

If I operate 5 percent more purposefully with my children—

If I operate 5 percent more purposefully with my friends—

If I am 5 percent more purposeful about my deepest yearnings—

If I am 5 percent more purposeful about taking care of my needs—

If I took more responsibility for fulfilling my wants—

If any of what I have been writing is true, it might be helpful if I—

Living purposefully is a fundamental orientation that applies to every aspect of our existence. It means that we live and act *by intention*. It is a distinguishing characteristic of those who enjoy a high level of control over their life.

The practice of living purposefully is the fifth pillar of self-esteem.

11

The Practice of Personal Integrity

As we mature and develop our own values and standards (or absorb them from others), the issue of personal integrity assumes increasing importance in our self-assessment.

Integrity is the integration of ideals, convictions, standards, beliefs— and behavior. When our behavior is congruent with our professed values, when ideals and practice match, we have integrity.

Observe that before the issue of integrity can even be raised we need principles of behavior—moral convictions about what is and is not appropriate—judgments about right and wrong action. If we do not yet hold standards, we are on too low a developmental rung even to be accused of hypocrisy. In such a case, our problems are too severe to be described merely as lack of integrity. Integrity arises as an issue only for those who profess standards and values, which, of course, is the great majority of human beings.

When we behave in ways that conflict with our judgment of what is appropriate, we lose face in our own eyes. We respect ourselves less. If the policy becomes habitual, we trust ourselves less or cease to trust ourselves at all.

No, we do not forfeit the right to practice self-acceptance in the basic sense discussed earlier; we have noted that self-acceptance is a precondition of change or improvement. But self-esteem necessarily suffers.

When a breach of integrity wounds self-esteem, only the practice of integrity can heal it.

When we behave in ways that conflict with our judgment of what is appropriate, we lose face in our own eyes.

At the simplest level, personal integrity entails such questions as: Am I honest, reliable, and trustworthy? Do I keep my promises? Do I do the things I say I admire and do I avoid the things I say I deplore? Am I fair and just in my dealings with others?

Sometimes we may find ourselves caught in a conflict between different values that clash in a particular context, and the solution may be far from self-evident. Integrity does not guarantee that we will make the best choice; it only asks that our effort to find the best choice be authentic— that we *stay conscious*, stay connected with our knowledge, call on our best rational clarity, take responsibility for our choice and its consequences, do not seek to escape into mental fog.

Congruence

Integrity means congruence. Words and behavior match.

There are people we know whom we trust and others we do not. If we ask ourselves the reason, we will see that congruence is basic. We trust congruency and are suspicious of incongruency.

Studies disclose that many people in organizations do not trust those above them. Why? Lack of congruence. Beautiful mission statements unsupported by practice. The doctrine of respect for the individual disgraced in action. Slogans about customer service on the walls unmatched by the realities of daily business. Sermons about honesty mocked by cheating. Promises of fairness betrayed by favoritism.

In most organizations, however, there are men and woman whom others trust. Why? They keep their word. They honor their commitments. They don't just promise to stick up for their people, they do it. They just don't preach fairness, they practice it. They don't just counsel honesty and integrity, they live it.

I gave a group of executives this sentence stem: **If I want people to** perceive me as trustworthy —. Here are typical endings: *"I must keep my word"; "I must be evenhanded in my dealings with everyone"; "I must walk my talk"; "I must follow through on my commitments"; "I must look after my people against the higher-ups"; "I must be consistent."* To any executive who wishes to be perceived as trustworthy, there is no mystery about what is required.

There are parents whom their children trust and there are parents whom their children do not trust. Why? The principle is the same as above: congruence. Children may not be able to articulate what they know, but they know.

When We Betray Our Standards

To understand why lapses of integrity are detrimental to self-esteem, consider what a lapse of integrity entails. If I act in contradiction to a moral value held by someone else but not by me, I may or may not be wrong, but I cannot be faulted for having betrayed my convictions. If, however, I act against what I myself regard as right, if my actions clash with my expressed values, then *I act against my judgment, I betray my mind.* Hypocrisy, by its very nature, is self-invalidating. It is mind rejecting itself. A default on integrity undermines me and contaminates my sense of self. It damages me as no external rebuke or rejection can damage me.

If I give sermons on honesty to my children yet lie to my friends and neighbors; if I become righteous and indignant when people do not keep their commitments to me but disregard my commitments to others; if I preach a concern with quality but indifferently sell my customers shoddy goods; if I unload bonds I know to be falling in value to a client who trusts my honor; if I pretend to care about my staff's ideas when my mind is already made up; if I outmaneuver a colleague in the office and appropriate her achievements; if I ask for honest feedback and penalize the employee who disagrees with me; if I ask for pay sacrifices from others on the grounds of hard times and then give myself a gigantic bonus—I may evade my hypocrisy, I may produce any number of rationalizations, but the fact remains I launch an assault on my self-respect that no rationalization will dispel.

If I am uniquely situated to raise my self-esteem, I am also uniquely situated to lower it.

One of the great self-deceptions is to tell oneself, "Only I will know."

Only I will know I am a liar; only I will know I deal unethically with people who trust me; only I will know I have no intention of honoring my promise. The implication is that *my judgment is unimportant and that only the judgment of others counts.* But when it comes to matters of self-esteem, I have more to fear from my own judgment than from anyone else's. In the inner courtroom of my mind, *mine is the only judgment that counts.* My ego, the "I" at the center of my consciousness, is the judge from whom there is no escape. I can avoid people who have learned the humiliating truth about me. I cannot avoid myself.

Most of the issues of integrity we face are not big issues but small ones, yet the accumulated weight of our choices has an impact on our sense of self.

I recall a news article I read some years ago about a medical researcher of high repute who was discovered to have been faking his data for a long time while piling up grant after grant and honor after honor. There was no way for self-esteem not to be a casualty of such behavior, even before the fakery was revealed. He knowingly chose to live in a world of unreality, where his achievements and prestige were equally unreal. Long before others knew, *he* knew. Impostors of this kind, who live for an illusion in someone else's mind, which they hold as more important than their own knowledge of the truth, do not enjoy good self-esteem.

Most of the issues of integrity we face are not big issues but small ones, yet the accumulated weight of our choices has an impact on our sense of self. I conduct weekly ongoing "self-esteem groups" for people who have come together for a specific purpose, to grow in self-efficacy and self-respect, and one evening I gave the group this sentence stem: **If I bring 5 percent more integrity into my life—**. As we went around the circle, here are the endings that were expressed:

If I bring 5 percent more integrity into my life—

I'd tell people when they do things that bother me.

I wouldn't pad my expense account.

I'd be truthful with my husband about what my clothes cost.

I'd tell my parents I don't believe in God.

I'd admit it when I'm flirting.

I wouldn't be so ingratiating to people I dislike.

I wouldn't laugh at jokes I think stupid and vulgar.

I'd put in more of an effort at work.

I'd help my wife more with chores, as I promised.

I'd tell customers the truth about what they're buying.

I wouldn't just say what people want to hear.

I wouldn't sell my soul to be popular.

I'd say no when I want to say no.

I would acknowledge my responsibility to people I've hurt.

I'd make amends.

I'd keep my promises.

I wouldn't pretend agreement.

I wouldn't deny it when I'm angry.

I'd make more of an effort to be fair and not just fly off the handle.

I'd admit it when others have helped me.

I'd admit it to my children when I know I'm wrong.

I wouldn't take supplies home from the office.

The ease and speed of people's responses point to the fact that these matters are not very far beneath the surface of awareness, although there is understandable motivation to evade them. (One of the reasons I find sentence-completion work so useful is its power to bypass most blocks and avoidances.) A tragedy of many lives is that people greatly underestimate the self-esteem costs and consequences of hypocrisy and dishonesty. They imagine that at worst all that is involved is some discomfort. But it is the spirit itself that is contaminated.

Dealing with Guilt

The essence of guilt, whether major or minor, is moral self-reproach. I did wrong when it was possible for me to do otherwise. Guilt always carries the implication of choice and responsibility, whether or not we are consciously aware of it. For this reason, it is imperative that we be clear on what is and is not in our power—what is and is not a breach of integrity. Otherwise, we run the risk of accepting guilt inappropriately.

The idea of Original Sin is anti-self-esteem by its very nature.

For example, suppose someone we love—a husband, a wife, a child—is killed in an accident. Even though we may know the thought is irrational, we may tell ourselves, "Somehow I should have prevented it." Perhaps this guilt is fed in part by our regrets over actions taken or not taken while the person was alive. In the case of deaths that seem senseless, such as when a person is hit by a careless automobile driver or dies during minor surgery, the survivor may experience an unbearable feeling of being out of control, of being at the mercy of an event that has no rational significance. Then self-blame or self-reproach can ameliorate the anguish, can diminish a sense of impotence. The survivor feels, "If only I had done such and such differently, this terrible accident would not have occurred." Thus, "guilt" can serve the desire for efficacy by providing an *illusion* of efficacy. We see the same principle when children blame themselves for their parents' wrongdoing. ("If I weren't bad, Daddy wouldn't have hit Mommy." "If I weren't bad, Mommy wouldn't have gotten drunk and set the house on fire.") This problem is examined in *Honoring the Self.*

The protection of self-esteem requires a clear understanding of the limits of personal responsibility. Where there is no power, there can be no responsibility, and where there is no responsibility, there can be no reasonable self-reproach. Regret, yes; guilt, no.

The idea of Original Sin—of guilt where there is no possibility of innocence, no freedom of choice, no alternatives available—is anti-self-esteem by its very nature. The very notion of guilt without volition or responsibility is an assault on reason as well as on morality.

Let us think about guilt and how it can be resolved in situations where we *are* personally responsible. Generally speaking, five steps are needed to restore one's sense of integrity with regard to a particular breach.

1. We must own the fact that it is we who have taken the particular action. We must face and accept the full reality of what we have

done, without disowning or avoidance. We own, we accept, we take responsibility.

2. We seek to understand why we did what we did. We do this compassionately (as discussed under the practice of self-acceptance), but without evasive alibiing.

3. If others are involved, as they often are, we acknowledge explicitly to the relevant person or persons the harm we have done. We convey our understanding of the consequences of our behavior. We acknowledge how they have been affected by us. We convey understanding of their feelings.

4. We take any and all actions available that might make amends for or minimize the harm we have done.

5. We firmly commit ourselves to behaving differently in the future.

Without all these steps, we may continue to feel guilty over some wrong behavior, even though it happened years ago, even though our psychotherapist might have told us everyone makes mistakes, and even though the wronged person may have offered forgiveness. None of that may be enough; self-esteem remains unsatisfied.

Sometimes we try to make amends without ever owning or facing what we have done. Or we keep saying "I'm sorry." Or we go out of our way to be nice to the person we have wronged without ever addressing the wrong explicitly. Or we ignore the fact that there are specific actions we could take to undo the harm we have caused. Sometimes, of course, there is no way to undo the harm, and we must accept and make our peace with that; we cannot do more than what is possible. But if we do not do what is possible and appropriate, guilt tends to linger on.

When guilt is a consequence of failed integrity, nothing less than an act of integrity can redress the breach.

What If Our Values Are Irrational?

While it is easy enough to recognize at a commonsense level the relationship between self-esteem and integrity, the issue of living up to our standards is not always simple. What if our standards are irrational or mistaken?

We may accept or absorb a code of values that does violence to our nature and needs. For example, certain religious teachings implicitly or explicitly damn sex, damn pleasure, damn the body, damn ambition, damn material success, damn (for all practical purposes) the enjoyment of life on earth. If children are indoctrinated with these teachings, what will the practice of "integrity" mean in their lives? Some elements of "hypocrisy" may be all that keeps them alive.

Once we see that living up to our standards appears to be leading us toward self-destruction, the time has come to question our standards.

Once we see that living up to our standards appears to be leading us toward self-destruction, the time has come to question our standards rather than simply resigning ourselves to living without integrity. We must summon the courage to challenge some of our deepest assumptions concerning what we have been taught to regard as the good. That courage may be needed is evident in the following sentence completions commonly heard in my therapy practice. Any psychotherapist who cares to experiment with these stems can discover for him- or herself how typical these endings are.

At the thought of going against my parents' values—

I feel frightened.

I feel lost.

I see myself as an outcast.

I no longer belong with my family.

I feel alone.

I'd have to think for myself.

I'd have to rely on my own mind.

What would I do then?

I'd lose my parents' love.

I'd have to grow up.

If I were to think for myself about the values I want to live by—

Mother would have a heart attack.

I'd be free.

I'd have to tell my parents I think they're wrong about a lot of things.

Is this what grown-ups do?

I'd need an awful lot of nerve.

Wouldn't that be arrogant?

I'd have to stand on my own feet.

I couldn't be Daddy's little girl anymore.

As examples of the confusion and conflict about what the practice of integrity might mean in daily living, I offer the following:

Women who struggle with the moral dilemmas created by the Catholic church's prohibition of birth control devices and abortion.

Employees in government agencies who, appalled by the magnitude of bureaucratic corruption among colleagues and superiors, feel themselves caught in conflict between their notion of patriotism and good citizenship on the one hand and the demands of individual conscience on the other.

Hard-working, ambitious businessmen who had been encouraged at the start of their careers to be productive and industrious but who, when they finally committed the sin of succeeding, were confronted with the disorienting biblical pronouncement that it shall be easier for a camel to pass through the eye of a needle than for a rich man to enter the kingdom of heaven.

Wives who sense that the traditional view of woman-as-servant-to-man is a morality of self-annihilation.

Young men struggling with the dilemma of complying with or fleeing from military conscription.

Former nuns and priests disenchanted with the religious institutions to which they had given their allegiance and striving to define their values outside the context of a tradition they can no longer accept.

Rabbis or former rabbis with precisely the same problem.

Young persons rebelling against the values of their parents and not knowing what vision of the good to live by instead.

In such conflicts we see how essential are other practices, such as living consciously and self-responsibly, to integrity. We cannot practice integrity in an intellectual vacuum.

To resolve any of the conflicts listed above, or countless others like them, one would have to rethink one's deepest values, commitments, and priorities—or perhaps think about them for the first time—and be willing, if necessary, to challenge any and all authorities.

One of the most positive aspects of the women's movement is its insistence that women think for themselves about who they are and what they want. But men need to learn this kind of independent thinking as much as women do.

One area in which living consciously and integrity clearly intersect is in the need to reflect on the values we have been taught, the shared assumptions of our family or culture, the roles we may have been assigned—and to question whether they fit our own perceptions and understanding, or whether they do violence to the deepest and best within us, to what is sometimes called "our true nature." One of the most positive aspects of the women's movement, as I see it, is its insistence that women think for themselves about who they are, what is possible and appropriate to them, and what they want (not what someone else wants them to want). But men need to learn this kind of independent thinking as much as women do. One of the penalties for living unconsciously— for both sexes—is that of enduring unrewarding lives in the service of self-stultifying ends never examined or chosen with awareness by the individuals involved.

The higher the level of consciousness at which we operate, the more we live by explicit *choice* and the more naturally does integrity follow as a consequence.

On Following Your Own Bliss

Discussing the complexities of moral decision making in a lecture once, I was asked what I thought of Joseph Campbell's counsel to "Follow your own bliss." Did I believe it was ethically appropriate? I answered that while I liked what I believed to be Campbell's basic intention, his statement could be dangerous if divorced from a rational context. I suggested this modification (if I were forced to condense my ideas on morality into a single sentence): "Live consciously—take responsibility for your choices and actions—respect the rights of others—and follow your own bliss." I added that as a piece of moral advice I loved the Spanish proverb " 'Take what you want,' said God, 'and pay for it.' " But of course complex moral decisions cannot be made simply on the basis of statements such as these, helpful though they may sometimes be. A moral life requires serious reflection.

Examples

Philip is the close friend of a famous actor. He is the actor's confidant. He listens emphatically when his friend calls him—sometimes in the middle of the night   to talk for hours about his personal and professional troubles. Philip's feelings of self-worth are nurtured by the intimacies this famous man shares with him. When he is with his other friends, Philip can not resist dropping remarks from time to time that stress the closeness of their connection. "I know millions of women adore him, but you'd be surprised at how insecure he is. He's always asking, 'Is it me they want, or my fame?' " "He has this awful feeling of being an impostor. Isn't that sad? He's such a wonderful person." "Sometimes—this is confidential, of course—he has trouble maintaining his erection." Philip insists that he loves his friend and is absolutely loyal. What does he tell himself, at three o'clock in the morning, about his dozens of betrayals, generated by his craving for status in the eyes of his other friends? Does he notice that each such betrayal lowers rather than raises his self-esteem? Does he make the connection?

Sally is a member of a book club whose monthly meetings she attends enthusiastically. They support her desire to feel cultured. The chairwoman is a charismatic, highly knowledgeable person whom everyone admires. Most of the women feel proud when she shares their literary assessments. They want to be on her "good side," because that enhances their feelings of personal worth. One day the chairwoman has a falling out with a member of the club, someone who had been a good friend of Sally's for years. No one knows what the dispute is about. The chairwoman chooses not to discuss its content except in very general terms. But she arranges for everyone to know that this person, who has dropped out of the club, is *persona non grata*. Now, no one wants to be known to be talking to her. When the woman telephones Sally, eager to discuss her perspective on the conflict, Sally finds an excuse to put her off. She is afraid that if she hears her friend's position and is moved by it, she will be flung into an impossible conflict. She does not want to lose status with her other friends or with the chairwoman. So she does not return her friend's phone calls. Inside her mind she begins to find more and more fault with her friend. Soon she is airing her own list of grievances, which she had never spoken of in the past. Her reward is the smile of approval on the chairwoman's face and their subsequent increased intimacy. She is aware of the reward but not comparably aware of its cost: diminished self-respect.

Until his electronics company begins to suffer from foreign competition, Irving was always an advocate of free trade. He scorned businessmen who sought the aid of government to grant them special privileges, favors, or various forms of protection. "That's not true capitalism," he said, correctly. Now he is frightened; he knows his products are not as good as those of his foreign competitors, who keep bringing innovation after innovation into the marketplace. He engages a public relations firm to help him write speeches favoring government restrictions on imports that threaten him. He hires a firm in Washington to lobby for legislation that would protect him. When associates try to point out that protected industries have a history of remaining permanently weak, he brushes their observations aside. He does not want to think about that; consciousness in this area has become irritating. "This is different," he asserts without explaining how or in what way. When he is told that people should be free to buy the best product available for the money, he answers righteously and irrelevantly, "Capitalism must be tempered by concern for the common good." When he is challenged with the observation that he buys foreign goods when they are superior to domestic, he answers, "Don't I have the right to get the best for my money?" When he is invited to give the commencement address at the university from which he graduated, he chooses as his theme "Living with Integrity."

A Personal Example

I have said that moral decisions are not always easy and that sometimes, rightly or wrongly, we experience our choices as agonizingly complex and difficult.

Many years ago I was married to a woman I was very attached to but no longer loved; my romance with Ayn Rand was fading but not "officially" terminated. Both relationships were painfully unresolved when I met and fell passionately in love with a third woman I would later marry: Patrecia, who would die at the age of thirty-seven. For a long time my mind was a chaos of conflicting loyalties, and I handled things very badly. I did not tell the truth to my wife or to Ayn as soon as I could have—never mind the reasons. "Reasons" do not alter facts.

=====

Lies do not work.

=====

It was a long road, but at its end was painfully acquired knowledge I had possessed at the beginning—that the truth had to be told and that by procrastinating and delaying I merely made the consequences for everyone more terrible. I succeeded in protecting no one, least of all myself. If part of my motive was to spare people I cared about, I inflicted a worse pain than they would otherwise have experienced. If part of my motive was to protect my self-esteem by avoiding a conflict among my values and loyalties, it was my self-esteem that I damaged. Lies do not work.

Sentence Completions to Facilitate the Practice of Integrity

If we examine our lives, we may notice that our practice of integrity exhibits inconsistencies. There are areas where we practice it more and areas where we practice it less. Rather than evade this fact, it is useful to explore it. It is worthwhile to consider: What stands in the way of my practicing integrity in every area of my life? What would happen if I lived my values consistently?

Here are sentence stems that can aid the process of exploration:

Integrity to me means—

If I think about the areas where I find it difficult to practice full integrity—

If I bring a higher level of consciousness to the areas where I find it difficult to practice full integrity—

If I bring 5 percent more integrity into my life—

If I bring 5 percent more integrity to my work—

If I bring 5 percent more integrity to my relationships—
If I remain loyal to the values I truly believe are right—
If I refuse to live by values I do not respect—
If I treat my self-esteem as a high priority—

A suggestion: Work with the first four of these stems for the first week, and the second four the following week. On the weekends work with the stem: **If any of what I am writing is true, it might be helpful if I—**. If you choose to bring a high level of awareness to what you produce, you may discover that living with greater integrity has become more realizable.

A Practical Application

"Do you think padding my expense account is really so awful?" a client asked me. "Everyone does it."

"I imagine," I said to him, "that something about it must disturb you or you wouldn't have brought it up."

"I've been doing these stems, 'If I bring 5 percent more integrity into my life,' and the other day when I began to fill out my expense sheet with padded items, I don't know, it didn't feel comfortable, it felt wrong."

"Lying gave you a bad feeling," I remarked.

"Yes, so I filled it out truthfully, and then, later, I wondered if I wasn't a sucker."

"You wondered, why be concerned with my integrity if other people aren't concerned with theirs?"

"Hell, no, if I'd thought about it like that, I'd—" He broke off and stared thoughtfully into space.

"What?"

"What you just said is what it all really comes to, doesn't it?"

"And if so, the question that naturally arises is: Do I take a poll on what I'll call acceptable behavior?"

"But I think lying about my expenses is *wrong!*" he said, almost perplexed.

"So, then, what's the question . . . ?"

"When I do something I think is wrong, it leaves, you know, a bad taste."

"I wonder what policy you'll adopt for the future."

"I feel cleaner when I'm honest."

"So you're saying, from the perspective of self-esteem, honesty is the best policy?"

"That's what it's looking like."

"I think that's a fairly important observation."

Keeping Your Integrity in a Corrupt World

In a world where we regard ourselves and are regarded by others as accountable for our actions, the practice of integrity is relatively easier than in a world where the principle of personal accountability is absent. A culture of accountability tends to support our moral aspirations.

The challenge for people today, and it is not an easy one, is to maintain high personal standards while feeling that one is living in a moral sewer.

If we live in a society where business associates, corporate heads, political figures, religious leaders, and other public personalities hold themselves to high standards of morality, it is relatively easier for an average person to practice integrity than in a society where corruption, cynicism, and amorality are the norm. In the latter kind of society, the individual is likely to feel that the quest for personal integrity is futile and unrealistic—unless he or she is extraordinarily independent and autonomous.

The challenge for people today, and it is not an easy one, is to maintain high personal standards while feeling that one is living in a moral sewer. Grounds for such a feeling are to be found in the behavior of our public figures, the horror of world events, and in our so-called art and entertainment, so much of which celebrates depravity, cruelty, and mindless violence. All contribute to making the practice of personal integrity a lonely and heroic undertaking.

If integrity is a source of self-esteem, then it is also, and never more so than today, an *expression* of self-esteem.

The Principle of Reciprocal Causation

Indeed, this leads to an important question. About all six pillars it might be asked, "To practice them, does one not need already to possess self-esteem? How then can they be the foundation of self-esteem?"

In answering, I must introduce what I call *the principle of reciprocal causation*. By this I mean that behaviors that generate good self-esteem are also expressions of good self-esteem. Living consciously is both a cause and an effect of self-efficacy and self-respect. And so is self-acceptance, self-responsibility, all the other practices I describe.

The more I live consciously, the more I trust my mind and respect my worth; and if I trust my mind and respect my worth, it feels natural to live consciously. The more I live with integrity, the more I enjoy good self-esteem; and if I enjoy good self-esteem, it feels natural to live with integrity.

Another noteworthy aspect of the dynamics involved here is that the practice of these virtues over time tends to generate a felt need for them. If I habitually operate at a high level of consciousness, unclarity and fog in my awareness will make me uncomfortable: I will usually experience a drive to dispel the darkness. If I have made self-responsibility second nature, passivity and dependency will be onerous to me. I will experience internal pressure to reassert the control over my existence possible only with autonomy. If I have been consistent in my integrity, I will experience dishonesty on my part as disturbing and will feel a thrust to resolve the dissonance and restore the inner sense of moral cleanliness.

Once we understand the practices I have described, we have the power (at least to some extent) to choose them. The power to choose them is the power to raise the level of our self-esteem, from whatever point we may be starting and however difficult the project may be in the early stages.

An analogy to physical exercise may be helpful. If we are in poor physical condition, exercise is typically difficult; as our condition improves, exercise becomes easier and more enjoyable. We begin where we are—and build our strength from there. Raising self-esteem follows the same principle.

These practices are ideals to guide us. And—this can hardly be overemphasized—they do not have to be lived "perfectly" 100 percent of the time in order to have a beneficent impact on our lives. Small improvements make a difference.

It might strike the reader, reflecting on this list of self-esteem practices, that they sound very much like a code of ethics—or part of one. That is true. The virtues that self-esteem asks of us are also ones that life asks of us.

The practice of personal integrity is the sixth pillar of self-esteem.

12

The Philosophy of Self-Esteem

To the extent that the six practices are integrated into our daily life, self-esteem is supported and strengthened. To the extent that they are not, self-esteem is undermined and subverted. This is the central thesis of Part II thus far. But what of an individual's beliefs, premises, ideas? Is it only practices that matter or do convictions also play a role in supporting self-esteem?

The answer is that convictions are important because they give rise to emotions and actions (practices). They are a crucial factor in the development of an individual's self-esteem. What people think, what they believe, what they tell themselves, influences what they feel and what they do. In turn, they experience what they feel and do as having meaning for who they are.

Part II began with a chapter entitled "The Focus on Action." Action has the last word, in that no living value can be achieved or sustained without it. Beliefs in a vacuum, beliefs divorced from action, mean nothing. But since beliefs do affect actions, since beliefs have action implications, we need to examine them in their own right.

There are beliefs that lead toward the practices I have been describing, and there are beliefs that lead away from them. When I speak of "beliefs" in this context, I mean convictions deeply grounded in our being. I do not mean notions to which we pay lip service or ideas we tell ourselves in the hope they will spark desired motivation. I mean premises that have the power to evoke emotion and to stimulate and guide behavior.

We are not always fully conscious of our beliefs. They may not exist in our minds as explicit propositions. They may be so implicit in our thinking that we are hardly aware of them or not aware of them at all. Yet they clearly lie behind our actions.

We can think of these ideas as "the philosophy of self-esteem"—a set of interrelated premises that inspire behaviors leading to a strong sense of efficacy and worth. We can also see in them an explication, in outline form, of the basic philosophy driving this book.

I place beliefs that have a bearing on self-esteem into two categories: beliefs about self and beliefs about reality. In each case the relevance of the idea to self-esteem is obvious.

Beliefs About the Self That Support Self Esteem

General

I have a right to exist.

I am of high value to myself.

I have a right to honor my needs and wants, to treat them as important.

I am not here on earth to live up to someone else's expectations; my life belongs to me. (And this is equally true of every other human being. Each person is the owner of his or her life; no one is here on earth to live up to my expectations.)

I do not regard myself as anyone else's property and I do not regard anyone else as my property.

I am lovable.

I am admirable.

I will usually be liked and respected by the people I like and respect.

I should deal with others fairly and justly and others should deal with me fairly and justly.

I deserve to be treated courteously and with respect by everyone.

If people treat me discourteously or disrespectfully, it is a reflection on them, not on me. It is only a reflection on me if I accept their treatment of me as right.

If someone I like does not return my feeling, it may be disappointing or even painful, but it is not a reflection on my personal worth.

No other individual or group has the power to determine how I will think and feel about myself.

I trust my mind.

I see what I see and know what I know.

I am better served by knowing what is true than by making myself "right" at the expense of the facts.

If I persevere, I can understand the things I need to understand.

No other individual or group has the power to determine how I will think and feel about myself.

If I persevere, and if my goals are realistic, I am competent to achieve them.

I am competent to cope with the basic challenges of life.

I am worthy of happiness.

I am "enough." (This does not mean that I have nothing more to learn and nowhere further to grow; it means that I have the right to primary self-acceptance, as discussed earlier.)

I am able to rise again from defeat.

I have a right to make mistakes; that is one of the ways I learn. Mistakes are not grounds for self-damnation.

I do not sacrifice my judgment, do not pretend my convictions are different than they are, to win popularity or approval.

It is not what "they" think; it is what I know. What I know is more important to me than a mistaken belief in someone else's mind.

No one has the right to force on me ideas and values I do not accept, just as I do not have the right to force my ideas and values on others.

If my goals are rational, I deserve to succeed at what I attempt.

Happiness and success are natural conditions to me—like health—not temporary aberrations of the real order of things; as with disease, it is disaster that is the aberration.

Self-development and self-fulfillment are appropriate moral goals.

My happiness and self-realization are noble purposes.

Living Consciously

The more conscious I am of that which bears on my interests, values, needs, and goals, the better my life will work.

It is joyful to exercise my mind.

I am better served by correcting my mistakes than by pretending they do not exist.

I am better served by holding my values consciously than unconsciously—and by examining them rather than by holding them uncritically as not-to-be-questioned "axioms."

I need to be on the lookout for temptations to evade unpleasant facts; I need to manage my avoidance impulses and not be ruled by them.

If I understand the wider context in which I live and act, I will be more effective; it is worth my while to seek to understand my environment and the wider world around me.

To remain effective, I need to keep expanding my knowledge; learning needs to be a way of life.

The better I know and understand myself, the better the life I can create. Self-examination is an imperative of a fulfilled existence.

Self-Acceptance

At the most fundamental level, I am for myself.

At the most fundamental level, I accept myself.

I accept the reality of my thoughts, even when I cannot endorse them and would not choose to act on them; I do not deny or disown them.

I can accept my feelings and emotions without necessarily liking, approving of, or being controlled by them; I do not deny or disown them.

I can accept that I have done what I have done, even when I regret or condemn it. I do not deny or disown my behavior.

I accept that what I think, feel, or do is an expression of myself, at least in the moment it occurs. I am not bound by thoughts, feelings, or actions I cannot sanction, but neither do I evade their reality or pretend they are not mine.

I accept the reality of my problems, but I am not defined by them. My problems are not my essence. My fear, pain, confusion, or mistakes are not my core.

At the most fundamental level, I am for myself.

Self-Responsibility

I am responsible for my existence.

I am responsible for the achievement of my desires.

I am responsible for my choices and actions.

I am responsible for the level of consciousness I bring to my work and other activities.

I am responsible for the level of consciousness I bring to my relationships.

I am responsible for my behavior with other people—co-workers, associates, customers, spouse, children, friends.

I am responsible for how I prioritize my time.

I am responsible for the quality of my communications.

I am responsible for my personal happiness.

I am responsible for choosing or accepting the values by which I live.

I am responsible for raising my self-esteem; no one else can give me self-esteem.

In the ultimate sense, I accept my aloneness. That is, I accept that no one is coming to make my life right, or save me, or redeem my childhood, or rescue me from the consequences of my choices and actions. In specific issues, people may help me, but no one can take over primary responsibility for my existence. Just as no one else can breathe for me, no one else can take over any of my other basic life functions, such as earning the experience of self-efficacy and self-respect.

The need for self-responsibility is natural; I do not view it as a tragedy.

Self-Assertiveness

In general, it is appropriate for me to express my thoughts, convictions, and feelings, unless I am in a context where I judge it objectively desirable not to.

I have a right to express myself in appropriate ways in appropriate contexts.

I have a right to stand up for my convictions.

I have a right to treat my values and feelings as important.

It serves my interests for others to see and know who I am.

Living Purposefully

Only I properly can choose the goals and purposes for which I live. No one else can appropriately design my existence.

If I am to succeed, I need to learn how to achieve my goals and purposes. I need to develop and then implement a plan of action.

If I am to succeed, I need to pay attention to the outcome of my actions.

I serve my interests by a high degree of reality checking—that is, looking for information and feedback that bears on my beliefs, actions, and purposes.

I must practice self-discipline not as a "sacrifice" but as a natural precondition of being able to achieve my desires.

Personal Integrity

I should practice what I preach.

I should keep my promises.

I should honor my commitments.

I should deal with other human beings fairly, justly, benevolently, and compassionately.

I should strive for moral consistency.

My self-esteem is more valuable than any short-term rewards for its betrayal.

I should strive to make my life a reflection of my inner vision of the good.

My self-esteem is more valuable than any short-term rewards for its betrayal.

Beliefs About Reality That Support Self-Esteem

That which is, is; a fact is a fact.

Self-chosen blindness does not make the unreal real or the real unreal.

Respect for the facts of reality (as best I understand them) yields more satisfying results than defiance of the facts of reality.

Survival and well-being depend on the appropriate exercise of consciousness. Avoidance of the responsibility of awareness is not adaptive.

In principle, consciousness is reliable; knowledge is attainable; reality is knowable.

Values that nurture and support the individual's life and fulfillment on earth are superior to values that endanger or threaten them.

Human beings are ends in themselves, not means to the ends of others, and ought to be treated as such. An individual human being belongs neither to family nor community nor church nor state nor society nor the world. A human being is not property.

All adult human associations should be chosen and voluntary.

We should not sacrifice self to others nor others to self; we should discard the idea of human sacrifice as a moral ideal.

Relationships based on an exchange of values are superior to those based on the sacrifice of anyone to anyone.

A world in which we regard ourselves and one another as accountable for our choices and actions works better than a world in which we deny such accountability.

A denial of personal accountability does not serve anyone's self-esteem, least of all the person doing the denying.

The moral, rationally understood, is the practical.

Commentary

To say of any of these ideas, "I agree with that," does not yet indicate that it is integral to the speaker's belief system. As I stated above, the ideas qualify as beliefs in the sense meant here only if they are experienced as true at a fairly deep level and are manifest in behavior.

This list of beliefs is not offered as exhaustive. Probably there are others that bear equally on the health of self-esteem. What I have named are those I am aware of that most clearly support the six practices. To the extent that they are genuinely experienced, they tend to inspire consciousness, self-acceptance, self-responsibility, self-assertiveness, purposefulness, and integrity.

I trust it is obvious that I regard these beliefs as rationally warranted. They are not mere arbitrary "postulates." But since I am not prepared in this context to offer a rigorous defense of each of them, I will simply observe that they are powerful motivators for the kind of actions that support psychological well-being. Looked at from the perspective of the six pillars, they clearly have functional utility. They are adaptive; they are the fuel of self-esteem.

A Standard of Value

Just as the six pillars provides a frame of reference from which to consider beliefs, so they provide a standard by which to consider child-rearing practices, educational practices, the policies of organizations, the value systems of different cultures, and the activities of psychotherapists. In each context we can ask: Is this practice, policy, value, or teaching one that supports and encourages the six pillars or one that discourages and undermines them? Is it more likely to lead toward increased self-esteem or away from it?

I do not wish to imply that self-esteem is the only criterion by which issues should be judged. But if the nurturing of self-esteem is our purpose, then it is appropriate to know how self-esteem is likely to be affected by different policies and teachings.

The practices and beliefs we have discussed pertain to "internal" factors that bear on self-esteem; that is, they exist or are generated from within the individual. We will turn now to an examination of "external" factors, that is, factors originating in the environment.

What is the role and contribution of other people? What is the potential impact of parents, teachers, managers, psychotherapists—and the culture in which one lives? These are the questions I will address in Part III.

PART III

External
Influences:
Self and Others

13

Nurturing a Child's Self-Esteem

The proper aim of parental nurturing is to prepare a child for independent survival as an adult. An infant begins in a condition of total dependency. If his or her upbringing is successful, the young man or woman will have evolved out of that dependency into a self-respecting and self-responsible human being who is able to respond to the challenges of life competently and enthusiastically. He or she will be "self-supporting"—not merely financially, but intellectually and psychologically.

A newborn infant does not yet have a sense of personal identity; there is no awareness of separateness, not, at any rate, as we who are adults experience such awareness. To evolve into selfhood is the primary human task. It is also the primary human challenge, because success is not guaranteed. At any step of the way, the process can be interrupted, frustrated, blocked, or sidetracked, so that the human individual is fragmented, split, alienated, stuck at one level or another of mental or emotional maturity. It is not difficult to observe that most people are stranded somewhere along this path of development. Nonetheless, as I discuss in *Honoring the Self*, the central goal of the maturational process is *evolution toward autonomy*.

It is an old and excellent adage that effective parenting consists first of giving a child roots (to grow) and then wings (to fly). The security of a firm base—and the self-confidence one day to leave it. Children do not grow up in a vacuum. They grow up in a social context. Indeed, much of the drama of unfolding individuation and autonomy occurs and can only occur in and through encounters with other human beings. In the first encounters of childhood, a child can experience the safety and security that allows a self to emerge—or the terror and instability that fractures the self before it is fully formed. In subsequent encounters, a child can experience being accepted and respected or rejected and demeaned. A child can experience the appropriate balance of protection and freedom or (1) the overprotectiveness that infantilizes or (2) the underprotective-ness that demands of the child resources that may not yet exist. Such experiences, as well as others we will discuss, contribute to the kind of self and self-esteem that develops over time.

---

*To evolve into selfhood is the primary human task. It
is also the primary human challenge, because
success is not guaranteed.*

The Antecedents of Self-Esteem

Some of the best work that psychologists have done concerning self-esteem has been in the area of child-parent relations. An example is Stanley Coopersmith's landmark study, *The Antecedents of Self-Esteem.* Coopersmith's goal was to identify the parental behaviors most often found where children grew up manifesting healthy self-esteem. I want to distill the essence of his report, as a prologue to the discussion that follows.

Coopersmith discovered no significant correlations with such factors as family wealth, education, geographic living area, social class, Father's occupation, or always having Mother at home. What he did find to be significant was the quality of the relationship between the child and the important adults in his or her life.

Specifically, he found five conditions associated with high self-esteem in children:

1. The child experiences total acceptance of thoughts, feelings, and the value of his or her person.

2. The child operates in a context of clearly defined and enforced limits that are fair, nonoppressive, and negotiable. The child is not given unrestricted "freedom." Consequently, the child experiences a sense of

security; there is a clear basis for evaluating his or her behavior. Further, the limits generally entail high standards, as well as confidence that the child will be able to meet them. Consequently, the child usually does.

3. The child experiences respect for his or her dignity as a human being. The parents do not use violence or humiliation or ridicule to control and manipulate. The parents take the child's needs and wishes seriously, whether or not they can accede to them in a particular instance. The parents are willing to negotiate family rules within carefully drawn limits. In other words, authority, but not authoritarianism, is operating.

As an expression of this overall attitude, parents are less inclined to punitive discipline (and there tends to be less need for punitive discipline), and more inclined to put the emphasis on rewarding and reinforcing positive behavior. They focus on what they do want rather than on what they do not want—on the positive rather than the negative.

The parents show an interest in the child, in his or her social and academic life, and they are generally available for discussion when and as the child wants it.

4. The parents uphold high standards and high expectations in terms of behavior and performance. Their attitude is not "anything goes." They have both moral and performance expectations that they convey in a respectful, benevolent, and nonoppressive manner; the child is challenged to be the best he or she can be.

5. The parents themselves tend to enjoy a high level of self-esteem. They model (what I call) self-efficacy and self-respect. The child sees living examples of that which he or she needs to learn. After carefully explaining such antecedents of self-esteem as his research could reveal, Coopersmith goes on to observe: "We should note that there are virtually no parental patterns of behavior or parental attitudes that are common to all parents of children with high self-esteem."

This last observation underscores our awareness that parental behavior alone does not decide the course of a child's psychological development. Apart from the fact that sometimes the most important influence in a child's life is a teacher, or a grandparent, or a neighbor, external factors are only part of the story, never the whole, as I have stressed repeatedly. We are causes, not merely effects. As beings whose consciousness is volitional, beginning in childhood and continuing throughout our life we make choices that have consequences for the kind of person we become and the level of self-esteem we attain.

To say that parents can make it easier or harder for a child to develop healthy self-esteem is to say that parents can make it easier or harder for a young person to learn the six practices and make them a natural and integral part of his or her life. The six practices provide a standard for assessing parental policies: Do these policies encourage or discourage consciousness, self-acceptance, self-responsibility, self-assertiveness, purposefulness, and integrity? Do they raise or lower the probability that a child will learn self-esteem-supporting behaviors?

Basic Safety and Security

Beginning life in a condition of total dependency, a child has no more basic requirement—as far as parental behavior is concerned—than that of safety and security. This entails the satisfaction of physiological needs, protection from the elements, and basic caretaking in all its obvious aspects. It entails the creation of an environment in which the child can feel nurtured and safe.

In this context the process of separation and individuation can unfold. A mind that can later learn to trust itself can begin to emerge. A person with a confident sense of boundaries can develop.

If the child is to learn to trust other human beings, and, in effect, to find confidence that life is not malevolent, the foundation is laid at this level.

Of course, the need for safety and security is not limited to the early years. The self is still forming during adolescence, and a home life of chaos and anxiety can place severe obstacles in the path of normal teenage development.

In my work with adults I often see the long-term effects of one form of trauma associated with the frustration of this need—a child's repeated experience of terror at the hands of adults. Certain therapy clients convey a quality of fear or anxiety that seems to reach back to the first months of life and to invade the deepest structure of the psyche. Such clients are distinguished not only by the intensity of their anxiety, nor by its pervasiveness, but by the fact that one senses that the person experiencing the anxiety is not the adult but rather a child or even an infant inside that adult's body—or, more precisely, inside the adult's psyche. These clients report that they have had feelings of basic terror as far back as they can remember.

Setting aside the possibility of birth trauma, there are two factors to be considered here. The first is the objective circumstances of their environment and the treatment they received as children. The second is the question of an innate disposition to experience anxiety: some individuals' threshold is almost certainly lower than others, so that what is not traumatic for one child is for another.

The terror might be of a physically violent father, a moody, unpredictable, emotionally disturbed mother, a menacing family member whose scowl conjures up images of unimaginable torture—a terror from which there is no escape and that plunges the child into unbearable feelings of helplessness.

> *The greater a child's terror, and the earlier it is experienced, the harder the task of building a strong and healthy sense of self.*

A nurse of thirty-eight, Sonia would involuntarily flinch if I inadvertently raised my voice slightly, especially while shifting in my chair. She claimed that her earliest memories were of her mother and father screaming at each other while she lay in her crib with her own cries ignored. Her sense that the world is a hostile and dangerous place was almost cellular. She was motivated by fear in almost all of her choices and actions, with negative consequences for her self-esteem. I suspected that she came into this world with a greater-than-average disposition to experience anxiety, made immeasurably worse by two parents under the sway of the irrational within themselves.

A thirty-four-year-old professor of philosophy, Edgar said his earliest memories were of being forced to stand on the bed while his father—a distinguished and respected physician in his community—beat him violently with a strap. "My cries could never make him stop. It was as if he were insane. He could destroy me and there was nothing I could do. That feeling has never left me. I'm thirty-four years old and I still feel that in the face of any kind of danger I have no means of defending myself. I'm afraid. I've always been afraid. I can't imagine who I would be without my fear."

The greater a child's terror, and the earlier it is experienced, the harder the task of building a strong and healthy sense of self. To learn the six practices on the foundation of an all-consuming sense of powerlessness—*traumatic* powerlessness—is very difficult. It is against this destructive feeling that good parenting aims to protect a child.

Nurturing Through Touch

Today we know that touch is essential for a child's healthy development. In its absence, children can die, even when other needs are met.

Through touch we send sensory stimulation that helps the infant's brain to develop. Through touch we convey love, caring, comfort, support, nurturing. Through touch we establish contact between one human being and another. Research shows that touch—such as massage—can profoundly affect health. At some level this is often known intuitively because in non-Western parts of the world the massaging of babies is standard practice. In the West it is not, and one reason that has been suggested is the bias against the body found in Christianity.

One of the most powerful ways parents can convey love is through touch. Long before a child can understand words, he or she understands touch. Declarations of love without touch are unconvincing and hollow. Our bodies cry out for the reality of the physical. We want to experience that our *person* is loved—valued—embraced—not some disembodied abstraction.

————

Long before a child can understand words,
he or she understands touch.

————

Children who grow up with little experience of being touched often carry an ache deep within them that never entirely vanishes. There is a hole in their self-regard. "Why could I never sit on my father's knee?" clients will say. "Why did Mother convey such reticence—even disgust—about physical touch?" The unspoken sentence is, "Why did they not love me enough to want to hold me?" And sometimes, "If my own parents didn't want to touch me, how can I expect anyone else to want to?"

The pain of this childhood deprivation is difficult to bear. Usually it is repressed. Consciousness contracts and psychic numbing is evoked—as a survival strategy, to make existence tolerable. Self-awareness is avoided. This is often the start of a pattern that lasts a lifetime.

Depending on other psychological factors, we can see two different responses to touch deprivation later in life. On one level they appear opposite, yet both express alienation and both are harmful to self-esteem. On the one hand we may see in an adult an avoidance of intimate contact with other human beings, a withdrawal from human encounters, expressing feelings of fear and unworthiness; a failure of self-assertiveness, among other things. Or we may see compulsive sexual promiscuity, an unconscious effort to heal the wound of touch starvation, but in a way that humiliates without resolving, and personal integrity and self-respect are two of the casualties. Both responses leave the individual isolated from authentic human contact.

Love

A child who is treated with love tends to internalize the feeling and to experience him- or herself as lovable. Love is conveyed by verbal expression, nurturing actions, and the joy and pleasure we show in the sheer fact of the child's being.

An effective parent can convey anger or disappointment without signaling withdrawal of love. An effective parent can teach without resorting to rejection. The value of the child as a human being is not on trial.

Love is not felt to be real when it is always tied to performance, tied to living up to Mother's or Father's expectations, and is withdrawn from time to time as a means of manipulating obedience and conformity. Love is not felt to be real when the child receives subtle or unsubtle messages to the effect, "You are not enough."

Unfortunately, many of us received such messages. You may have potential, but you are unacceptable as you are. You need to be fixed. One day you may be enough, but not now. You will be enough only if you fulfill our expectations.

"I am enough" does not mean "I have nothing to learn and nowhere to grow to." It means "I accept myself as a value as I am." We cannot build self-esteem on a foundation of "I am not enough." To convey to a child "You are not enough" is to subvert self-esteem at the core. No child feels loved who receives such messages.

Acceptance

A child whose thoughts and feelings are treated with acceptance tends to internalize the response and to learn self-acceptance. Acceptance is conveyed, not by agreement (which is not always possible) but by listening to and acknowledging the child's thoughts and feelings, and by not chastising, arguing, lecturing, psychologizing, or insulting.

If a child is repeatedly told that he or she must not feel this, must not feel that, the child is encouraged to deny and disown feelings or emotions in order to please or placate parents. If normal expressions of excitement, anger, happiness, sexuality, longing, and fear are treated as unacceptable or wrong or sinful or otherwise distasteful to parents, the child may disown and reject more and more of the self to belong, to be loved, to avoid the terror of abandonment. We do not serve a child's development by making self-repudiation the price of our love.

Few attitudes of parents can be so helpful for the child's healthy development as the child's experience that his or her nature, temperament, interests, and aspirations are accepted—*whether or not parents share them.* It is unrealistic in the extreme to imagine that parents will enjoy or be comfortable with a child's every act of self-expression. But acceptance in the sense described in this book does not require enjoyment or comfort—or agreement.

---

*We do not serve a child's development by making
self-repudiation the price of our love.*

A parent may be athletic, a child may not be—or the reverse. A parent may be artistic, a child may not be—or the reverse. A parent's natural rhythms may be fast, a child's may be slow—or the reverse. A parent may be orderly, a child may be chaotic—or the reverse. A parent may be extroverted, a child may be introverted—or the reverse. A parent may be very "social," a child may be less so—or the reverse. A parent may be competitive, a child may not be—or the reverse. *If differences are accepted, self-esteem can grow.*

Respect

A child who receives respect from adults tends to learn self-respect. Respect is conveyed by addressing a child with the courtesy one normally extends to adults. (As child psychologist Haim Ginott used to observe, if a visiting guest accidentally spills a drink, we do not say, "Oh, you're so sloppy! What's the matter with you?" But then why do we think such statements are appropriate for our children, who are much more important to us than the visitor? Surely it would be more appropriate to say to the child something like, "You've spilled your drink. Will you get some paper towels from the kitchen?")

I recall a client once saying to me, "My father talks to any busboy with more courtesy than he's ever extended to me." "Please" and "thank you" are words that acknowledge dignity—that of the speaker as well as the listener.

Parents need to be informed: "Be careful what you say to your children. They may agree with you." Before calling a child "stupid" or "clumsy" or "bad" or "a disappointment," consider the question, "Is this how I want my child to experience him or herself?"

If a child grows up in a home where everyone deals with everyone else with natural, good-natured courtesy, he or she learns principles that apply both to self and to others. Respect of self and others feels like the normal order of things—which, properly, it is.

The fact that we love a child does not guarantee that respect will be automatic. Lapses of consciousness are always possible, no matter how loving our feelings. Once when my granddaughter Ashley was five I was whirling her around, laughing with her, and enjoying myself so much that I did not stop when she said, "I want to be put down now, Grandpa." But I caught myself an instant later when she said solemnly, "Grandpa, you're not listening to me." "Sorry, sweetheart," I answered, and obeyed.

Visibility

Especially important for the nurturing of a child's self-esteem is the experience of what I have called *psychological visibility*. I wrote about the human need for visibility, as it applies to all human relationships, in *The Psychology of Romantic Love*. Here I want to touch on just a few basics as they pertain to a child's interactions with parents. But first, some general comments about visibility.

If I say or do something and you respond in a way that I perceive as congruent in terms of my own behavior—if I become playful and you become playful in turn, or if I express joy and you show understanding of my state, or if I express sadness and you convey empathy, or if I do something I am proud of and you smile in admiration—I feel seen and understood by you. I feel visible. In contrast, if I say or do something and you respond in a way that makes no sense to me in terms of my own behavior—if I become playful and you react as if I were being hostile, or if I express joy and you display impatience and tell me not to be silly, or if I express sadness and you accuse me of pretending, or if I do something I am proud of and you react with condemnation—I do not feel seen and understood, I feel invisible.

To feel visible to you I do not require your agreement with what I am saying. We might be having a philosophical or political discussion, and we might hold different viewpoints, but if we show understanding of what the other is saying, and if our responses are congruent in terms of that, we can continue to feel visible to each other and even, in the midst of arguing, be having a thoroughly good time.

When we feel visible, we feel that the other person and I are in the same reality, the same universe, metaphorically speaking. When we don't, it is as if we were in different realities. But all satisfying human interactions require congruence at this level; if we do not experience ourselves as in the same reality, we cannot relate in a mutually satisfying way.

The desire for visibility is the desire for a form of objectivity. I cannot perceive myself, cannot perceive my person, "objectively," only internally, from a perspective that is uniquely private. But if your responses make sense in terms of my internal perceptions, you become a mirror allowing me the experience of objectivity about my person. I see myself reflected in your (appropriate) responses.

Visibility is a matter of degree. From childhood on, we receive from human beings some measure of appropriate feedback; without it, we could not survive. Throughout our life there will be people whose responses will allow us to feel superficially visible and, if we are fortunate, a few people with whom we will feel visible in a more profound way.

As an aside, let me say that it is in romantic love, at its best, that psychological visibility tends to be most fully realized. Someone who loves us passionately is motivated to know and understand us to a greater depth than someone with whom our relationship is more casual. What does one often hear from people who are in love? "He (she) *understands* me as I have never felt understood before."

A child has a natural desire to be seen, heard, understood, and responded to appropriately. To a self that is still forming, this need is particularly urgent. This is one of the reasons a child will look to a parent for a response after having taken some action. A child who experiences his or her excitement as good, as a value, but is punished or rebuked for it by adults undergoes a bewildering experience of invisibility and disorientation. A child who is praised for "always being an angel" and knows this is not true also experiences invisibility and disorientation.

Working with adults in psychotherapy, I see the frequency with which the pain of invisibility in their home life as children is clearly central to their developmental problems and to their insecurities in adult relationships. Thus:

If I had felt visible to my parents—

I wouldn't feel so alienated from people today.

I would have felt like a member of the human race.

I would have felt safe.

I would have felt visible to myself.

I would have felt loved.

I would have felt there was hope.

I would have felt like one of the family.

I would have felt connected.

I would be sane.

I would have been helped to understand myself.

I would have felt I had a home.

I would have felt I belonged.

If a child says, unhappily, "I didn't get the part in my school play," and Mother answers, empathically, "That must hurt," the child feels visible. What does a child feel if Mother answers sharply, "Do you think you'll always get what you want in life?"

If a child bursts into the house, full of joy and excitement, and Mother says, smiling, "You're happy today," the child feels visible. What does a child feel if Mother screams, "Do you have to make so much noise? You're so selfish and inconsiderate! What is the matter with you?"

If a child struggles to build a tree house in the backyard, and Father says, admiringly, "Even though it's hard, you're sticking with it," the child feels visible. What does a child feel if Father says, impatiently, "God, can't you do anything?"

If a child is out for a walk with Father and comments on a wide variety of things he sees along the way, and Father says, "You really notice a lot," the child feels visible. What does a child feel if Father says, irritably, "Don't you ever stop talking?"

When we convey love, appreciation, empathy, acceptance, respect, we make a child visible. When we convey indifference, scorn, condemnation, ridicule, we drive the child's self into the lonely underground of invisibility.

Psychologists and educators, reflecting on the childhood elements that support self-esteem, often speak of giving the child an appreciation of his or her uniqueness and also of giving the child a sense of affiliation or belonging (the sense of roots). Both goals are achieved to the extent that the child is given the experience of visibility.

When we convey love, appreciation, empathy,
acceptance, respect, we make a child visible.

Visibility should not be equated with praise. Watching a child struggle with a homework assignment and saying "Math seems hard for you" is not praise. Saying "You're looking upset right now—want to talk?" is not praise. Saying "You wish you didn't have to go to the dentist" is not praise. Saying "You really seem to enjoy chemistry" is not praise. But such statements do evoke the sense of being seen and understood.

If we are to love effectively—whether the object is our child, our mate, or a friend—the ability to provide the experience of visibility is essential. This presupposes the ability to see. And this presupposes the exercise of consciousness.

And in giving this to our child—visibility, consciousness—we model a practice that he or she may learn to emulate.

Age-Appropriate Nurturing

That children require nurturing is obvious. What is sometimes less obvious is the need for nurturing to be age-appropriate or, more precisely, appropriate to the child's level of development.

Some forms of nurturing that are right for a three-month-old infant would clearly be infantilizing for a six-year-old child. The infant is dressed by an adult; a six-year-old properly dresses him or herself. Some forms of nurturing that are right for a six-year-old would subvert growth toward autonomy in a sixteen-year-old. When a six-year-old asks a question, it can be nurturing to take the question seriously and answer it. When a teenager asks a question it may be nurturing to draw out his or her own thoughts on the subject or recommend a book to read or a library to go to for research.

I recall a twenty-six-year-old woman who came to me in a state of crisis because her husband had left her *and she did not know how to shop for herself.* For the first nineteen years of life, her mother had purchased all her clothes; when she married at nineteen, her husband took over that responsibility—and not only for clothing but for all household goods, including food. Emotionally, she felt herself to be a child, with a child's level of self-sufficiency. The thought of having to make independent choices and decisions, even about the simplest, most mundane matters, terrified her.

If a parent's goal is to support the child's independence, one of the ways this is achieved is to offer a child choices in keeping with the child's level of development. A mother may not think it advisable to ask her five-year-old whether he or she wants to wear a sweater; but she can offer a choice of two sweaters. Some children are eager for an adult's advice when it is not necessary. It is helpful to respond, "What do *you* think?"

One wants to turn over choice and decision making to a child as fast as the child can comfortably handle them. This is a judgment call, requiring consciousness and sensitivity from the adult. The point is: Be aware of the ultimate objective.

Praise and Criticism

Loving parents, concerned to support the self-esteem of their children, may believe that the way to do it is with praise. But inappropriate praise can be as harmful to self-esteem as inappropriate criticism.

Many years ago I learned from Haim Ginott an important distinction: that between evaluative praise and appreciative praise. It is evaluative praise that does not serve a child's interests. Appreciative praise, in contrast, can be productive both in supporting self-esteem and in reinforcing desired behavior.

To quote from Ginott's *Teacher and Child:*

In psychotherapy a child is never told, "You are a good little boy." "You are doing great." "Carry on your good work." Judgmental praise is avoided. Why? Because it is not helpful. It creates anxiety, invites dependency, and evokes defensiveness. It is not conducive to self-reliance, self-direction, and self-control. These qualities demand freedom from outside judgment. They require reliance on inner motivation and evaluation. To be himself, one needs to be free from the pressure of evaluative praise.

If we state what we like and appreciate about the child's actions and accomplishments, we remain factual and descriptive; we leave it to the child to do the evaluating. Ginott offers these examples of the process:

Marcia, age twelve, helped the teacher rearrange the books in the class library. The teacher avoided personal praise. ("You did a good job. You are a hard worker. You are a good librarian.") Instead she described what Marcia accomplished: "The books are all in order now. It'll be easy for the children to find any book they want. It was a difficult job. But you did it. Thank you." The teacher's words of recognition allowed Marcia to make her own inference. "My teacher likes the job I did. I am a good worker."

Phyllis, age ten, wrote a poem describing her reaction to the first snow of the season. The teacher said, "Your poem reflected my own feelings; I was delighted to see my winter thoughts put into poetic phrases." A smile crossed the little poet's face. She turned to her friend and said, "Mrs. A. really *likes* my poem. She thinks I am terrific."

Ruben, age seven, had been struggling to make his handwriting neat. He found it difficult to keep his letters on the line. Finally, he managed to create a neat page with well-constructed letters. The teacher wrote on his paper: "The letters are neat. It was a pleasure to read your page." When the papers were returned, the children eagerly read the notes the teacher had written. Suddenly, the teacher heard the smacking of lips. There was Ruben *kissing* his paper! "I am a good writer," he announced.

The more specifically targeted our praise, the more meaningful it is to the child. Praise that is generalized and abstract leaves the child wondering what exactly is being praised. It is not helpful.

Not only does praise need to be specific, it needs to be commensurate with its object. Overblown or grandiose praise tends to be overwhelming and anxiety provoking—because the child knows it does not match his or her self-perceptions (a problem that is avoided by descriptions of behavior, plus expressions of appreciation, that omit these unrealistic evaluations).

Some parents are intent on helping their children's self-esteem, but they praise globally, indiscriminately, and extravagantly. At best, this does not work. At worst, it backfires: the child feels invisible and anxious. In addition, this policy tends to produce "approval addicts"—children who cannot take a step without looking for praise and who feel disvalued if it is not forthcoming. Many devoted parents, with the best intentions in the world but without the appropriate skills, have turned their children into such approval addicts by saturating the home environment with their "loving" evaluations

———

Inappropriate praise can be as harmful to self-esteem
as inappropriate criticism.

———

If we wish to nurture autonomy, *always leave space for the child to make his or her own evaluations*, after we have described behavior. Leave the child free of the pressure of our judgments. Help create a context in which independent thinking can occur.

When we express our pleasure in and appreciation of a child's questions or observations or thoughtfulness, we are encouraging the exercise of consciousness. When we respond positively and respectfully to a child's efforts at self-expression, we encourage self-assertiveness. When we acknowledge and show appreciation for a child's truthfulness, we encourage integrity. Catch a child doing something right and convey pleasure at the sight of it. Trust the child to draw the appropriate conclusions. That is the simplest statement of effective reinforcement.

As to criticism, it needs to be directed only at the child's behavior, never at the child. The principle is: Describe the behavior (hitting a sibling, breaking a promise), describe your feelings about it (anger, disappointment), describe what you want done (if anything)—*and omit character assassination.*[1]

When I speak of describing your feelings, I mean statements like "I feel disappointed," or "I feel dismayed," or "I feel angry." I do *not* mean statements like "I feel you are the most rotten kid who ever lived," which is not a description of a feeling but of a thought, judgment, or evaluation concealed in the language of feeling. There is no such emotion as "You are the most rotten kid who ever lived." The actual emotion here is rage and the desire to inflict pain.

No good purpose is ever served by assaulting a child's self-esteem. This is the first rule of effective criticism. We do not inspire better behavior by impugning a child's worth, intelligence, morality, character, intentions, or psychology. No one was ever made "good" by being informed he or she was "bad." (Nor by being told, "You're just like [someone already viewed as reprehensible].") Attacks on self-esteem tend to increase the likelihood that the unwanted behavior will happen again—"Since I am bad, I will behave badly."

No one was ever made "good" by being informed
he or she was "bad."

Many an adult in psychotherapy complains of still hearing the internalized voices of Mother or Father telling them they are "bad," "rotten," "stupid," "worthless." Often they struggle toward a better life against the gravitational pull of those abusive terms, fighting not to succumb to their parents' dark view of them. They do not always succeed. Since self-concept tends to turn into destiny through the principle of self-fulfilling prophecies, we need to consider what self-concept we wish to promote.

If we can rebuke without violating or demeaning a child's dignity, if we can respect a child's self-esteem even when we are angry, we have mastered one of the most challenging and important aspects of competent parenting.

Parental Expectations

I have already commented on Coopersmith's findings with regard to parental expectations. It is no service to children to expect nothing of them. Rational parents uphold ethical standards to which they hold children accountable. They also uphold standards of performance: they expect children to learn, master knowledge and skills, and move toward increasing maturity.

Such expectations need to be calibrated to the child's level of development and be respectful of the child's unique attributes. One does not overwhelm a child with expectations that take no cognizance of his or her context and needs. But neither does one assume that a child will always operate at a high level "naturally," guided by sheer emotional impulse.

Children clearly show a desire to know what is expected of them and do not feel secure when the answer is "nothing."

Recommendations for Further Reading

Of all the books written on the art of child-rearing, there are six that I personally found extraordinarily useful because of the wisdom and clarity they bring to the "nuts-and-bolts" problems of everyday family living. Although they rarely mention self-esteem as such, they are superb guidebooks to nurturing the self-esteem of the young. I mention them here because they develop so artfully and imaginatively the specifics of conveying love, acceptance, respect, and appropriate praise and criticism in the face of the countless challenges that children present to parents and other adults.

Three of these books are by Haim Ginott: *Between Parent and Child, Between Parent and Teenager,* and *Teacher and Child.** The other three titles are by two former students of Ginott, Adele Faber and Elaine Mazlish: *Liberated Parents, Liberated Children; How To Talk So Kids Will Listen and Listen So Kids Will Talk;* and *Siblings without Rivalry.*

Yet another outstanding book is *Parent Effectiveness Training* by Dr. Thomas Gordon. One of its great merits is that it offers fairly detailed principles combined with specific skills and techniques for resolving a wide variety of child-parent conflicts. Gordon's approach is largely congruent with that of Ginott, although there appear to be some differences. For one, Ginott insists that parents must in some circumstances set limits and rules; Gordon criticizes this idea and seems to argue that all conflicts should be resolved "democratically." In this issue I side with Ginott,

---

* My only reservations concerning the first two of these books are (1) a psychoanalytic orientation in some of Ginott's comments that I do not share; (2) a puzzlingly evasive treatment of the issue of masturbation, and (3) a dated, traditional perspective on male and female roles. These issues are minor, however, in light of what the books have to offer.

although I am not certain how real this difference is, since Gordon would not allow a small child to play in the streets at his or her discretion. What both men share (along with Faber and Mazlish) is a passionate aversion to disciplining by physical punishment. I applaud this because I am convinced that fear of physical punishment is deadly for the growth of a child's self-esteem.

Dealing with Mistakes

How parents respond when children make mistakes can be fateful for self-esteem.

A child learns to walk through a series of false moves. Gradually he or she eliminates the moves that don't work and keeps the moves that do; making mistakes is integral to the process of learning to walk. Making mistakes is integral to a great deal of learning.

If a child is chastised for making a mistake, or ridiculed, humiliated, or punished—or if the parent steps in impatiently and says, "Here, let me do it!"—he or she cannot feel free to struggle and learn. A natural process of growth is sabotaged. To avoid mistakes becomes a higher priority than to master new challenges.

A child who does not feel accepted by parents if he or she makes a mistake may learn to practice *self*-rejection in response to mistakes. Consciousness is muted, self-acceptance is undermined, self-responsibility and self-assertiveness are suppressed.

Given the chance, children will usually learn from their mistakes naturally and spontaneously. Sometimes it can be useful to ask, noncritically and nonpedantically, "What did you learn? What might you do differently next time?"

Making mistakes is integral to a great deal of learning.

It is more desirable to stimulate the search for answers than to provide answers. However, to think of stimulating the mind of the child usually requires a higher level of consciousness (and of patience) of the parent than does the practice of handing down ready-made solutions. Impatience is often the enemy of good parenting.

Working with adults who received destructive messages about mistakes as children, I often use a series of sentence stems. Here are a typical sequence and typical endings:

When my mother saw me making a mistake —

She became impatient.

She conveyed that I was hopeless.

She called me her big baby.

She became angry and said, "Here, let me show you!"

She laughed and looked contemptuous.

She yelled for my father.

When my father saw me making a mistake —

He got angry.

He gave a sermon.

He swore.

He compared me to my superior brother.

He sneered.

He launched into a half-hour lecture.

He talked about how brilliantly he did things.

He said, "You're your mother's son."

He walked out of the room.

When I catch myself making a mistake —

I tell myself I'm stupid.

I call myself a klutz.

I feel like a loser.

I feel frightened.

I wonder what will happen when I'm found out.

I tell myself it's pointless to try.

I tell myself it's unforgivable.

I feel self-contempt.

If someone had told me it's all right to make mistakes—

I'd be a different person.

I wouldn't make so many mistakes.

I wouldn't be so afraid to try anything.

I wouldn't be so self-critical.

I'd be more open.

I'd be more adventuresome.

I'd accomplish more.

What I hear myself saying is—

I'm doing everything to myself my mother and father once did to me.

My parents are still inside my head.

I have no more compassion for myself than my father did.

I berate myself worse than Mother did.

If I can't make mistakes, I can't grow.

I'm stifling myself.

My self-esteem is devastated by mistakes.

If I had the courage to allow myself mistakes—

I would not make as many mistakes.

I'd be careful but more relaxed.

I could enjoy my work.

I would take more chances with new ideas.

I'd have more ideas.

I could be more creative.

I'd be happier.

I would not be irresponsible.

If I were more compassionate about my mistakes—

I wouldn't feel doomed and I would try harder.

I would give more.

I'd like myself more.

I wouldn't be depressed.

I would be more conscious.

I wouldn't struggle with all this fear.

I'd be my own man and not my parents' little boy.

As I learn a better attitude toward making mistakes—

I will feel less tense.

My work will improve.

I think I will try new things.

I will have to say good-bye to an old script.

I will become a better parent to myself.

I will find it hard.

I will have to learn that it's not self-indulgence.

I will have to practice.

It will take getting used to.

I feel hopeful.

I feel excited.

The last six stems listed above point to one of the ways we can begin to undo negative programming. In therapy or in my self-esteem groups I might ask a client to write six to ten endings for several of these last stems every day for two or three weeks—as a potent device of deprogramming. The principle is that we keep "radiating" the destructive ideas with highly concentrated awareness (which is very different from worrying or "stewing" or obsessing or complaining about them).

The Need for Sanity

There is perhaps nothing more important to know about children than that they need to make sense out of their experience. In effect, they need to know that the universe is rational—and that human existence is knowable, predictable, and stable. On that foundation, they can build a sense of efficacy; without it, the task is worse than difficult.

Physical reality tends to be far more "reliable" than most human beings. Consequently, children who feel ineffective in the human realm often turn for a sense of power to nature or machinery or engineering or physics or mathematics, all of which offer a degree of consistency and "sanity" rarely found among human beings.

But "sanity" in family life is one of a child's most urgent needs if healthy development is to be possible.

What does *sanity* mean in this context? It means adults who, for the most part, say what they mean and mean what they say. It means rules that are understandable, consistent, and fair. It means not being punished today for behavior that was ignored or even rewarded yesterday. It means being brought up by parents whose emotional life is more or less graspable and predictable—in contrast to an emotional life punctuated by bouts of anxiety or rage or euphoria unrelated to any discernible cause or pattern. It means a home in which reality is appropriately acknowledged—in contrast to a home in which, for instance, a drunken father misses the chair he meant to sit on and crashes to the floor while Mother goes on eating and talking as though nothing had happened. It means parents who practice what they preach. Who are willing to admit when they make mistakes and apologize when they know they have been unfair or unreasonable. Who appeal to a child's wish to understand rather than the wish to avoid pain. Who reward and reinforce consciousness in a child rather than discourage and penalize it.

---

*There is perhaps nothing more important to know
about children than that they need to make sense
out of their experience.*

If, instead of obedience, we want cooperation from our children; if, instead of conformity, we want self-responsibility—we can achieve it in a home environment that supports the child's *mind*. We cannot achieve it in an environment intrinsically hostile to the exercise of mind.

The Need for Structure

Children's security and growth needs are in part met by the presence of an appropriate structure.

"Structure" pertains to the rules, implicit or explicit, operative in a family, rules about what is or is not acceptable and permissible, what is expected, how various kinds of behavior are dealt with, who is free to do what, how decisions affecting family members are made, and what kind of values are upheld.

A good structure is one that respects the needs, individuality, and intelligence of each family member. Open communication is highly valued. Such a structure is flexible rather than rigid, open and discussible rather than closed and authoritarian. In such a structure, parents offer explanations, not commandments. They appeal to confidence rather than to fear. They encourage self-expression. They uphold the kind of values we associate with individuality and autonomy. Their standards inspire rather than intimidate.

Children do not desire unlimited "freedom." Most children feel safer and more secure in a structure that is somewhat authoritarian than in no structure at all. Children need limits and feel anxious in their absence. This is one of the reasons they test limits to be certain they are there. They need to know that *someone is flying the plane.*

Overly "permissive" parents tend to produce highly anxious children. By this I mean parents who back away from any leadership role; who treat all family members as equal not only in dignity but also in knowledge and authority; and who strive to teach no values and uphold no standards for fear of "imposing" their "biases" on their children. A client once said to me, "My mother would have thought it 'undemocratic' to tell me that getting pregnant at the age of thirteen is not a good idea. Do you know how terrifying it is to grow up in a house where no one acts like they know what's true or right?"

When children are offered rational values and standards, self-esteem is nurtured. When they are not, self-esteem is starved.

A Family Dinner

With both parents working, sometimes long hours, it is often difficult for parents to spend with children all the time they would like. Sometimes parents and children do not even take meals together. Without entering into all the complexities of this issue and all the problematic aspects of contemporary life-styles, I want to mention one simple suggestion that clients of mine have found helpful.

I ask parents who consult me to make a commitment to have at least one major family dinner a week at which all members are present.

I ask that dinner be slow and leisurely and that everyone be invited to talk about his or her activities and concerns. No lectures, no sermons, no patronizing, just sharing of experiences, everyone treated with love and respect. The theme is self-expression and self-disclosure—and the sustaining of connections.

Many parents who agree with the project in principle find they need considerable discipline in its execution. The urge to condescend, patronize, pontificate, can be powerful. They can stifle self-expression even while "demanding" it. If, however, they can overcome the impulse to be "authorities," if they can express thoughts and feelings simply and naturally with their children and invite the same self-expression in return, they offer a profound psychological gift to their children and to themselves. They help create a sense of "belonging" in the best sense of that word—that is, they create a sense of *family*. They create an environment in which self-esteem can grow.

Child Abuse

When we think of child abuse we think of children who are physically abused or sexually molested. That such abuse can be catastrophic for a child's self-esteem is widely recognized. It evokes the experience of traumatic powerlessness, the feeling of nonownership of one's own body, and a sense of agonizing defenselessness that can last a lifetime.

However, a more comprehensive examination of what constitutes child abuse would have to include the following items, all of which throw up severe obstacles to the growth of a child's self-esteem. Parents perpetrate child abuse when they . . .

Convey that the child is not "enough."

Chastise the child for expressing "unacceptable" feelings.

Ridicule or humiliate the child.

Convey that the child's thoughts or feelings have no value or importance.

Attempt to control the child by shame or guilt.

Overprotect the child and consequently obstruct normal learning and increasing self-reliance.

Underprotect the child and consequently obstruct normal ego development.

Raise a child with no rules at all, and thus no supporting structure; or else rules that are contradictory, bewildering, undiscussable, and oppressive—in either case inhibiting normal growth.

Deny a child's perception of reality and implicitly encourage the child to doubt his or her mind.

Terrorize a child with physical violence or the threat of it, thus instilling acute fear as an enduring characteristic at the child's core.

Treat a child as a sexual object.

Teach that the child is bad, unworthy, or sinful by nature.

When a child's basic needs are frustrated, as they invariably are when subjected to the above treatment, the result is acute pain. Often embedded in that pain is the feeling: *Something is wrong with me. Somehow I am defective.* And the tragedy of a destructive self-fulfilling prophecy is set in motion.

Urgent Issues

As I said earlier, my goal in this chapter has not been to offer a course on child-rearing. My goal has been to isolate certain issues that my experience as a psychotherapist has taught me are often fateful for a young person's self-esteem.

When we listen to the stories of adults in therapy, noting the historical circumstances under which tragic decisions were sometimes made, it is not difficult to see what was missing and needed during the childhood years. By extrapolating from wounds, as it were, we can deepen our understanding of what prevents wounds from occurring.

Over two decades ago, in *Breaking Free,* I published a list of questions I used in psychotherapy to facilitate explorations into the childhood origins of poor self-esteem. I include here a revised and slightly expanded version of that list, as a kind of summing up of some, although not all, of the issues we have been addressing. They can be useful stimulants to self-examination for individuals as well as evocative guides for parents.

1. When you were a child, did your parents' manner of behaving and of dealing with you give you the impression that you were living in a world that was rational, predictable, intelligible? Or a world that was

contradictory, bewildering, unknowable? *In your home, did you have the sense the evident facts were acknowledged and respected or avoided and denied?*

2. Were you taught the importance of learning to think and of cultivating your intelligence? Did your parents provide you with intellectual stimulation and convey the idea that the use of your mind can be an exciting adventure? Did anything in your home life suggest such a perspective, if only implicitly? *Was consciousness valued?*

Were you encouraged toward obedience or toward self-responsibility?

---

3. Were you encouraged to think independently, to develop your critical faculty? Or were you encouraged to be obedient rather than mentally active and questioning? (Supplementary questions: Did your parents project that it was more important to conform to what other people believed than to discover what is true? When your parents wanted you to do something, did they appeal to your understanding and give you reasons, when possible and appropriate, for their request? Or did they communicate, in effect, "Do it because I say so?") *Were you encouraged toward obedience or toward self-responsibility?*

4. Did you feel free to express your views openly, without fear of punishment? *Were self-expression and self-assertiveness safe?*

5. Did your parents communicate their disapproval of your thoughts, desires, or behavior by means of humor, teasing, or sarcasm? *Were you taught to associate self-expression with humiliation?*

6. Did your parents treat you with respect? (Supplementary questions: Were your thoughts, needs, and feelings given consideration? Was your dignity as a human being acknowledged? When you expressed ideas or opinions, were they taken seriously? Were your likes and dislikes, whether or not they were acceded to, treated with respect? Were your desires responded to thoughtfully and, again, with respect?) *Were you implicitly encouraged to respect yourself, to take your thoughts seriously, to take the exercise of your mind seriously?*

7. Did you feel that you were psychologically visible to your parents, seen and understood? Did you feel real to them? (Supplementary questions: Did your parents seem to make a genuine effort to understand you? Did your parents seem authentically interested in you as a person? Could

you talk to your parents about issues of importance and receive concerned, meaningful understanding from them?) *Was there congruence between your sense of who you were and the sense of who you were conveyed by your parents?*

8. Did you feel loved and valued by your parents, in the sense that you experienced yourself as a source of pleasure to them? Or did you feel unwanted, perhaps a burden? Did you feel hated? Or did you feel that you were simply an object of indifference? *Were you implicitly encouraged to experience yourself as lovable?*

9. Did your parents deal with you fairly and justly? (Supplementary questions: Did your parents resort to threats to control your behavior— either threats of immediate punitive action on their part, threats in terms of long-range consequences for your life, or threats of supernatural punishments, such as going to hell? Were you appreciated when you did well, or merely criticized when you did badly? Were your parents willing to admit it when they were wrong? Or was it against their policy to concede that they were wrong?) *Did you feel yourself to be living in a rational, just, and "sane" environment?*

10. Was it your parents' practice to punish you or discipline you by striking or beating you? *Was fear or terror intentionally evoked in you as a means of manipulation and control?*

11. Did your parents project that they believed in your basic competence and goodness? Or that they saw you as disappointing, ineffectual, worthless, or bad? *Did you feel that your parents were on your side, supporting the best within you?*

12. Did your parents convey the sense that they believed in your intellectual and creative potentialities? Or did they project that they saw you as mediocre or stupid or inadequate? *Did you feel that your mind and abilities were appreciated?*

13. In your parents' expectations concerning your behavior and performance, did they take cognizance of your knowledge, needs, interests, and circumstances? Or were you confronted with expectations and demands that were overwhelming and beyond your ability to satisfy? *Were you encouraged to treat your wants and needs as important?*

14. Did your parents' behavior and manner of dealing with you tend to produce guilt in you? *Were you implicitly (or explicitly) encouraged to see yourself as bad?*

15. Did your parents' behavior and manner of dealing with you tend to produce fear in you? *Were you encouraged to think, not in terms of*

gaining values or satisfaction, but in terms of avoiding pain or disapproval?

16. Did your parents respect your intellectual and physical privacy? *Were your dignity and rights respected?*

17. Did your parents project that it was desirable for you to think well of yourself—in effect, to have self-esteem? Or were you cautioned against valuing yourself, encouraged to be "humble"? *Was self-esteem a value in your home?*

18. Did your parents convey that what a person made of his or her life and what you, specifically, made of your life, was important? (Supplementary questions: Did your parents project that great things are possible for human beings, and specifically that great things were possible for you? Did your parents give you the impression that life could be exciting, challenging, a rewarding adventure?) *Were you offered an uplifting vision of what was possible in life?*

19. Did your parents instill in you a fear of the world, a fear of other people? *Were you given the sense that the world is a malevolent place?*

20. Were you urged to be open in the expression of your emotions and desires? Or were your parents' behavior and manner of treating you such as to make you fear emotional self-assertiveness and openness or to regard it as inappropriate? *Were emotional honesty, self-expression, and self-acceptance supported?*

21. Were your mistakes accepted as a normal part of the learning process? Or as something you were taught to associate with contempt, ridicule, punishment? *Were you encouraged in a fear-free approach to new challenges and new learning?*

22. Did your parents encourage you in the direction of having a healthy, affirmative attitude toward sex and toward your own body? A negative attitude? Or did they treat the entire subject as nonexistent? *Did you feel supported in a happy and positive attitude toward your physical being and evolving sexuality?*

23. Did your parents' manner of dealing with you tend to develop and strengthen your sense of your masculinity or femininity? Or to frustrate and diminish it? *If you were male, did your parents convey that that was desirable? If you were female, did they convey that that was desirable?*

24. Did your parents encourage you to feel that your life belonged to you? Or were you encouraged to believe that you were merely a family asset and that your achievements were significant only insofar as they

brought glory to your parents? (Supplementary question: Were you treated as a family resource, or as an end in yourself?) *Were you encouraged to understand that you are not here on earth to live up to someone else's expectations?*

Strategic Detachment

Many children undergo experiences that place enormous obstacles in the way of the development of self-esteem. Everyone knows this. A child may find the world of parents and other adults incomprehensible and threatening. The self is not nurtured but attacked. The will to be conscious and efficacious is assaulted. After a number of unsuccessful attempts to understand adult policies, statements, and behavior, many children give up—and take the blame for their feelings of helplessness.

Often they sense, miserably, desperately, and inarticulately, that something is terribly wrong—with their elders, or with themselves, or with *something.* What they often come to feel is: "I'll never understand other people. I'll never be able to do what they expect of me. I don't know what's right or wrong, and I'm never going to know."

To persevere with the will to understand in the face of obstacles is the heroism of consciousness.

The heroic child who continues to struggle to make sense out of the world and the people in it, however, is developing a powerful source of strength, no matter what the anguish or bewilderment experienced along the way. Caught in a particularly cruel, frustrating, and irrational environment, he or she will doubtless feel alienated from many of the people in the immediately surrounding world, and legitimately so. But the child will not feel alienated from reality, will not feel, at the deepest level, incompetent to live—or at least he or she has a decent chance to avoid that fate. To persevere with the will to understand in the face of obstacles is the heroism of consciousness.

Often children who survive extremely adverse childhoods have learned a particular survival strategy. I call it "strategic detachment." This is not the withdrawal from reality that leads to psychological disturbance, but an intuitively calibrated *disengagement* from noxious aspects of their family life or other aspects of their world. They somehow know, *This is not all there is.* They hold the belief that a better alternative exists *somewhere* and that *someday they will find their way to it.* They persevere in that idea. They somehow know *Mother is not all women, Father is not all men, this family does not exhaust the possibilities of human relationships—there is life beyond this neighborhood.* This does not spare them suffering in the present, but it allows them not to be destroyed by it. Their strategic detachment does not guarantee that they will never know feelings of powerlessness, but it helps them not to be stuck there.

We admire such children. But as parents we would like to offer our own children happier options.

Parenting as a Vehicle of Personal Evolution

In an earlier chapter I outlined the key ideas or beliefs most consequential for self-esteem. It follows that a family in which these ideas are communicated, as well as exemplified in the adult's practice, is one in which children's self-esteem is nurtured. A child who grows up in this philosophical context has an enormous developmental advantage.

However, ideas and values are most powerfully communicated when they are embedded into family life, rooted in the being of the parents. Regardless of what we think we're teaching, we teach what we are.

This fact can be turned around and looked at from another perspective.

Almost any important task can be used as a vehicle for personal development. Work can be a path for personal growth and development; so can marriage; so can child-rearing. We can choose to make any of them a spiritual discipline—a discipline in the service of our own evolution. We can take the principles that build self-esteem and use our work as an arena in which to apply them—with the result that both performance and self-esteem will rise. We can take the same principles and apply them in our marriage—with the result that the relationship will flourish (other things being equal) and self-esteem will rise. We can take the principles that raise self-esteem in ourselves, and apply them to our interactions with our children.

We need not pretend to our children that we are "perfect." We can acknowledge our struggles and admit our mistakes. The likelihood is that the self-esteem of everyone in the family will benefit.

If we choose to bring a (5 percent!) higher level of consciousness to dealings with our children—to what we say and how we respond—what might we do differently?

If we choose to bring a higher level of self-acceptance to our life, what might we convey to our children about self-acceptance?

If we choose to bring a higher level of self-responsibility to our parenting (rather than always blaming our mate or our children), what example might we set?

If we are more self-assertive, more authentic, what might our children learn about being genuine?

If we operate at a higher level of purposefulness, what might our children learn about goal achievement and an active orientation toward life?

If we bring a higher level of integrity to the task of parenting, in what ways might our children benefit?

And if we do all of this, in what ways might *we* benefit?

The answer to this last is simple: In supporting and nurturing the self-esteem of our children, we support and nurture our own.

14

Self-Esteem in the Schools

To many children, school represents a "second chance"—an opportunity to acquire a better sense of self and a better vision of life than was offered in their home. A teacher who projects confidence in a child's competence and goodness can be a powerful antidote to a family in which such confidence is lacking and in which perhaps the opposite perspective is conveyed. A teacher who treats boys and girls with respect can provide enlightenment for a child struggling to understand human relationships who comes from a home where such respect is nonexistent. A teacher who refuses to accept a child's negative self-concept and relentlessly holds to a better view of the child's potential has the power—sometimes—to save a life. A client once said to me, "It was my fourth-grade teacher who made me aware a different kind of humanity existed than my family—she gave me a vision to inspire me."

But for some children, school is a legally enforced incarceration at the hands of teachers who lack either the self-esteem or the training or both to do their jobs properly. These are teachers who do not inspire but humiliate. They do not speak the language of courtesy and respect but of ridicule and sarcasm. With invidious comparisons they flatter one student at the expense of another. With unmanaged impatience they deepen a child's terror of making mistakes. They have no other notion of discipline than threats of pain. They do not motivate by offering values but by evoking fear. They do not believe in a child's possibilities; they believe only in limitations. They do not light fires in minds, they extinguish them.

Who cannot recall encountering at least one such teacher during one's school years?

Of any professional group it is teachers who have shown the greatest receptivity to the importance of self-esteem.

Most teachers want to make a positive contribution to the minds entrusted to their care. If they sometimes do harm, it is not by intention. And today most are aware that one of the ways they can contribute is by nurturing the child's self-esteem. They know that children who believe in themselves, and whose teachers project a positive view of their potential, do better in school than children without these advantages. Indeed, of any professional group it is teachers who have shown the greatest receptivity to the importance of self-esteem. But what nurtures self-esteem in the classroom is not self-evident.

I have stressed that "feel good" notions are harmful rather than helpful. Yet if one examines the proposals offered to teachers on how to raise students' self-esteem, many are the kind of trivial nonsense that gives self-esteem a bad name, such as praising and applauding a child for virtually everything he or she does, dismissing the importance of objective accomplishments, handing out gold stars on every possible occasion, and propounding an "entitlement" idea of self-esteem that leaves it divorced from both behavior and character. One of the consequences of this approach is to expose the whole self-esteem movement in the schools to ridicule.

By way of illustration, consider an article appearing in *Time* (February 5, 1990) that stated:

> A standardized math test was given to 13-year-olds in six countries last year. Koreans did the best, Americans did the worst, coming in behind Spain, Ireland, and Canada. Now the bad news. Besides being shown triangles and equations, the kids were shown the statement "I am good at mathematics." . . . Americans were No. 1, with an impressive 68% in agreement.
>
> American students may not know their math, but they have evidently absorbed the lessons of the newly fashionable self-esteem curriculum wherein kids are taught to feel good about themselves.

Some American educators have argued that these figures are misleading because whereas other countries measured the performance of only the top 10 percent of students, the U.S. figures represent a much broader sampling, which brought our average down. They have also argued that in the Korean culture, for instance, it is far less acceptable to say complimentary things about oneself than in the American culture. Just the same, within the limits of his naive and primitive understanding of self-esteem, the criticisms of "self-esteem curricula" the author of this article goes on to make are entirely justified. He is attacking, in effect, the "feel good" approach, and the attack is deserved.

Therefore, let me stress once again that when I write of self-efficacy or self-respect, I do so in the context of reality, not of feelings generated out of wishes or affirmations or gold stars granted as a reward for showing up. When I talk to teachers, I talk about *reality-based* self-esteem. Let me say further that one of the characteristics of persons with healthy self-esteem is that they tend to assess their abilities and accomplishments realistically, neither denying nor exaggerating them.

Might a student do poorly in school and yet have good self-esteem? Of course. There are any number of reasons why a particular boy or girl might not do well scholastically, from a dyslexic condition to lack of adequate challenge and stimulation. Grades are hardly a reliable indicator of a given individual's self-efficacy and self-respect. But rationally self-esteeming students do not delude themselves that they are doing well when they are doing poorly.

Self-esteem pertains to that which is open to our volitional choice. It cannot properly be a function of the family we were born into, or our race, or the color of our skin, or the achievements of our ancestors.

We do not serve the healthy development of young people when we convey that self-esteem may be achieved by reciting "I am special" every day, or by stroking one's own face while saying "I love me," or by identifying self-worth with membership in a particular group ("ethnic pride") rather than with personal character. Let us remember that self-esteem pertains to *that which is open to our volitional choice*. It cannot properly be a function of the family we were born into, or our race, or the color of our skin, or the achievements of our ancestors. These are values people sometimes cling to in order to avoid responsibility for achieving authentic self-esteem. They are sources of pseudo self-esteem. Can one ever take legitimate pleasure in any of these values? Of course. Can they ever provide temporary support for fragile, growing egos? Probably. But they are not substitutes for consciousness, responsibility, or integrity. They are not sources of self-efficacy and self-respect. They can, however, become sources of self-delusion.

On the other hand, the principle of self-acceptance can have an important application here. Some students who come from different ethnic backgrounds but who are eager to "fit in" may in effect deny and disown their distinctive ethnic context. In such cases it is clearly desirable to help students to appreciate the unique aspects of their race or culture, to "own" their history, as it were, and not treat their heritage as unreal or shameful.

What makes the challenge of fostering children's self-esteem particularly urgent today is that many young people arrive in school in such a condition of emotional distress that concentrating on learning can be extraordinarily difficult. Robert Reasoner, former superintendent of the Moreland School District in California, writes:

Sixty-eight percent of children entering school today in California have both parents in the work force, which means relatively little time spent with either parent. Over 50 percent of students have already seen a family change—a separation, a divorce, or a remarriage; in many districts, by high school 68 percent are not living with their two original parents. Twenty-four percent are born out of wedlock and have never known a father. Twenty-four percent are born bearing the residual effects of their mother's abuse of drugs. In California, 25 percent will be either sexually or physically abused before they finish high school. Twenty-five percent come from families with alcohol or drug problems. Thirty percent are living in conditions considered substandard. Fifteen percent are recent immigrants adjusting to a new culture and a new language. Whereas in 1890 90 percent of the children had grandparents living in the home, and in 1950 40 percent living in the home, today the figure is down to 7 percent; so there is far less of a support system. As to the emotional life of young people, consider these figures. Thirty to 50 percent will contemplate suicide. Fifteen percent will make a serious attempt to kill themselves. Forty-one percent drink heavily every two-three weeks. Ten percent of girls will become pregnant before they finish high school. Thirty percent of boys and girls will drop out of school by the age of eighteen.[1]

Schools cannot be expected to provide solutions for all the problems in students' lives. But good schools—which means good teachers—can make an enormous difference. In attempting to raise self-esteem in the classroom, what are the issues? In this chapter I want to address—in broad strokes—the fundamentals that need to be considered.

The Goals of Education

Perhaps the place to begin is with how the teacher conceives the goals of education.

Is the primary goal to train young people to be "good citizens"? Then a high premium may be placed not on fostering autonomy or encouraging independent thinking but on memorizing a shared body of knowledge and belief, on absorbing "the rules" of the particular society, and often on learning obedience to authority. Earlier in our history, this clearly was the goal of our public educational system.

In *Breakpoint and Beyond*, George Land and Beth Jarman make an interesting observation worth quoting in this context:

> As late as October of 1989, the Association of California School Administrators, operating from a viewpoint of [traditional] thinking, announced, "The purpose of the school system is not to provide students with an education." Individual education is "a means to the true end of education, which is to create a viable social order." Here the leaders of one of the largest school systems in the world have declared that students can enter the twenty-first century supported by schools that do not have education as their central purpose![2]

I vividly recall my own experiences in grade school and high school during the 1930s and 1940s. The two most important values conveyed to me in that world were the ability to remain silent and motionless for long periods of time and the ability to march with my fellow students in a neat row from one classroom to another. School was not a place to learn independent thinking, to have one's self-assertiveness encouraged, to have one's autonomy nourished and strengthened. It was a place to learn how to fit into some nameless system created by some nameless others and called "the world" or "society" or "the way life is." And "the way life is" was not to be questioned. Since I questioned everything and found silence and stillness unbearable, I was quickly identified as a trouble-maker.

Many brilliant minds have commented on their dismal experiences in school, their boredom, their lack of appropriate intellectual stimulation and nourishment, their sense that the last thing the educational system was designed for was the cultivation of minds. Schools were interested not in autonomy but in the manufacture of someone's notion of "good citizens."

"In education," wrote Carl Rogers in *On Becoming a Person*, "we tend to turn out conformists, stereotypes, individuals whose education is 'completed,' rather than freely creative and original thinkers."

Commenting on this disposition of teachers (and parents) to demand obedience and conformity as primary values, to discourage rather than support normal and healthy progress toward autonomy, Jean Piaget wrote in *The Moral Judgment of the Child*, "If one thinks of the systematic resistance offered by people to the authoritarian method, and the admirable ingenuity employed by children the world over to evade disciplinarian constraint, one cannot help regarding as defective a system which allows so much effort to be wasted instead of using it in cooperation."

What is needed and demanded today, in the age of the knowledge worker, is not robotic obedience but persons who can think.

There is reason to hope that this orientation is changing. The assembly line has long since ceased to be the appropriate symbol of the workplace, as we have made the transition from a manufacturing to an information society and mind work has largely replaced muscle work. What is needed and demanded today, in the age of the knowledge worker, is not robotic obedience but persons who can think; who can innovate, originate, and function self-responsibly; who are capable of self-management; who can remain individuals while working effectively as members of teams; who are confident of their powers and their ability to contribute. What the workplace needs today is self-esteem. And what the workplace needs sooner or later of necessity becomes the agenda of the schools.

In earlier forms of industrial organization, where a great deal of work was repetitive and near mindless, obedience may have been a prized value. It is hardly the first trait a manager looks for today. A superb teacher of teachers and a specialist in educational technology that supports autonomy, Jane Bluestein observes in *21st Century Discipline*, "There is evidence that children who are too obedient may have difficulty functioning in today's work world."[3] Today, a high premium is put on initiative and self-responsibility because that is what a rapidly changing, intensely competitive economy requires.

If schools are to be adaptive, the goals of education need to embrace more than merely mastering a particular body of knowledge that students are expected to regurgitate on exams. The aim must be to teach children how to think, how to recognize logical fallacies, how to be creative, *and how to learn.* This last is emphasized because of the speed with which yesterday's knowledge becomes inadequate to today's demands: most work now requires a commitment to lifelong learning. Among other things, young people need to learn how to use computers and libraries to access the ever-expanding new knowledge essential to their progress in the workplace.

Schools are criticized at present because it is possible to graduate high school without knowing how to write a coherent paragraph or add up one's restaurant check. But a mastery of simple English composition or arithmetic, while essential, does not begin to touch what a person must know today at any level above the most menial job.

So the fostering of self-esteem must be integrated into school curricula for at least two reasons. One is to support young people in persevering with their studies, staying off drugs, preventing pregnancy, abstaining from vandalism, and gaining the education they need. The other is to help prepare them psychologically for a world in which *the mind* is everyone's chief capital asset.

I confess to cringing a little when I hear colleagues in the self-esteem/education field announce that teachers must help young people to trust their "intuition"—while not saying a word about teaching them to think, or understand the principles of logic, or have a respect for reason—thus implying that "intuition" is all they need. "Intuition" has a place in the scheme of things, to be sure, but without rationality it is dangerously unreliable. At best, it is not enough, and it is irresponsible to suggest to young people that it is. No one has ever suggested that Charles Manson did not operate "intuitively."

If the proper goal of education is to provide students with a foundation in the basics needed to function effectively in the modern world, then nothing is more important than building courses on the art of critical thinking into every school curriculum. And if self-esteem means confidence in our ability to cope with the challenges of life, is anything more important than learning how to use one's mind?

We are thinking beings and we are creative beings. Recognition of this fact needs to be at the center of any educational philosophy. When we place the value of these functions at the forefront of our curriculum, we nurture self-esteem.

Individual teachers and designers of curricula must ask themselves: How does my work contribute to the process of young people becoming thinking, innovative, creative human beings?

The Teacher's Self-Esteem

As with parents, it is easier for a teacher to inspire self-esteem in students if the teacher exemplifies and models a healthy, affirmative sense of self. Indeed, some research suggests that this is the primary factor in the teacher's ability to contribute to a student's self-esteem.[4]

Teachers with low self-esteem tend to be more punitive, impatient, and authoritarian. They tend to focus on the child's weaknesses rather than strengths. They inspire fearfulness and defensiveness. They encourage dependency.[5]

Low-self-esteem teachers are typically unhappy teachers.

Teachers with low self-esteem tend to be overdependent on the approval of others. They tend to feel that others are the source of their "self-esteem." Therefore, they are hardly in a position to teach that self-esteem must be generated primarily from within. They tend to use their own approval and disapproval to manipulate students into obedience and conformity, since that is the approach that works when others apply it to them. They teach that self-esteem comes from "adult and peer approval." They convey an external approach to self-esteem rather than an internal one, thereby deepening whatever self-esteem problems students already have.

Further, low-self-esteem teachers are typically unhappy teachers, and unhappy teachers often favor demeaning and destructive tactics of classroom control.

Children watch teachers in part to learn appropriate adult behavior. If they see ridicule and sarcasm, often they learn to use it themselves. If they hear the language of disrespect, and even cruelty, it tends to show up in their own verbal responses. If, in contrast, they see benevolence and an emphasis on the positive, they may learn to integrate that into their own responses. If they witness fairness, they may absorb the attitude of fairness. If they receive compassion and see it offered to others, they may learn to internalize compassion. If they see self-esteem, they may decide it is a value worth acquiring.

Furthermore, as Robert Reasoner notes:

> Teachers with high self-esteem are ... more apt to help children develop problem-solving strategies than to give advice or deny the significance of what children perceive to be problems. Such teachers build a sense of trust in students. They base their classroom control on understanding, joint cooperation and involvement, working through problems, caring, and mutual respect. This positive relationship allows children to learn and to grow in their confidence and ability to function independently.[6]

What a great teacher, a great parent, a great psychotherapist, and a great coach have in common is a deep belief in the potential of the person with whom they are concerned—a conviction about what that person is capable of being and doing—plus the ability to transmit the conviction during their interactions. "I always did poorly in math in school," a client said to me, "and I always knew I could never do well—until I met a teacher who refused to believe me. She *knew* I could do math, and her certainty had so much power it was irresistible." The ability to inspire students in this way is not usually found among teachers who have little belief in themselves.

Teachers with good self-esteem are likely to understand that if they wish to nurture the self-esteem of another, they need to relate to that person from their vision of his or her worth and value, providing an experience of acceptance and respect. They know that most of us tend to underestimate our inner resources, and they keep that knowledge central in their awareness. Most of us are capable of more than we believe. When teachers remain clear about this, others can acquire this understanding from them almost by contagion.

Sometimes it can be difficult to go on believing in another person when that person seems not to believe in him or herself. Yet one of the greatest gifts a teacher can offer a student is the refusal to accept the student's poor self-concept at face value, seeing through it to the deeper, stronger self that exists within if only as a potential. (This is accomplished, in part, by making the student aware of choices and options the student had not noted and by breaking problems down into smaller, more manageable units that fall within the student's present competence and thus give him or her a base on which to build.) A teacher's own self-esteem can make this task easier.

---

*One of the greatest gifts a teacher can offer a student
is the refusal to accept the student's poor
self-concept at face value.*

For this reason, when I speak at teachers' conferences, I often spend much of my time talking about what educators can do to raise the level of their own self-esteem rather than about what they can do for the self-esteem of students. Remember the guru with the weakness for sweets.

Expectations

To give a child the experience of acceptance does not mean, as we have already noted, to signal "I expect nothing of you." Teachers who want children to give their best must convey that that is what they expect.

Research tells us that a teacher's expectations tend to turn into self-fulfilling prophecies. If a teacher expects a child to get an A—or a D—either way, expectations tend to become realities. If a teacher knows how to convey "I am absolutely convinced you can master this subject, and I expect you to and will give you all the help you need," the child feels nurtured, supported, and inspired.

A classroom in which what is wanted and expected is that one will give one's best is a classroom that develops both learning and self-esteem.

The Class Environment

If the primary goal of the educational system is one factor that has consequences for a child's self-esteem, and if the teacher's own self-esteem is another, yet a third is the classroom environment. This means the way the child is treated by the teacher and sees other children being treated.

1. *A child's dignity.* One of the painful things about being a child is that one tends not to be taken seriously by adults. Whether one is dismissed discourteously or praised for being "cute," most children are not used to having their dignity as human beings respected. So a teacher who treats all students with courtesy and respect sends a signal to the class: You are now in an environment where different rules apply than those you may be used to. In this world, your dignity and feelings matter. In this simple way a teacher can begin to create an environment that supports self-esteem.

I recall an incident many years ago when I was invited to speak at a school for gifted children. During my presentation I invited the students to talk about what it was like to be labeled "a gifted child." They spoke enthusiastically about the pluses, but they also spoke about minuses. Some talked about the discomfort of being treated as a "family resource." Some talked about the high expectations of their parents that did not necessarily relate to their own interests and needs. They talked about wanting to be treated "like normal human beings." And they talked about the ways even loving adults did not necessarily treat them seriously. Present in the room, in addition to the students, were most of the teachers, the assistant principal, and the school psychologist. After the talk, a number of students gathered around to ask me further questions. Then the assistant principal joined in and asked some question of a boy who looked to be about eleven. Halfway through his answer, the school psychologist walked over and started talking to the assistant principal— who turned her back on the boy and left him standing there in midsentence. Astonished, he looked at me and spread his arms, as if to say, "What can you do when you deal with grown-ups? They still don't get it." I smiled in understanding and spread my arms, copying his gesture, as if to say, "Yeah, what can you do?" If this assistant principal had been talking to an adult rather than a child and her colleague had interrupted as he did, without a word of apology or explanation, and if she had turned her back on the adult speaking, without even an "Excuse me," they both would have been perceived as flagrantly rude. Except that, since an adult was involved, they almost certainly wouldn't have done it. Why is discourtesy acceptable if directed against a young person? What message is conveyed? That respect is only appropriate for older people?

2. *Justice in the classroom.* Children are extremely sensitive to issues of fairness. If they see the same rules applied consistently to everyone; if, for instance, they see that their teacher has the same attitude and policy whether talking to a boy, a girl, a Caucasian, a black American, a Hispanic, or an Asian—they register the appropriate lesson, they perceive the teacher as having integrity, and their sense of safety and security is enhanced. On the other hand, favoritism (and disfavoritism) poisons a classroom atmosphere. It encourages feelings of isolation and rejection and diminishes children's sense that this is a world with which they will be able to deal. A teacher cannot help enjoying one student more than another, but professionals know how to manage their feelings. They hold themselves accountable to objective standards of behavior. A child needs the sense that in the classroom, justice will prevail. A teacher who does not understand this can turn an eight-year-old into a cynic who no longer cares to give his or her best.

3. *Self-appreciation.* When teachers help a child feel visible by offering appropriate feedback, they encourage self-awareness. When they offer not judgments but descriptions of what they see, they help the child to see him or herself. When they draw attention to a child's strengths, they encourage self-appreciation.

However, teachers often tend to concentrate not on strengths but on weaknesses. Johnny is good at English but poor in math, so the whole focus is put on math. Since math does have to be learned, this is understandable, but it is a mistake nonetheless. The mistake is not that the teacher says math needs more attention—it does; the mistake is that the teacher treats this as more important than Johnny's skill in English. If Johnny is good in English, that is a reason to encourage him to do *more* writing and reading, not less. Teachers tend to call parents when a child is doing poorly. There is reason to believe that calling them when the child is doing well could be more productive; in the latter case one can still address negatives but not treat them as the most important element in the situation. Help Johnny to be aware of and appreciate his assets. They may indicate where his passion lies and point the way to his future.

And even when dealing with weaknesses, a teacher can focus on Johnny's deficiency in ways that hurt self-esteem: "You'll never get anywhere in life if you can't learn such-and-such—what's the matter with you?" Or the teacher can inspire him to extend his mastery to a new field, so that working on math becomes self-esteem building—"You stick with it, even though it's tough." The focus should remain on the positive.

Sometimes a child is not fully aware of his or her assets. It is the teacher's job to facilitate that awareness. This has nothing to do with phony compliments. Every child does some things right. Every child has some assets. They must be found, identified, and nurtured. A teacher should be a prospector, looking for gold. Try to think back to what it would have been like to be in a class where the teacher felt there was no more urgent task than to discover the good in you—your strengths and virtues—and to help you become more aware of them. Would that have inspired the best in you? Would that be an environment in which you were motivated to grow and learn?

A teacher should be a prospector, looking for gold.

---

4. *Attention.* Every child needs attention, and some children need more attention than others. There is one kind of student who is often ignored. This is the student who does his or her work extremely well but who is shy, retiring, and very silent in class. A teacher needs to make an extra effort to bring this child out. This might be accomplished by asking, as often as necessary, "Clara, what's your opinion?" Or, "What do you think about that, Charley?" Sometimes it is useful to ask such a child to help some other student who is having difficulties with the work, so that the child has an opportunity to "come out" and experience being effective with another person. (The point is not altruism; the point is that the child gets to experience being socially competent. "Peer facilitation," observes educator Kenneth Miller, "is one of the best things happening in schools today."[7] Sometimes it is useful to ask the shy student to stay for a few minutes after class to form more of a personal connection—to send the signal that he or she is noticed and cared about.

This is a signal that every student needs and deserves. Above all, what is needed is the message that what the child thinks and feels *matters.* The tragedy for many children is when year after year they do not get this message from adults, at some point what they think and feel matters less to themselves. The problem is compounded when children who treat themselves as if they did not matter are praised for their "unselfishness."

5. *Discipline.* In every classroom there are rules that must be re-spected if learning is to progress and tasks are to be accomplished. Rules

can be *imposed,* by dint of the teacher's power, or they can be *explained* in such a way as to engage the mind and understanding of the student. Jane Bluestein writes:

> When we ask our students to do something, we usually have a better reason than *because I said so.* Telling them the real, logical, and intrinsic reason for a limit or a rule—so the markers do not dry out, so that we do not disturb anyone on our way down the hall, so that no one trips and falls—builds commitment and cooperation even from rebellious students.[8]

A teacher can think about rules in one of two ways. She or he can wonder: How can I *make* students do what needs to be done? Or: How can I inspire students to *want* to do what needs to be done? The first orientation is necessarily adversarial and at best achieves obedience while encouraging dependency. The second orientation is benevolent and achieves cooperation, while encouraging self-responsibility. The first approach threatens pain. The second offers values—and power, too. Which approach a teachers feels more comfortable with has a good deal to do with his or her sense of efficacy as a person.

Sometimes a teacher may feel that there is no choice but to motivate by a student's desire to avoid a negative rather than to gain a positive. Perhaps so. But as an exclusive or dominant policy it is psychologically disempowering. It makes escape from pain more important than experiencing joy—which leads to self-contraction (the contraction of thought and feeling) rather than self-expression and self-development.

In *Teacher Effectiveness Training,* Tom Gordon proposes that students participate in the process of rule setting—that they be invited to think through what an effective classroom requires—and this has the advantage not only of stimulating superior cooperation but also of fostering greater autonomy.

"The essence of discipline," writes Haim Ginott in *Teacher and Child,* "is finding effective alternatives to punishment." His chapter on discipline in this book is outstanding in the strategies he offers for motivating students in ways that enhance rather than diminish self-esteem.

Discipline problems often result when children come to school with negative expectations concerning the behavior of adults based on their experiences at home. Without conscious awareness of their motives, they may be disruptive or hostile in class to evoke the kind of punishment they are used to; they may provoke anger because anger is what they "know" is in store for them. The challenge to a teacher is not to be "hooked" by this strategy and fulfill the student's worst expectations. It can be difficult to preserve respect and compassion when dealing with such students, but teachers wise and mature enough to do so can have an extraordinary impact.

> *Compassion and respect do not imply*
> *lack of firmness.*

An examination of the strategies of maintaining classroom discipline is not my purpose here. An excellent treatment of that issue, apart from the Ginott book, may be found in Jane Bluestein's *21st Century Discipline*. Bluestein displays great ingenuity in illustrating how teachers can maintain discipline while strengthening the autonomy of the student.

She addresses, for instance, the well-known but often ignored principle that misconduct is better corrected by allowing a student to experience its logical consequences than by punishment. When a class was sluggish and uncooperative—repeatedly—about completing a lesson, she announced that class would not be dismissed for lunch until the lesson was completed. By the time the students got to the lunchroom the food was cold and much of it was gone. Next day, every lesson was completed and every desk was neatly cleared two minutes before dismissal time. "I'm still amazed that they all learned to tell time overnight." She writes:

> In . . . authority relationships, misconduct is an invitation for the teacher to exercise power and control. Our immediate response, in this type of arrangement, is *How can I teach him or her a lesson?* In a 21st-century classroom, the lessons to be learned from one's misconduct come from the consequences of this misconduct, not the power of the teacher. . . . In the example [of the sluggish class], the students missed lunch because of a poor choice they had made, not as a punishment for misbehaving. As soon as the students got themselves ready on time, there was no reason for the negative consequence (delaying lunch) to continue.

One last word on this subject. If low self-esteem can impel some teachers to rigid, punitive, even sadistic behavior, it can impel others to the kind of mushy "permissiveness" that signals a complete absence of authority—with classroom anarchy as the result. Compassion and respect do not imply lack of firmness. A capitulation to disruptive elements in the class means abdication of the teacher's responsibilities. Competent teachers understand the need for standards of acceptable behavior. But they also understand that toughness need not and should not entail insults or responses aimed at demeaning anyone's sense of personal value. One of the characteristics of a superior teacher is mastery of this challenge.

To achieve the results they want, teachers sometimes have to exercise imagination. Problems cannot be reduced to a list of formula strategies that will fit every occasion. One teacher I know solved a classroom problem by gravely asking the biggest, noisiest boy in the class, when they were alone, if he could help her by exercising his natural leadership abilities to persuade some of the others to be more orderly. The boy looked a bit disoriented, evidently not knowing how to answer; but peacefulness quickly prevailed, and the boy responsible felt proud of himself.

Understanding Emotions

If a proper education has to include an understanding of thinking, it also has to include an understanding of feelings.

Unfortunately, many parents implicitly teach children to repress their feelings and emotions—or those which parents find disturbing. "Stop crying or I'll really give you something to cry about!" "Don't you dare get angry!" "Don't be afraid! Do you want people to think you're a sissy?" "No decent girl has such feelings!" "Don't be so excited! *What's the matter with you?*"

Emotionally remote and inhibited parents tend to produce emotionally remote and inhibited children. This is accomplished not only through their overt communications but also by their own behavior, which signals to a child what is "proper," "appropriate," "socially acceptable."

Further, parents who accept certain teachings of religion are likely to convey the unfortunate notion that there are such things as "evil thoughts" or "evil emotions." "It's a sin to feel that!" The child may learn moral terror of his or her inner life.

An emotion is both a mental and a physical event. It is an automatic psychological response, involving both mental and physiological features, to our subconscious appraisal of what we perceive as beneficial or harmful to ourself.* Emotions reflect the perceiver's value response to different aspects of reality: "for me or against me," "good for me or harmful," "to be pursued or to be avoided," and so forth. A discussion of the psychology of emotions may be found in *The Disowned Self.*

To cease to know what we feel is to cease to experience what things mean to us. This unconsciousness is often actively encouraged in children. A child may be led to believe that emotions are potentially dangerous, that sometimes it is necessary to deny them, to make oneself unaware of them. The child can learn to disown certain emotions and cease to experience them consciously. On the psychological level, a child deflects awareness, thereby ceasing to recognize or acknowledge certain feelings. On the physical level, a child inhibits breathing, tenses his or her body, induces muscular tensions, and blocks the free flow of feelings, thereby inducing a partial state of numbness.

I do not wish to imply that parents are the only source of childhood repression. They are not. Children can learn on their own to protect their equilibrium by disowning certain of their feelings, as I discuss in *Honoring the Self.* However, it is undeniable that too many parents encourage the practice of emotional repression by making it a tacit condition of their approval.

As the child grows, he or she may slash away more and more feelings, more and more parts of the self, in order to be accepted, loved, and not abandoned. The child may practice self-repudiation as a survival strategy. He or she cannot be expected to understand the unfortunate long-range consequences.

A teacher is in a position to teach children a rational respect for feelings coupled with an awareness that one can accept a feeling without having to be ruled by it.

We can learn to own when we are afraid, and accept it, and (for instance) still go to the dentist when it is necessary to do so. We can learn to admit when we are angry, and talk about it, and not resort to fists. We can learn to recognize when we hurt, and own the feeling, and not put on a phony act of indifference. We can learn to witness our feelings of impatience and excitement, and breathe into them, and yet not go out to play until we have finished our homework. We can learn to recognize our sexual feelings, and accept them, and not be controlled by them in self-destructive ways. We can learn to recognize and accept our emotions

---

* I omit here certain experiences of anxiety and depression whose roots may be biological and may not fully fit this definition.

without losing our minds. We can learn to wonder: What might my feelings be trying to tell me? What might I need to consider or think about?

We can learn that a pain or fear confronted is far less dangerous than a pain or fear denied.

We can learn that we are accountable for what we choose to do, but that feelings as such are neither moral nor immoral—they simply *are*.

Today, this is the kind of understanding some people gain only in psychotherapy. But in the schools of the future, no one will finish the twelfth grade without having been exposed to these ideas. They will be an integral part of everyone's education because of their clear importance to the achievement of a decent life.

―――

**We can learn to recognize and accept our emotions
without losing our minds.**

―――

It need hardly be added that if a teacher is to succeed in teaching self-acceptance, he or she must be comfortable in accepting the feelings of students, must create an environment in which such acceptance is felt by everyone. Children who feel accepted find it easier to accept themselves.

This point was made previously in our discussion of effective parenting and of necessity it is made again here. Indeed, virtually all of the principles identified in the preceding chapter have application in the classroom. For example, handling mistakes with benevolence rather than as if they were shameful; for reasons I trust are clear, how a teacher responds to a student's mistakes can have an impact on the rest of the student's life.

Few schools today teach the art of thinking and fewer still teach the things I have been saying about emotions. But the schools of the future will have to.

Dealing with Others

Another subject will have to be added at the grade and high school level: the art of interpersonal competence.

If self-esteem is confidence in our ability to cope with the basic challenges of life, one of these challenges is to relate effectively with other human beings. This means to relate in such a way that our interactions, more often than not, are experienced as positive and successful both for ourselves and for the other person(s). Consider that today about 95 percent of people who work for a living do so in an organization—they work with other people. If they lack the security and skills to relate competently, they are usually badly limited in what they will be able to accomplish. Any list of the four or five most important attributes for success in an organization mentions the ability to work well in cooperation with associates. True, people who relate poorly to others are sometimes successful, but it is the hard way around and the odds are against it.

We know a lot about the skills that make for competence in human interactions, and this knowledge needs to be part of a young person's education.

We know a lot about the skills that make for competence in human interactions, and this knowledge needs to be part of a young person's education.

We know, for example, that the best relationships rest on a foundation of respect for self and respect for the other. We know that win-win (mutually beneficial) negotiations, in which both parties gain values, are superior to win-lose negotiations, in which one person's gain is another's loss (a theme, incidentally, that is encountered more and more often in business literature). We know that dealing with people fairly and justly provides the security they need to give their best. We know that a spirit of benevolence, compassion, and mutual aid—without self-sacrifice—serves the interests of everyone. We know that people who keep their word and honor their promises and commitments evoke trust and cooperation, and those who don't, don't. We know that winners look for solutions and losers look for someone to blame. We know that verbal and written communication skills are of the highest importance, especially in the workplace—and are in fact one of the most significant determinants of career success. We know about active listening and appropriate feedback and the role of empathy—and also about what happens when these elements are missing. We know that the individual practice of self-responsibility and the willingness to be accountable can give teams a synergistic power obtainable in no other way. We know that appropriate self-assertiveness can enrich, not subvert, team efforts, and that fear of assertiveness can sabotage them. We know that *no* human interaction can be optimally successful if one or both parties are afraid of normal self-assertiveness and self-expression.

Is this knowledge of less importance to a young person's education than information about geography?

In providing training in interpersonal effectiveness, we accomplish two goals simultaneously: We nurture self-esteem, and we build competence in that which life asks of us.

Competence and Skills

We see, then, that what students need from teachers if they are to grow in self-esteem is respect, benevolence, positive motivation, and education in essential knowledge and vital skills.

Necessarily, children arrive in any class with significant differences in ability. Effective teachers know that one can learn only by building on strengths, not by focusing on weaknesses. Consequently, they build competence (and self-esteem) by giving the student tasks geared to his or her present level of ability. The successes that this approach makes possible allow the student to progress to the next step.

A teacher's job is to make victories possible—and then build on them.

Since the experience of mastering new challenges is essential to the growth of self-esteem, a teacher's artfulness in knowing how to calibrate this progression is vital.

The Grade Curve

One of the most unfortunate practices in schools today is marking students on a grade curve. This places every student in an adversarial relationship to every other student. Instead of wishing to be among bright students, one is given reason to wish to be among dull ones—since the competence of others is a threat to one's grades. Obviously there need to be criteria for measuring progress and for ascertaining level of mastery of a subject. I am not criticizing grades as such. But these criteria need to be objective. A standard that has no objective reference to knowledge or mastery and that makes every student the enemy of every other is no friend to self-esteem.

If I cannot write a two-page essay without half a dozen grammatical errors, the fact that everyone else in the class made over a dozen errors does not make me an A student in English Composition. If I am to grow and learn as I need to, I must be held to reasonable standards of competence. To provide those standards is one of the responsibilities of educators. Resorting to the grade curve is a default on this responsibility.

Cognitive Individuality

In the past it was assumed that everyone learned the same way and one teaching method could be right for everyone. Today we know that people learn in different ways, have different "cognitive styles," and that teaching at its best is adapted to the specific learning needs of individual students.[9] The better schools have begun to integrate this understanding into their teaching methods.

To quote Howard Gardner, a pioneering theorist in cognitive science:

Each person has a unique mixture of intelligences, or ways of understanding the world—linguistic, logical, mathematical, spatial, musical, physical (the use of the body to solve problems or make things), understanding of others and understanding of self.

Also, each person has a different learning style. Some may respond best to visual information, others to language (lectures, reading), others must touch or engage the physical world for things to make sense.

Once we understand this, it becomes malpractice to treat kids as if their minds were all the same.[10]

Systems have been developed that identify the three or four major learning styles of people, so that course material can be presented in the way most likely to be effective. It is safe to predict that this is going to be enormously important to the self-esteem of young people who in the past would have had to struggle to adopt to a cognitive style less natural to them than their own.

The Obedient Student Versus the Responsible Student

Let us contrast more traditional ways of teaching with the kind of teaching that nurtures self-esteem by way of a set of comparisons. What we are comparing are the characteristics of the obedient student with those of the responsible student—the student who experiences "the locus of control" as external to self versus the student who experiences "the locus of control" as internal. The contrast helps us understand some of the goals of "the new education." I have adapted this material from Jane Bluestein's *21st Century Discipline.*

The Obedient Student is characterized by the following traits:

1. Motivated by external factors, such as the need to please authority and win extrinsic approval.

2. Follows orders.

3. May lack confidence to function effectively in absence of authority figures; lacks initiative; waits for orders.

4. Self-esteem is defined externally; feels worthwhile only when receiving approval.

5. Feels "I am my behavior" (and somebody else probably made me this way).

6. Difficulty seeing connection between behavior and its consequences.

7. Difficulty seeing choices and options; finds it hard to make decisions.

8. Feelings of helplessness and teacher dependency are common.

The Responsible Student is characterized by the following traits:

1. Motivated by internal factors, such as the need to weigh choices and experience personal consequences.

2. Makes choices.

3. More confident to function effectively in the absence of authority; takes initiative.

4. Self-esteem: defined internally—worthwhile with or without approval (or even with disapproval).

5. Knows "I am not my behavior, although I am responsible for how I behave."

6. Better able to see the connection between behavior and its consequences.

7. Better able to see choices and options and to make decisions.

8. Personal sense of empowerment and independence is common.

9. Operates from an external value system (usually that of someone important to him or her, that is, "significant others") that may not be personally appropriate and may even be harmful.

9. Operates from internal value system (what is best or safest for him or her), while being considerate of the needs and values of others.

10. Obeys; may think.

10. Thinks; may obey.

11. Lacks confidence in internal signals and in ability to act in own self-interest.

11. Has confidence in internal signals and in ability to act in own self-interest.

12. Has difficulty predicting outcomes or consequences of actions.

12. Better able to predict outcomes or consequences of actions.

13. Has difficulty understanding or expressing personal needs.

13. Better able to understand and express personal needs.

14. Limited ability to get needs met without hurting self or others.

14. Better able to take care of own needs without hurting self or others.

15. Limited negotiation skills; orientation is "You win–I lose."

15. Better developed negotiation skills; orientation is "You win–I win."

16. Compliant.

16. Cooperative.

17. Oriented to avoid punishment, "keeping teacher off my back."

17. Commitment to the task, experiencing outcome of positive choosing.

18. May experience conflict between internal and external needs (what I want versus what teacher wants); may experience guilt or rebelliousness.

18. Better able to resolve conflict between internal and external needs (what I want versus what the teacher wants); less inclined to guilt or rebelliousness.

19. May make poor choices to avoid disapproval or abandonment (to make my friends like me more).

19. May make poor choices to experience personal consequences and to satisfy curiosity.

Moral Implications

To anticipate one of the conclusions toward which I am heading, I want to draw attention to one *moral* aspect of the shift from the ideal of obedience to the ideal of responsibility.

Whereas the obedient student will, under different circumstances, sacrifice self or others (this has been the practice of obedient people throughout all of human history), the responsible student, ideally, will be taught to operate outside the sacrifice paradigm. This is implicit in the "win-win" philosophy, although, unfortunately, it has not been identified explicitly. At best, the responsible student may learn a new concept of human relationships *that rejects the propriety of practicing human sacrifice.*

On the one hand, he or she will be far less ready to sacrifice others in pursuit of personal goals. On the other hand, he or she will be far less willing to *be sacrificed* for the alleged greater good of some alleged higher value—that is, for *someone else's goals.* He or she will be far less willing, for instance, to sacrifice a personal life for the good of the company (or the tribe) and will be far less willing to die (or kill) in a war dreamed up by leaders for reasons that offend human intelligence.

The obedient student was taught not to challenge authority. The responsible student is prepared to question—and if need be, to challenge—anything. As we will see more clearly in the next chapter, *that is what the marketplace now requires.* More broadly, it is what civilization requires.

The Treatment of Girls

Thus far in the book I have discussed issues of self-esteem with no reference to gender issues. Every recommendation I have made applies equally to males and females, since I see the basic principles of self-esteem as reflecting and addressing our common humanity. The importance of living consciously, for example, is not more urgent for one gender than for another. The six pillars are offered as universals for both genders and for all races, allowing for the fact that some *forms of expression* (of, say, self-assertiveness) may vary from culture to culture.

Yet a recent study has produced some alarming findings regarding self-esteem setbacks among adolescent girls. The American Association of University Women (AAUW), working with Greenberg-Lake: The Analysis Group, recently (1990) completed a national survey research project to study the interaction of self-esteem and education and career aspirations in adolescent girls and boys.[11] The study included three thousand children between grades four and ten, in twelve locations nationwide. One of its key findings was that while both boys and girls find adolescence a difficult time, and on average suffer a significant loss of self-esteem during this period, the loss is most dramatic and has the most long-lasting effect for girls.

Girls who at eight and nine are confident, assertive, and feel authoritative about themselves often emerge from adolescence with a poor self-concept, constrained views of their future, and much diminished confidence in themselves and their abilities.

The obedient student was taught not to challenge authority. The responsible student is prepared to question—and if need be, to challenge—anything.

The biggest difference between boys and girls shows up in the area of "doing things." Boys' sense of confidence in doing a lot of things well correlates with general self-esteem. Girls typically feel competent in far fewer areas, which correlates with poorer self-esteem. (Competence has survival value, therefore is basic to the experience of being appropriate to life.)

In class, boys speak out more than girls and are more likely to argue with the teacher if they feel they are right. In this area girls are less self-assertive.

None of this is surprising. Most girls are raised to regard intelligence and competence as much less important to their future than being pleasing and accommodating. A boy gets straight A's in school and his parents are jubilant; they feel this augers well for his future ability to earn a living. A girl gets straight A's and her parents may be indifferent: What has intelligence got to do with catching a husband? I know two children both of whom are assertive and outgoing and both of whom are physically beautiful. The boy receives smiles of approval for his boisterousness, but no one tells him constantly (or hardly at all) how beautiful he is. The girl receives little or no acknowledgment of her assertiveness but hears endlessly how pretty she is. (In the AAUW study girls are nearly twice as likely as boys to mention a physical characteristic as the thing they like most about themselves. Boys are nearly twice as likely as girls to mention a talent as the thing about themselves they like most.)

The problem of dramatic inequality in self-esteem is most likely to show up during adolescence because this is the period when young people are preparing for action in the adult world. To quote from the AAUW report:

> The higher self-esteem of young men translates into bigger career dreams. Boys start out at a higher level than do girls when it comes to career aspirations. . . . Finding it difficult to dream and constrained by gender rules, girls start out with lower hopes for their careers, and are already less confident in their talents and abilities. Girls are much more likely than boys to say they are "not smart enough" or "not good enough" for their dream careers.

The question of concern here is: Family and cultural considerations aside (and their influence is enormous), what might be the role of educators in this problem among adolescent girls?

Teachers are influenced by the same gender stereotypes as others in our culture. If our culture regards intelligence and achievement as less important in females than in males, teachers will often carry (and project) this perspective. If teachers expect girls to do less well than boys in general or in specific subjects (such as math and science), it is a foregone conclusion that this expectation tends to become a self-fulfilling prophesy.

Unsurprisingly, math and science figure prominently in the AAUW report. Skill in math and science auger well for success in many of our most-admired professions.

> One of the most dramatic and easily measured effects of schools and teachers on their adolescent students is in the teaching of math and science. The survey finds a strong relationship between math and science and adolescent self-esteem. Math and science have the strongest relationship to self-esteem for young women, and as they "learn" that they are not good at these topics their sense of self-worth and aspirations for themselves deteriorate. . . . 81 percent of elementary school girls like math. By high school, 61 percent say they like math . . . [but] significantly fewer believe they are "good at math."

It would be a misguided feminism to protest that the error here is in overvaluing such "masculine" subjects as math and science. Given their objective importance to a wide range of activities and professions, it would be a poor defense of women to assert that math and science are not "feminine" subjects and therefore not subjects in which women should be encouraged to excel. Can anyone familiar with the literature of psychological research doubt that if a group of teachers were informed that new studies had conclusively demonstrated "the natural superiority of females in math," their next set of female students would discover in themselves a miraculous ability to excel at math?

———

For a teacher, one of the meanings of living consciously is being aware of the implications of one's classroom behavior.

———

The challenge for teachers, then, is to work consciously at ridding themselves of gender stereotypes that generate different expectations for boys and girls. This would mean, among other things, calling on both sexes equally, helping each sex equally (as needed), conveying confidence in the potential of both sexes equally. This would require a high level of vigilant self-awareness (and perhaps feedback from peer observers). For a teacher, one of the meanings of living consciously is being aware of the implications of one's classroom behavior, the nonverbal messages one conveys to students concerning their abilities, potentials, and worth.

We will return to the subject of women and self-esteem when we examine the role of culture.

Self-Esteem Curricula

A number of educators have designed specific programs for the school system aimed at building the self-esteem of students. I will only mention two of which I have personal knowledge and that I admire.

I have already quoted from one designed by Robert Reasoner: *Building Self-Esteem: A Comprehensive Program for Schools*. This program has been adopted by a sizable number of California schools, and its success has been impressive—measured in terms of improved grades and attendance, significantly reduced dropouts, teenage pregnancy, and drug addiction, and a massive drop in vandalism. Indeed, most of the schools where the program is used were subsequently ranked by an independent agency to be among the finest in California.

Another powerful program is Constance Dembrowsky's *Personal and Social Responsibility.*[12] The aim of this course is not self-esteem explicitly but the cultivation of self-responsibility and the development of the kind of skills that generate the experience of self-efficacy—which means it *is* a self-esteem program in everything but name. Designed for teenagers, it can be especially effective with teenagers who are at risk. Ms. Dembrowsky is in the front ranks of those in the self-esteem movement who understand that the roots of healthy self-esteem are internal rather than external. Her focus is on what the young person must learn and do to become empowered.

One of my hopes for this book is that it will contribute to the creation of new self-esteem programs for the schools designed specifically to develop the practice of the six pillars in young people.

The frustrations, pressures, and challenges teachers face test their self-esteem, energy, and dedication every day. To preserve throughout their careers the vision with which the best of them started—to hold fast to the idea that the business they are in is that of setting minds on fire—is a heroic project.

The work they are doing could not be more important. Yet to do it well, they need to embody (at least to a decent extent) that which they wish to communicate.

A teacher who does not operate at an appropriate level of consciousness cannot model living consciously for his or her students.

A teacher who is not self-accepting will be unable successfully to communicate self-acceptance.

A teacher who is not self-responsible will have a difficult time persuading others of the value of self-responsibility.

A teacher who is afraid of self-assertiveness will not inspire its practice in others.

A teacher who is not purposeful is not a good spokesperson for the practice of living purposefully.

A teacher who lacks integrity will be severely limited in the ability to inspire it in others.

If their goal is to nurture self-esteem in those entrusted to their care, teachers—like parents, like psychotherapists, like all of us—need to begin by working on their own. One arena in which this can be done is the classroom itself. Just as parenting can be a spiritual discipline, a path for personal development, so can teaching. The challenges each present can be turned into vehicles for personal growth.

15
Self-Esteem and Work

Self-esteem, which has always been an urgent personal need, has gained new significance in the last decades of this century. Changed social and economic realities have created new challenges to our trust in ourselves.

Let us remember the primary meaning of self-esteem. It is confidence in the efficacy of our mind, in our ability to think. By extension, it is confidence in our ability to learn, make appropriate choices and decisions, and manage change. The survival value of such confidence is obvious; so is the danger when that trust is missing. Studies of business failure tell us that a common cause is executive fear of making decisions. But it is not just executives who need trust in their judgment; everyone needs it, and never more so than now.

The Context

We live in a period when we are faced with an extraordinary number of choices concerning our values, religious or philosophical orientations, and general life-style. We are very far from being a monolithic culture to which everyone more or less conforms. As I pointed out earlier, the greater the number of choices and decisions we need to make at a conscious level, the more urgent our need for self-esteem. But here I want to focus not on the culture at large but on the world of work—the challenges to economic adaptiveness both for individuals and organizations.

In clarifying why I assert that the economic need for large numbers of people with decent levels of self-esteem is unprecedented and represents a turning point in our evolution, I must ask the reader to follow me through a number of brief historical excursions. Without this historical understanding, I do not believe one can fully appreciate the moment in history at which we have arrived—nor its significance for self-esteem.

The economic need for large numbers of people with decent levels of self-esteem is unprecedented and represents a turning point in our evolution.

Everyone knows that there have been major developments in the past few decades in the national and global economy. These developments have all contributed to making the need for self-esteem more urgent for all those who participate in the process of production, from the leader of an enterprise to entry-level personnel. They include:

1. The shift from a manufacturing to an information economy; the diminishing need for manual or blue-collar workers and the rapidly growing need for knowledge workers with advanced verbal, mathematical, and social skills.
2. The continuing and escalating explosion of new knowledge, new technology, and new products and services, which keep raising the requirements of economic adaptiveness.
3. The emergence of a global economy of unprecedented competitiveness, which is yet another challenge to our ingenuity and belief in ourselves.
4. The increasing demands on individuals at every level of a business enterprise, not just at the top but throughout the system, for self-management, personal responsibility, self-direction, a high level of consciousness, and a commitment to innovation and contribution as top priorities.
5. The entrepreneurial model and mentality becoming central to our thinking about economic adaptiveness.
6. The emergence of *mind* as the central and dominant factor in all economic activity.

Let us briefly consider each of these points.

1. *The shift from a manufacturing to an information economy; the diminishing need for manual or blue-collar workers and the rapidly growing need for knowledge workers with advanced verbal, mathematical, and social skills.*

We are manufacturing more goods by far than ever before in our history, but with far fewer people. In earlier decades roughly half the working population was employed in blue-collar jobs; today the figure is less than 18 percent, and estimates are that in not too many years it will be 10 percent. Manufacturing has become much less labor intensive; the cost of labor in the overall process of production has dropped and will drop further. This means, among other things, that the availability of a cheap labor supply has become increasingly irrelevant in terms of competitive advantage. In the United States, the market for unskilled labor has shrunk appallingly—appallingly, that is, for those whose lack of education, training, and basic reading, writing, and arithmetical skills leave them with little to contribute. The demand today is for people with *knowledge*.

This point is essential to understanding the problem of unemployment among the uneducated and untrained, the so-called underclass of our society. No longer is it enough to have only muscles or to have mastered variations on the kind of physical skills that have been known for hundreds and even thousands of years; not if one wants access to a good job. Today one needs an education. One needs formal training. Or else one needs to be extraordinarily gifted at self-education. And one needs to understand that the process can never stop, because new knowledge begins to make one's training obsolete almost as soon as one completes it.

The situation was very different in the early days of business. Then, the boss knew everything that was necessary to run his business. He might need the assistance of a few other people to carry out the work, but not because they had mastered knowledge of which he was ignorant. As businesses grew and technology advanced, companies began to employ managers and engineers with particular areas of mastery outside the boss's. But still, knowledge was confined to the very few.

Thinking and decision making were done at the top of the hierarchy and passed down the chain of command. (The army was the only model for a large-scale organization anyone had. Creating the first modern steel mill, Andrew Carnegie sent his second-in-command to study the organization and communication system of the Prussian military and adapted many of its principles to his industry. Previously, the largest ironworks had employed six hundred people; Carnegie's challenge was to integrate and manage the efforts of six thousand.) A few key executives projected the goals and formulated the strategies and tactics the organization was to follow. A few bright engineers made their own contribution. Any knowledge or information about the business or about the wider economic context was the prerogative of this small group.

As to the overwhelming majority of employees in an organization, they were told what was expected of them and their sole responsibility was scrupulously to carry out instructions. An ideal employee would be one whose actions matched the consistency and reliability of machines. Frederick Winslow Taylor, pioneer of scientific management, summed up this idea to Harvard students in 1909: A worker's job "is to find out what boss wants and give it to him exactly as he wants." It was assumed that the worker could have nothing valuable or creative to contribute to the process of production or marketing. The system at this stage of development did not require for its operation great numbers of persons with firm self-esteem, just as it did not require a highly educated, highly skilled work force.

Today, what we see is no longer "management" and "workers" but an integration of specialists.

Looked at from the perspective of today, it is easy enough to criticize what is now called "classical management." Understood in its own context, we can appreciate its logic and benefits. A man in 1912 working, say, on an assembly line, might be unable to read or write English—he might be an immigrant from the Old World—but by conscientiously carrying out the task he had been trained to do he could earn a living for himself and his family—a better and more reliable living than had ever been possible before. Frederick Taylor's great innovation was to analyze production tasks into simple, discrete, easily mastered steps, which no one had thought of doing before, and which allowed people to work "smarter" rather than harder. Raising workers' productivity, he raised their wages. A blue-collar employee of even modest self-esteem could learn to function effectively in an environment created for him, as it were, by those whose self-confidence and ambition were higher.

As technology evolved, the demand for more advanced levels of skill in the operation of equipment increased. But there was no demand for higher education or creative thinking or self-management—or autonomy. Such values might make a substantial *personal* contribution to the average individual's life, in terms of enjoyment and satisfaction, but *not in terms of income.* Not in the 1950s or 1960s, at the climax of the industrial phase of our development, when the blue-collar worker was at the pinnacle of success. Then, most college-educated men and women did not earn more than a skilled machinist who was a high school dropout of very limited intellectual development. It is a very different story now, when access to decent jobs requires education and training.

Today, in a complex business organization that orchestrates the knowledge and skills of financial, marketing, and sales people, engineers, lawyers, systems analysts, mathematicians, chemists, physicists, researchers, computer specialists, designers, health care professionals, experts of every kind what we see is no longer "management" and "workers" but an integration of *specialists.* Each of these specialists has knowledge and expertise not possessed by the others in the organization. Each is relied on to think, to create, to be innovative, to contribute. "Workers" become "associates" in an atmosphere that is becoming increasingly collegial rather than hierarchical.

In such a setting, interpersonal competence is a high priority. And low self-esteem tends to stand in the way of such competence.

2. *The continuing and escalating explosion of new knowledge, new technology, and new products and services, which keep raising the requirements of economic adaptiveness.*

In the 1990s, successful business organizations know that to remain competitive in world markets they need a steady stream of innovations in products, services, and internal systems that must be planned for as a normal part of their operations. Conscious individuals know that if they wish to advance in their careers they cannot rest on yesterday's knowledge and skills. An overattachment to the known and familiar has become costly and dangerous; it threatens both organizations and individuals with obsolescence.

Scientific breakthroughs and technological discoveries are pouring from our laboratories and research and development departments at an unprecedented rate. Ninety percent of the scientists who have ever lived are alive now.

Until very recently, for the hundreds of thousands of years that human beings have existed on this planet, people saw existence as essentially unchanging. They believed that the knowledge possible to humans was already known. As I observed earlier, the idea of human life as a process of advancing from knowledge to new knowledge, from discovery to discovery, is only a couple of seconds old, measured in evolutionary time.

It can be argued that this new development puts the energy of economic necessity behind our continuing evolutionary progress—compelling us to reconceive what human beings are capable of.

3. *The emergence of a global economy of unprecedented competitiveness, which is yet another challenge to our ingenuity and belief in ourselves.*

In the decades immediately following World War II, the United States was the undisputed industrial leader of the world. We were at the height of our economic power. With the other industrial nations struggling to recover from the wreckage of war, we had no competitors. Our workers were the highest paid. Our standard of living was beyond most of the world's imagination, if not beyond its envy. Communist and socialist countries were promising someday to surpass us, but that was only a promise for the future, with nothing to support it in the present, although it was a promise that many American intellectuals believed and propagated.

========

An overattachment to the known and familiar has become costly and dangerous; it threatens both organizations and individuals with obsolescence.

========

Business itself—large business—had become heavily bureaucratic, weighted down with many levels of management. It depended more on economies of scale than on innovation to maintain economic supremacy, indulging much undetected financial waste and moving further and further away from the entrepreneurial spirit of an earlier age. (Government policies played a major role in bringing this development about, but that is another story.) Alfred Sloan, famed head of General Motors, once summed up the carmaker's strategy by saying that "it was not necessary to lead in technical design or run the risk of untried experiments, provided that our cars were at least equal in design to the best of our competitors in a grade."[1] One of the last great innovations of the American automobile industry was the automatic transmission—introduced in 1939.

The 1950s and 1960s were the time of the "Organization Man." Not independent thinking, but faithful compliance to the rules, was the road to success. Not to stand out, but to fit in, was the formula for those who wanted to rise. Just enough self-esteem to maintain a decent level of competence within the framework that existed—but not so much self-esteem as to challenge basic company values or policies. What the company promised in exchange was lifetime protection and security. "Be a company man and the company will take care of you" was the promise.

Self-denial for the good of the company was a value that found a ready audience, since, for thousands of years, human beings had been taught that self-denial was the essence of morality: self-denial for the tribe, for God, for king, state, country, society.[2]

Unions were at the height of their influence and power. Their leaders had little apprehension of the changes that lay ahead. Certainly they did not foresee that by the 1980s, with virtually all their goals achieved, they would be threatened with economic irrelevance, and, like a hemophiliac, would see an increasing percentage of their membership draining away.

Freedom means change; the ability to manage change is at least in part a function of self-esteem.

"American industry runs on muscle," a union executive announced. I was sitting beside him on an airplane when he said it. The year was 1962. He began to decry the "disaster" of automation, asserting that thousands of workers would be permanently unemployed because of new machines and that "something ought to be done about it." I answered that this was a fallacy that had been exploded often; that the introduction of new machines and new technology invariably resulted in *increasing* the demand for labor as well as raising the general standard of living. I remarked that automation increased the demand for skilled labor relative to unskilled labor, and that doubtless many workers would have to learn new skills; companies would have to train them. "But," he asked indignantly, "what about the people who don't *want* to learn new skills? Why should they have troubles? Aren't they entitled to security?" This meant, I pointed out, that the ambition, the farsightedness, the drive to do better and still better, the living energies of creative individuals were to be throttled and suppressed—for the sake of those who had "thought enough" and "learned enough" and did not wish to be imposed on further or to think about what their jobs depended on. Is that what he was proposing? His response was silence. I thought: Freedom means change; the ability to manage change is at least in part a function of self-esteem. Sooner or later, all roads lead to self-esteem.

But change was coming, whether anyone's self-esteem was ready or not.

At first, no one took the Japanese seriously. For a long time Japanese products had been associated with low quality, shoddy imitativeness, and total unreliability. It was inconceivable in the 1950s or 1960s that one day Japan would surpass the United States in automobiles, superconductors, and consumer electronics—or displace the Swiss as the number one producer of watches.

When, by 1953, Japan completed its postwar reconstruction, it embarked on an extraordinary pattern of growth that averaged 9.7 percent annually over the next twenty years. Leading this explosion was the triumph of the Japanese automobile. Between the 1950s and the 1970s, Japanese car production increased one hundred times, catching up with the United States in 1979, then rushing on to surpass it. Japan became the leading producer of radios in the 1960s and of television sets in the 1970s. In a total break with the past, Japanese products became associated with high quality and dependability, most notably in high-technology areas such as jets, machine tools, robots, semiconductors, calculators and copiers, computers and telecommunications, advanced energy systems, including nuclear power, and rocketry. Above all, it was a victory of superior management strategy—and the irony was that most of that strategy had been learned from the United States, where it was rarely practiced.

By the 1980s the United States was facing competition not only from Japan but other Pacific Rim nations as well: South Korea, Singapore, Taiwan, and Hong Kong. That was from the East. From the opposite direction there was a reborn and regenerated Europe—above all, an industrially powerful and fast-growing West Germany.

The reaction on the part of American business at first was dismay, disbelief, and denial. Global competitiveness of this intensity was a new and disorienting experience. True enough, there had been competition among the "Big Three" in the U.S. automobile industry, but General Motors, Ford, and Chrysler all played by the same rules and shared the same basic assumptions; none challenged the others to rethink their basic premises. The Japanese and the Germans did.

Global competition is a far more powerful stimulant to innovation than domestic competition. Other cultures have other perspectives, other ways of seeing things. Their ideas bring a richer mix to business thinking. But for this reason, a higher level of self-esteem—and competence—is required to play in this arena. At first, American workers and executives refused to acknowledge the Japanese might be pursuing practices worth emulating. The notion of learning from them was perceived as demeaning; instead, their initial response was to dig in their heels and cling more tenaciously to the familiar way of doing things.[3] Sometimes, an additional response was to denounce the Japanese and demand political protection against them. This parallels exactly what one sees in the practice of psychotherapy, when a self-doubting, insecure person blindly persists in counterproductive behavior, clings to the illusory safety of compulsive inflexibility, and blames all misfortune on someone else.

Only the shock of devastating competition from Japan and Germany awakened the U.S. automobile industry from its complacent slumber. Whether it awakened in time remains unknown. With no significant innovations of its own for decades, it resisted radial tires, disk brakes, and fuel injection, first put into production cars in Europe. Now it is fighting back, and the quality of American automobiles has greatly improved; but it still lags behind in innovation.

———

Global competition is a far more powerful stimulant to innovation than domestic competition.

———

Nor was this American industry unique in its slowness to grasp that the context had changed and that new policies were needed. When the Swiss were shown the first digital watches, their response was: "But this isn't a watch; a watch has springs and gears." When they woke up, they had lost their leadership position.

The United States is still—by far—the most powerful industrial nation on earth. With 5 percent of the world's population, we generate 25 percent of the world's industrial production. No knowledgeable person ever imagined that we would retain the percentage of world production that we enjoyed in the years following the Second World War, when other economies were in ruins. Nor would it have been considered desirable. We *wanted* other countries to resurrect themselves and helped to make it happen. Our output of goods and services, overall, is much greater than it has ever been; as a percentage of gross national product, it has remained constant for over four decades. In response to changing conditions we have already introduced major changes into our business institutions—from restructuring and "slimming down" (getting rid of superfluous layers of management, for instance) to much greater concentration on quality and customer service, to new systems of organization and management that better support innovation and adaptiveness to a fast-changing environment.

We are now operating in a context of constantly escalating challenge.

We do face problems of major magnitude: an inadequate rate of economic growth; an educational system that does not meet our needs; a deteriorating infrastructure; a declining standard of living. To what extent these problems will be resolved or get worse in the next decade remains to be seen.

The point now is not that we are in irreversible decline. The point is simply that one of the major changes in the world, with ramifications for business in general and our need of self-esteem in particular, is that we are now operating in a context of *constantly escalating challenge.* The challenge is to our creativity, flexibility, speed of responsiveness, ability to manage change, ability to think outside the square, ability to get the best out of people. Economically, the challenge is to our innovativeness—and, behind that, to our management ability. Psychologically, the challenge is to our self-esteem.

4. *The increasing demands on individuals at every level of a business enterprise, not just at the top but throughout the system, for self-management, personal responsibility, self-direction, a high level of consciousness, and a commitment to innovation and contribution as top priorities.*

The older bureaucratic command-and-control pyramid, modeled after the military, has progressively given way to flatter structures (fewer levels of management), flexible networks, cross-functional teams, ad hoc combinations of talents coming together for particular projects and then disbanding. The requirements of the flow of knowledge and information are determining organization, rather than preconceived mechanical layers of authority.

The ranks of middle management have been radically thinned, not merely as a cost-cutting strategy but because computers have taken over the task of relaying information throughout the system, making the role of manager-as-information-relay-station superfluous. Knowledge is more widely disseminated and freely available than ever before, making it much easier for people to operate at higher levels of consciousness in their work and consequently to be more productive.

Without the old and familiar chains of command, many managers are going through what might be termed a self-esteem crisis: with lines of authority and power no longer clear-cut, they are challenged to find new definitions of their roles. Their need now is to disengage feelings of self-worth from traditional forms of status, or from the performance of particular tasks, and to base it instead on their ability to think, to learn, to master new ways of functioning, to respond appropriately to change. From the boardroom to the factory floor, work is understood more and more clearly as an expression of thought. As equipment and machinery have become more sophisticated, the knowledge and skill required to operate them has risen accordingly. Employees are expected to monitor them, service them, repair them if necessary, anticipate needs, solve problems—in a word, function as self-respecting, self-responsible professionals.

From the boardroom to the factory floor, work is understood more and more clearly as an expression of thought.

The better organizations understand that the man or woman on the floor is likely to know more about what improvements are possible and necessary—in goods, services, internal systems—than the people above who are more remote from the immediate action. Books on business and management are filled with stories of contributions made by workers to the improvement of processes, services, and products. There are stories of men and women going far beyond their job description in response to unexpected problems they take responsibility for solving. Enterprise and initiative are no longer perceived as the monopoly of a few "special people." They are perceived as traits appropriate to everyone.

Not that everyone manifests them. We are still in the early stages of the knowledge revolution. But—increasingly—there is in companies the opportunity for people to do so and the hope that they will do so. This in itself is a call to higher self-esteem.

A modern organization elevates the practice of teamwork to new heights of virtuosity, while simultaneously requiring a core of individualism in each participant—because *thinking* is an activity of an individual mind, and so is *self-trust,* and so are *tenacity, perseverance,* and all the other mind-traits that make achievement possible.

To quote Charles Garfield in his study of the new policies and philosophy of some of our leading-edge corporations, *Second to None:*

> In an area that demands partnership [at every level], a time when our emphasis must shift toward cooperative efforts, the individual paradoxically takes on far greater importance. We can no longer afford to operate companies in which masses of "hired hands" are chronically underutilized while a few "heads" at the top do all thinking. . . . Competing in an era that demands continuous innovation requires us to harness the brain-power of *every* individual in the organization.[4]

The pressure to remain competitive is forcing a rethinking of every aspect of internal business activity—structures, policies, reward systems, divisions of responsibility, managerial practices (mind work cannot be managed like muscle work), and relationships among all those who participate in achieving productive goals.

One of the lessons business has needed to learn is the importance of entrepreneurship, not just for beginners, but also for well-established industries.

5. *The entrepreneurial model and mentality becoming central to our thinking about economic adaptiveness.*

When we think of entrepreneurship, our first association is with independent entrepreneurs who start new businesses or pioneer new industries. And yet entrepreneurship is essential to the continued success of "big business." This was the lesson of the 1980s.

It is useful to think back to the early days of American business and to innovators who launched this country on its meteoric growth—as a frame of reference for understanding in what sense "the entrepreneurial mentality" is needed within large business organizations that have existed for years.

With the advent of capitalism and the emergence of the early American entrepreneurs, a number of shifts in people's consciousness took place. It is noteworthy that all have a direct bearing on our need for self-esteem.

The question, "What has your birth determined you to be?" was replaced by the question, "What have you made of yourself?" In other words, identity was no longer something one inherited but something one created.

The idea of *progress* caught people's imagination. The premise was that intelligence, ingenuity, and enterprise could generate a continuing improvement in the standard of living—that new discoveries, new products, new expressions of human creativity could without limit keep raising the quality of existence. While mind was not yet fully understood to be the supreme capital asset, it had begun to move from background to foreground, sometimes under such names as "competence" or "ability."

Self-reliance and self-responsibility were seen as supremely appropriate in this new order of things, in contrast to the conformity and obedience more valued in earlier, tribal societies. Independence became an economically adaptive virtue.

New ideas with commercial application were valued. The ability to perceive and actualize new wealth-producing possibilities was valued. The entrepreneurial mentality was rewarded.

Not that these perspectives were understood and embraced equally by everyone. Far from it. Even among some of the best business innovators, traces of the authoritarian mind-set inherited from an earlier age were not fully expunged. Old perspectives and old ways of thinking do not vanish overnight or without resistance. The battle for full acceptance of this new vision is still being fought.

The new economic system disrupted the old order of things. It was no respecter of authority. It often disregarded tradition. It did not dread change but greatly accelerated it. Freedom could be intoxicating but it also could be frightening.

Entrepreneurship is by its nature antiauthority. It is anti–status quo. It is always moving in the direction of making what exists obsolete. Early in this century the economist Joseph Schumpeter wrote of the work of the entrepreneur as that of "creative destruction."

The essence of entrepreneurial activity is that of endowing resources with new wealth-producing capabilities—of seeing and actualizing productive possibilities that have not been seen and actualized before. This presupposes the ability to think for oneself, to look at the world through one's own eyes—a lack of excessive regard for the-world-as-perceived-by-others—at least in some respects.

In the early decades of capitalism, men came out of nowhere, starting with nothing but brains and ambition, created industries, and earned fortunes. Almost all these men started out as workers and almost none graduated high school (few even entered it). They were a challenge and a rebuke to the remnants of feudal aristocracy, to "old money" anchored in social position and disdainful of work, who looked at these new wealth producers with dismay and resentment. The entrepreneur was an impudent upstart, they told one another, whose activities generated social disequilibrium. In fact, he represented a threat not only to their social position but also to their self-esteem. What would become of them in a system geared to merit and achievement, as judged by the market, rather than to inherited status?

If capitalism offered a broader arena for self-esteem to operate in than had ever existed before, it also offered challenges that had no precedent in earlier, tribal societies—challenges to self-reliance, self-assertiveness, self-responsibility, and personal accountability. Capitalism created a market for the independent mind.

The large organizations that we associate with modern capitalism emerged in the United States only after the Civil War, and in Europe after the Franco-Prussian War—only in roughly the last 130 years. Throughout the nineteenth century, we remained predominantly an agricultural economy: most people earned their living on farms, and land was the chief source of wealth, as it had been for thousands of years. We began as a nation of farmers and small shopkeepers. No one then could have imagined the large industrial concerns and the extraordinary economic development that began to emerge in the last quarter of the nineteenth century, beginning with the railroads, as human energy was unleashed and began to gather momentum.

Capitalism created a market for the
independent mind.

The average farmer or shopkeeper was not an innovator. He was typically more self-reliant than his predecessors, to be sure, more independent and more resourceful—evidenced by the facts, among others, that he may have left his homeland in Europe to make a new life in America, and that the looser social structure in the New World, the greater freedom, threw him more on his own and demanded greater self-direction and therefore greater self-esteem. But, within the knowledge context of the period, economic adaptiveness demanded of him neither high levels of education nor innovativeness. His mind, learning ability, and decision-making capabilities were not constantly challenged.

The individuals who saw themselves thus challenged and were inspired to meet the challenge—the entrepreneurs and inventors—were an almost infinitesimal minority. It is they who were responsible for the transition from an agricultural to a manufacturing society. This led to U.S. leadership in steel, electricity, the telephone and telegraph, farm equipment and agronomy, office equipment, the first household appliances, and, a little later, automobiles and aviation.

At the height of its success in this century, American business was jolted out of its complacency by foreign competition, and—against the resistance of its own entrenched bureaucracy—forced to think again about the continuing importance of entrepreneurship. Part of the stimulation for this new thinking came from the achievements of smaller organizations, which were pointing the way to the future.

In the last two decades there has been an explosion of entrepreneurship, almost entirely in small- and medium-sized business. By the late 1980s, between 600,000 and 700,000 new enterprises were started every year, as against one sixth or one seventh of these figures during the best years of the 1950s and 1960s. While the Fortune 500 companies have been losing workers steadily since the early 1970s, and many of these companies have been struggling for survival, small- and medium-sized business was able to create roughly eighteen million new jobs; the majority of these jobs were in firms with fewer than twenty employees. Small- and medium-sized business has displayed an innovativeness and flexibility—an ability to respond to market changes and opportunities with lightning speed—too often lacking in larger, more cumbersome organizations.

They led the way in showing the path big business must follow if it is to remain competitive. While many companies are still struggling with the problems of balancing traditional, administrative management, on the one hand, and entrepreneurial management on the other—the first is focused on protecting and nurturing that which already exists, the second on making it obsolete—it is increasingly obvious that entrepreneurship cannot be the prerogative of small or new businesses. It is imperative all the way up to organizations the size of General Motors—and right now GM is struggling with just this challenge.

In the context of big business, to become entrepreneurial means to learn to think like small business at its most imaginative and aggressive: to cultivate lightness, lack of encumbrance, swiftness of response, constant alertness to developments that signal new opportunities. This means, among other things, radically reducing bureaucracy and freeing units to operate entrepreneurially.

In response to this need, increasing numbers of large organizations have established autonomous or semiautonomous entrepreneurial units internally. Their intention is to free innovators from the obstructions of multitiered, change-resisting, bureaucratic management.

More broadly, they are committed to making innovation a planned for and systematic part of normal operations. They are learning to treat it is a discipline—something that can be learned, organized, and practiced.*

> *The more unstable the economy and the more rapid the rate of change—the more urgent the need for large numbers of self-esteeming individuals.*

If low self-esteem correlates with resistance to change and clinging to the known and familiar, then never in the history of the world has low self-esteem been as economically disadvantageous as it is today. If high self-esteem correlates with comfort in managing change and in letting go of yesterday's attachments, then high self-esteem confers a competitive edge.

There is a principle we can identify here. In the earlier years of American business, when the economy was fairly stable and change relatively slow, the bureaucratic style of organization worked reasonably well. As the economy became less stable and the pace of change quickened, it became less and less adaptive, unable to respond swiftly to new developments. Let us relate this to the need for self-esteem. The more stable the economy and the slower the rate of change, the less urgent the need for large numbers of individuals with healthy self-esteem. *The more unstable the economy and the more rapid the rate of change—which is clearly the world of the present and future—the more urgent the need for large numbers of self-esteeming individuals.*

---

* Peter Drucker has written the classic text on how this is to be done: *Innovation and Entrepreneurship.*

6. *The emergence of* mind *as the central and dominant factor in all economic activity.*

The meaning of this statement is implicit in all of the foregoing points, but a few further observations are in order.

In an agricultural economy wealth is identified with land. In a manufacturing economy, it is identified with the ability to make things: capital assets and equipment; machines and the various materials used in industrial production. In either of these societies, wealth is understood in terms of matter, not mind; physical assets, not knowledge and information.

In a manufacturing society, intelligence is the guiding force behind economic progress, to be sure, but when people think of wealth they think of raw materials, such as nickel and copper, and physical property, such as steel mills and textile looms.

Wealth is created by transforming the materials of nature to serve human purposes—by transforming a seed into a harvest; by transforming a waterfall into a source of electricity; by transforming iron ore, limestone, and coal into steel, and steel into the girders of apartment buildings. If all wealth is the product of mind and labor, of thought directing action, then one way to understand the transition from an agricultural to an industrial society is to say that the balance between mind and physical effort is profoundly altered. Physical labor began to move along a declining arc of importance, *while mind began to climb.*

As an extension of human intelligence, a machine substitutes the power of thought for the power of muscles. While making physical labor less demanding, it makes it more productive. As technological development keeps evolving, the ratio keeps shifting in favor of mind. And as mind becomes more important, self-esteem becomes more important.

The climax of this process of development is the emergence of an information economy in which material resources count for less and less and knowledge and new ideas count for almost everything.

The value of a computer, for instance, lies not in its material constituents but in its design, in the thinking and knowledge it embodies—and in the quantity of human effort it makes unnecessary. Microchips are made out of sand; their value is a function of the intelligence encoded within them. A copper wire can carry forty-eight telephone conversations; a single fiber-optic cable can carry more than eight thousand conversations; yet fiber-optic cables are cheaper, more efficient, and much less energy consuming to produce than copper.

Each year since 1979 the United States has produced more with less energy than the year before. The worldwide drop in the price of raw materials is a consequence of the ascendancy of mind in our economic life.

The mind always has been our basic tool of survival. But for most of our history, this fact was not understood. Today it is obvious to (almost) the whole world.

Challenges

In an economy in which knowledge, information, creativity—and their translation into innovation—are transparently the source of wealth and of competitive advantage, there are distinct challenges both to individuals and to organizations.

To individuals, whether as employees or as self-employed professionals, the challenges include:

> To acquire appropriate knowledge and skills, and to commit oneself to a lifetime of continuous learning, which the rapid growth of knowledge makes mandatory.

> To work effectively with other human beings, which includes skill in written and oral communication, the ability to participate in nonadversarial relationships, understanding of how to build consensus through give and take, and willingness to assume leadership and motivate coworkers when necessary.

> To manage and respond appropriately to change.

> To cultivate the ability to think for oneself, without which innovativeness is impossible.

Such challenges entail the need to bring a high level of consciousness to one's working life, to its demands in terms of knowledge and skills—and also its opportunities, the possibilities for growth and self-development it offers. A commitment to lifelong learning is a natural expression of the practice of living consciously.

In dealing with other people, there is the need for that level of self-respect that underlies respect for others; freedom from gratuitous fear, envy, or hostility; expectation of being dealt with fairly and decently; and the conviction that one can have genuine values to contribute. Again we are led to the importance of self-esteem.

As an example, consider how poor self-esteem might show up in communication. People with troubled self-esteem often belittle their ideas, even while expressing them. They can turn fact into opinion, confusingly, by starting sentences with "I think" or "I feel." They apologize before presenting a new idea. They make self-deprecating remarks. They laugh to release nervous energy, thus laughing at inappropriate times. They suddenly freeze in confusion and uncertainty because they anticipate disagreement and "rejection." They make statements that sound like questions by raising the tone of the voice at the end of a sentence. Not all communication problems are the result of inadequate education; sometimes the cause is a self-concept that generates self-sabotage.

A commitment to lifelong learning is a natural expression of the practice of living consciously.

Or consider the issue of benevolence, goodwill, and the ability to interact with others constructively, which relate to a positive sense of self. Men and women of healthy self-esteem do not seek to prove their worth by making others wrong. They do not approach relationships with gratuitous belligerence. It is self-doubt and insecurity that see all encounters—with staff, superiors, subordinates, customers, clients—as overt or covert war.

Cooperative endeavors rest on the willingness of participants to be accountable, which is a corollary of the practice of self-responsibility. Such endeavors rest on the willingness of people to keep their promises, honor their commitments, think about the consequences of their actions to others, and manifest reliability and trustworthiness, which are all expressions of the practice of personal integrity.

If more is offered to individuals than ever before in our history, in opportunities for fulfillment, achievement, and self-expression, more is asked of them in terms of psychological development.

Self-esteem is far from being the only asset one needs, of course—let there be no mistake about this—but without it the individual is severely impaired and is in effect at a competitive disadvantage.

To organizations, the challenges include:

To respond to the need for a constant stream of innovation by cultivating a discipline of innovation and entrepreneurship into the mission, strategies, policies, practices, and reward system of the organization.

To go beyond paying lip service to "the importance of the individual" by designing a culture in which initiative, creativity, self-responsibility, and contribution are fostered and rewarded.

To recognize the relationship between self-esteem and performance and to think through and implement policies that support self-esteem. This demands recognizing and responding to the individual's need for a sane, intelligible, noncontradictory environment that a mind can make sense of; for learning and growth; for achievement; for being listened to and respected; for being allowed to make (responsible) mistakes.

Since, in the 1990s and beyond, the demand for such mind workers will be greater than the supply, they will be in a position to demand such treatment and to favor the companies that offer it, thus giving these companies an economic advantage. When prospective employees ask themselves, "Is this an organization where I can learn, grow, develop myself, enjoy my work?" they are implicitly asking, whether they identify it or not, "Is this a place that supports my self-esteem—or does violence to it?"

The successful organization of the future will be an organization geared to self-esteem.

It is said that the successful organization of the future will be above all a learning organization. It can equally be said that it will be an organization geared to self-esteem.

Bringing Out the Best in People

Leaders do not usually ask themselves, "How can we create a self-esteem-supporting culture in our organization?" But the best (the most conscious) of them do ask, "What can we do to stimulate innovation and creativity? How can we make this the kind of place that will attract the best people? And what can we do to earn their continuing loyalty?"

These questions are all different, and yet the answers to them are largely the same or at least significantly overlap. It would be impossible to have an organization that nurtured innovation and creativity and yet did not nurture self-esteem in some important ways. It would be impossible to have an organization that nurtured self-esteem, rationally understood, and yet did not stimulate innovation, creativity, excitement, and loyalty.

An example: Some businesses are experimenting with tying pay raises to the acquisition of new knowledge and skills; employees are paid to learn, paid to master new areas of expertise. The assumption is that the more knowledgeable and skilled they are, the greater the contribution to the company they will be able to make. But will not a growth in competence very likely lead to an increase in the experience of self-efficacy?

From the point of view of the individual, it is obvious that work can be a vehicle for raising self-esteem. The six pillars all have clear application here. When we bring a high level of consciousness, responsibility, and so on to our tasks, self-esteem is strengthened—just as, when we avoid them, self-esteem is weakened.

When I am invited by companies to teach how self-esteem principles and technology can be utilized to stimulate higher performance, I often work with the sentence-completion technique, asking participants in the program to write six to ten endings every day, over a period of some weeks, for sentence stems such as the following:

If I bring 5 percent more awareness to my work today—
If I bring 5 percent more self-acceptance to my daily activities—
If I operate 5 percent more self-responsibly today—
If I operate 5 percent more self-assertively today—
If I operate 5 percent more purposefully today—
If I bring 5 percent more integrity to my work today—

Stems such as these and dozens of others like them invariably stimulate a direct experience of what the practice of the six pillars means, not only for self-esteem, but also for productivity and interpersonal effectiveness.

In this section I want to focus on self-esteem from the perspective of the organization—the kind of policies and practices that either undermine or support the self-efficacy and self-respect of people.

An organization whose people operate at a high level of consciousness, self-acceptance (and acceptance of others), self-responsibility, self-assertiveness (and respect for the assertiveness of others), purposefulness, and personal integrity would be an organization of extraordinarily empowered human beings. These traits are supported in an organization to the extent that the following conditions are met:

1. People feel safe: secure that they will not be ridiculed, demeaned, humiliated, or punished for openness and honesty or for admitting "I made a mistake" or for saying "I don't know, but I'll find out."

2. People feel accepted: treated with courtesy, listened to, invited to express thoughts and feelings, dealt with as individuals whose dignity is important.

3. People feel challenged: given assignments that excite, inspire, and test and stretch their abilities.

4. People feel recognized: acknowledged for individual talents and achievements and rewarded monetarily and nonmonetarily for extraordinary contributions.

5. People receive constructive feedback: they hear how to improve performance in nondemeaning ways that stress positives rather than negatives and that build on their strengths.

6. People see that innovation is expected of them: their opinions are solicited, their brainstorming is invited, and they see that the development of new and usable ideas is desired of them and welcomed.

7. People are given easy access to information: not only are they given the information (and resources) they need to do their job properly, they are given information about the wider context in which they work—the goals and progress of the company—so that they can understand how their activities relate to the organization's overall mission.

8. People are given authority appropriate to what they are accountable for: they are encouraged to take initiative, make decisions, exercise judgment.

9. People are given clear-cut and noncontradictory rules and guidelines: they are provided with a structure their intelligence can grasp and count on and they know what is expected of them.

10. People are encouraged to solve as many of their own problems as possible: they are expected to resolve issues close to the action rather than pass responsibility for solutions to higher-ups, and they are empowered to do so.

11. People see that their rewards for successes are far greater than any penalties for failures: in too many companies, where the penalties for mistakes are much greater than the rewards for success, people are afraid to take risks or express themselves.

12. People are encouraged and rewarded for learning: they are encouraged to participate in internal and external courses and programs that will expand their knowledge and skills.

13. People experience congruence between an organization's mission statement and professed philosophy, on the one hand, and the behavior of leaders and managers, on the other: they see integrity exemplified and they feel motivated to match what they see.

14. People experience being treated fairly and justly: they feel the workplace is a rational universe they can trust.

15. People are able to believe in and take pride in the value of what they produce: they perceive the result of their efforts as genuinely useful, they perceive their work as worth doing.

To the extent that these conditions are operative in an organization, it will be a place in which high-self-esteem people will want to work. It will also be one in which people of more modest self-esteem will find their self-esteem raised.

What Managers Can Do

When I sat with a group of managers once, outlining the above set of conditions, one of them remarked, "You talk about self-esteem, but what you have described are conditions that stimulate active and creative employee participation—that stimulate innovation." Precisely.

For executives who want to build a high-self-esteem organization I would structure a different but inevitably overlapping list of proposals:

1. Work on your own self-esteem: commit yourself to raising the level of consciousness, responsibility, and integrity you bring to your work and your dealings with people—staff, subordinates, associates, higher-ups, customers, and suppliers.

2. When you talk with your people, be present to the experience: make eye contact, listen actively, offer appropriate feedback, give the speaker the experience of being heard.

3. Be empathic: let the speaker know that you understand his or her feelings as well as statements, which is a way of giving the speaker an experience of visibility.

4. Regardless of who you are speaking to, maintain a tone of respect: do not permit yourself a condescending, superior, sarcastic, or blaming tone.

5. Keep encounters regarding work task-centered, not ego-centered:

never permit a dispute to deteriorate into a conflict of personalities; the focus needs to be *on reality*—"What is the situation?" "What does the work require?" "What needs to be done?"

6. Give your people opportunities to practice self-responsibility: give them space to take the initiative, volunteer ideas, attempt new tasks, expand their range.

7. Speak to your people's understanding: give the reasons for rules and guidelines (when they are not self-evident), explain why you cannot accommodate certain requests; don't merely hand down orders from on high.

8. If you make a mistake in your dealings with someone, are unfair or short-tempered, admit it and apologize: do not imagine (like some autocratic parents) that it would demean your dignity or position to admit taking an action you regret.

9. Invite your people to give you feedback on the kind of boss you are: I agree with someone who once said that "you are the kind of manager your people say you are," so check it out and let your people see that you are open to learning and self-correction, and set an example of nondefensiveness.

10. Let your people see that it's safe to make a mistake or say "I don't know, but I will find out": to evoke fear of error or ignorance is to invite deception, inhibition, and an end to creativity.

11. Let your people see that it's safe to disagree with you: convey respect for differences of opinion and do not punish dissent.

12. Describe undesirable behavior without blaming: let someone know if his or her behavior is unacceptable, point out its consequences, communicate what kind of behavior you want instead, and omit character assassination.

13. Let your people see that you talk honestly about your feelings: if you are hurt or angry or offended, say so with honesty and dignity (and give everyone a lesson in the strength of self-acceptance).

14. If someone does superior work or makes an excellent decision, invite him or her to explore how and why it happened: do not limit yourself simply to praise; by asking appropriate questions, help raise the person's consciousness about what made the achievement possible and thereby increase the likelihood that others like it will occur in the future.

15. If someone does unacceptable work or makes a bad decision, practice the same principle as above: do not limit yourself to corrective feedback; invite an exploration of what made the error

possible, thus raising the level of consciousness and minimizing the likelihood of a repetition.

16. Give clear and unequivocal performance standards: let people understand your nonnegotiable expectations regarding the quality of work.

17. Praise in public and correct in private: acknowledge achievements in the hearing of as many people as possible while letting a person absorb corrections in the safety of privacy.

18. Let your praise be realistic: like parents who make compliments meaningless by praising extravagantly for trivia, you can make your positive acknowledgments devoid of force if they are over-blown and not calibrated to the reality of what has been accomplished.

19. When the behavior of someone creates a problem, ask him or her to propose a solution: whenever possible, avoid handing down solutions but give the problem to the responsible party, thereby encouraging self-responsibility, self-assertiveness, and intensified awareness.

20. Convey in every way possible that you are not interested in blaming, you are interested in solutions, and exemplify this policy personally: when we look for solutions, we grow in self-esteem; when we blame (or alibi), we weaken self-esteem.

21. Give your people the resources, information, and authority to do what you have asked them to do: remember that there can be no responsibility without power, and nothing so undermines morale as assigning the first without giving the second.

22. Remember that a great manager or leader is not one who comes up with brilliant solutions but who sees to it that his people come up with brilliant solutions: a manager, at his or her best, is a coach, not a problem solver for admiring children.

23. Take personal responsibility for creating a culture of self-esteem: no matter what "self-esteem training" they might be given, subordinates are unlikely to sustain the kind of behavior I am recommending if they do not see it exemplified by the higher-ups.

24. Work at changing aspects of the organization's culture that undermine self-esteem: traditional procedures, originating in an older model of management, may stifle not only self-esteem but also any creativity or innovation (such as requiring that all significant decisions be passed up a chain of command, thus leaving those close to the action disempowered and paralyzed).

25. Avoid overdirecting, overobserving, and overreporting: excessive "managing" ("micromanaging") is the enemy of autonomy and creativity.

26. Plan and budget appropriately for innovation: do not ask for people's innovative best and then announce there is no money (or other resources), because the danger is that creative enthusiasm will dry up and be replaced by demoralization.

27. Find out what the central interests of your people are and, whenever possible, match tasks and objectives with individual dispositions: give people an opportunity to do what they enjoy most and do best; build on people's strengths.

28. Ask your people what they would need in order to feel more in control of their work and, if possible, give it to them: if you want to promote autonomy, excitement, and a strong commitment to goals, empower, empower, empower.

29. Reward such natural expressions of self-esteem as self-assertiveness, (intelligent) risk taking, flexible behavior patterns, and a strong action orientation: too many companies pay lip service to such values while rewarding those who conform, don't ask difficult questions, don't challenge the status quo, and remain essentially passive while performing the motions of their job description.

30. Give assignments that stimulate personal and professional growth: without an experience of growth, self-esteem—and enthusiasm for the job—tends to be undermined.

31. Stretch your people: assign tasks and projects slightly beyond their known capabilities.

32. Educate your people to see problems as challenges and opportunities; this is one perspective clearly shared by high achievers and by people of high self-esteem.

33. Support the talented non–team player: in spite of everything we can say about the necessity for effective teamwork, there needs to be a place for the brilliant hermit who is moving to different music, and even team players benefit from seeing this respect for individuality.

34. Teach that errors and mistakes are opportunities for learning: "What can you learn from what happened?" is a question that promotes self-esteem; it also promotes not repeating mistakes; and sometimes it points the way to a future solution.

35. Challenge the seniority tradition and promote from any level on

the basis of merit: recognition of ability is one of the great inspirers of self-respect.

36. Reward generously for outstanding contributions, such as new products, inventions, services, and money-saving projects: profit-sharing programs, deferred compensation plans, cash or stock bonuses, and royalties can all be used to reinforce the signal that your organization wants innovation and respects intelligent self-assertion and self-expression.

37. Write letters of commendation and appreciation to high achievers and ask the CEO to do likewise: when people see that their company values their *mind*, they are motivated to keep pushing at the limits of what they feel capable of achieving.

38. Set a standard of personal integrity: keep your promises, honor your commitments, deal with everyone fairly (not just insiders, but suppliers and customers as well), and acknowledge and support this behavior in others; give your people the pride of working for a *moral* company.

I doubt that there is one principle listed above that thoughtful executives are not aware of—in the abstract. The challenge is to practice them consistently and weave them into the fabric of daily procedures.

A Leader's Role

Everything I have said above clearly applies to leaders—the CEO or company president—as much as to managers. But I want to say a few additional words about the leader.

The primary function of a leader in a business enterprise is (1) to develop and persuasively convey a vision of what the organization is to accomplish, and (2) to inspire and empower all those who work for the organization to make an optimal contribution to the fulfillment of that vision and to experience that, in doing so, they are acting in alignment with their self-interest. The leader must be an inspirer and a persuader.

The higher the self-esteem of the leader, the more likely it is that he or she can perform that function successfully. A mind that distrusts itself cannot inspire the best in the minds of others. Neither can leaders inspire the best in others if their primary need, arising from their insecurities, is to prove themselves right and others wrong.

It is a fallacy to say that a great leader should be egoless. A leader needs an ego sufficiently healthy that it does not experience itself as on the line in every encounter—so that the leader is free to be task and results oriented, not self-aggrandizement or self-protection oriented.

If degrees of self-esteem are thought of on a scale from 1 to 10, with 10 representing optimal self-esteem and 1 almost the lowest imaginable, then is a leader who is a 5 more likely to hire a 7 or a 3? Very likely he or she will feel more comfortable with the 3, since people often feel intimated by others more confident than themselves. Multiply this example hundreds or thousands of times and project the consequences for a business.

Warren Bennis, our preeminent scholar of leadership, tells us that the basic passion in the best leaders he has studied is for self-expression.[5] Their work is clearly a vehicle for self-actualization. Their desire is to bring "who they are" into the world, into reality, which I speak of as the practice of self-assertiveness.

It is a fallacy to say that a great leader should be egoless.

Leaders often do not fully recognize the extent to which "who they are" affects virtually every aspect of their organization. They do not appreciate the extent to which they are role models. Their smallest bits of behavior are noted and absorbed by those around them, not necessarily consciously, and reflected via those they influence throughout the entire organization. If a leader has unimpeachable integrity, a standard is set that others feel drawn to follow. If a leader treats people with respect— associates, subordinates, customers, suppliers, shareholders—that tends to translate into company culture.

For these reasons, a person who wants to work on his or her "leadership ability" should work on self-esteem. Continual dedication to the six pillars and their daily practice is the very best training for leadership—as it is for life.

The Power to Do Good

Can the right organizational environment transform a person of low self-esteem into one of high self-esteem? Not very likely—although I can think of instances where a good manager or supervisor drew out of a person what no one had ever drawn out before and at least laid a foundation for improved self-respect.

Clearly there are troubled individuals who need a more focused kind of professional help—I am speaking of psychotherapy, which we will discuss in the following chapter—and it is not the function of a business organization to be a psychological clinic.

The policies that support self-esteem are also the policies that make money.

But for the person of average self-esteem, an organization dedicated to the value and importance of the individual has an immense potential for doing good at the most intimate and personal level, even though that is not, of course, its purpose for being. And in doing so, it contributes to its own life and vitality in ways that are not remote and ethereal but are ultimately bottom line. The policies that support self-esteem are also the policies that make money. The policies that demean self-esteem are the policies that sooner or later cause a company to lose money—simply because, when you treat people badly and disrespectfully, you cannot possibly hope to get their best. And in today's fiercely competitive, rapidly changing global economy, nothing less than their best is good enough.

16

Self-Esteem and Psychotherapy

In the 1950s, when I began the practice of psychotherapy, I became convinced that low self-esteem was a common denominator in all the varieties of personal distress I encountered in my practice. I saw low self-esteem as a predisposing causal factor of psychological problems and also a consequence. The relationship was reciprocal. As I said in the Introduction, this was the realization that ignited my fascination with the subject.

Sometimes problems could be understood as direct expressions of an underdeveloped self-esteem—for example, shyness, timidity, and fear of self-assertion or intimacy. Sometimes problems could be understood as consequences of the *denial* of poor self-esteem, that is, as defenses built against the reality of the problem—for example, controlling and manipulative behavior, obsessive-compulsive rituals, inappropriate aggressiveness, fear-driven sexuality, destructive forms of ambition—all aiming to produce some experience of efficacy, control, and personal worth. It seemed clear that problems that were manifestations of poor self-esteem were also contributors to the continuing deterioration of self-esteem.

Consequently, it was my view from the beginning that a primary task of psychotherapy is to help build self-esteem. This was not the perspective of my colleagues. Self-esteem was rarely considered at all, and insofar as it was, the traditional assumption was (and is) that self-esteem will benefit indirectly and implicitly, as a by-product of psychotherapy:

as other problems are solved, the client will naturally feel better about him- or herself. It is true that when anxiety and depression are diminished, the client feels stronger. It is also true that developing self-esteem diminishes anxiety and depression. I thought that self-esteem can and should be addressed explicitly; that it should set the context of the entire therapeutic enterprise; and that even when one is not working on it as such, even when one is focused instead on solving specific problems, one can do so by framing or contextualizing the process in such a way as to make it explicitly self-esteem strengthening. For example, almost all schools of therapy help clients to confront previously avoided conflicts or challenges. But I typically ask, "How do you *feel about yourself* when you avoid an issue you know, at some level, needs to be dealt with? And how do you feel about yourself when you master your avoidance impulses and confront the threatening issue?" I frame the process in terms of its consequences for self-esteem. I want clients to notice how their choices and actions affect their experience of themselves. I see this awareness as a powerful motivator for growth; it often helps in managing and transcending fear.

It was my view from the beginning that a primary task of psychotherapy is to help build self-esteem.

My purpose in this chapter is not to discuss the technique of psychotherapy as such, but merely to offer a few general observations about building self-esteem in a psychotherapeutic context and to suggest something of my approach. This chapter is addressed not only to the clinician or to students of therapy but to anyone thinking about therapy who would like to understand the self-esteem orientation as a frame of reference.

The Goals of Psychotherapy

Psychotherapy has two basic goals. One is the alleviation of suffering. The other is the facilitation and enhancement of well-being. While the two projects overlap, they are not the same. To reduce or eliminate anxiety is not equivalent to generating self-esteem, although it can contribute to that end. To reduce or eliminate depression is not equivalent to generating happiness, although, again, it can contribute to that end.

On the one hand, psychotherapy aims to reduce irrational fears, depressive reactions, and troublesome feelings of every kind (perhaps from past traumatic experiences). On the other hand, it encourages the learning of new skills, new ways of thinking about and looking at life, better strategies for dealing with self and others, and an expanded sense of one's possibilities. I place both these goals in the context of aiming to strengthen self-esteem.

Raising self-esteem is more than a matter of eliminating negatives; it requires the attainment of positives. It requires a higher level of consciousness in the way one functions. It requires greater self-responsibility and integrity. It requires the willingness to move through fear to confront conflicts and discomfiting realities. It requires learning to face and master rather than withdraw and avoid.

Raising self-esteem is more than a matter of eliminating negatives; it requires the attainment of positives.

If someone enters therapy and at the end of the process does not live more consciously than at the beginning, the work has failed. If in the course of treatment the client does not grow in self-acceptance, self-responsibility, and all the other practices that support self-esteem, we would also have to question the therapeutic experience. Regardless of school, any effective therapy promotes growth along these dimensions, at least to some extent. But if a therapist understands the importance of the six practices and cultivates them as a conscious project, he or she is more likely to produce consistent results. He or she is challenged to develop means—cognitive, behavioral, experiential—that will promote self-esteem.

If one therapeutic goal is to encourage a higher level of consciousness in the client, so that the client lives more mindfully and with better reality contact, then through conversation, psychological exercises and processes, body and energy work, and homework assignments, one can work at removing blocks to awareness, on the one hand, and stimulate and energize higher consciousness, on the other.

If another goal is to inspire greater self-acceptance, then one can create a climate of acceptance in the office, lead the client to identify and reown blocked and disowned parts of the self, and teach the importance of being in a nonadversarial relationship to oneself and its parts (see my discussion of subpersonalities below).

If another goal is to strengthen self-responsibility, then one can frustrate the client's maneuvers to transfer responsibility to the therapist, facilitate through exercises the client's appreciation of the rewards of self-responsibility, and convey by every means possible that no one is coming to the rescue and that each of us is responsible for our choices and actions and for the attainment of our desires.

If another goal is to encourage self-assertiveness, then one can create an environment in which self-assertion will be safe, teach self-assertion through exercises such as sentence-completion, psychodrama, role-playing, and the like—work to defuse or neutralize fears of self-assertiveness—and actively encourage the client in facing and dealing with threatening conflicts and challenges.

If another goal is to support living purposefully, then one can convey the role and importance of purpose in life, assist in the client's clarification and articulation of goals, explore action plans, strategies, and tactics and their necessity for goal attainment, and work to awaken the client to the rewards of a life that is proactive and purposeful rather than reactive and passive.

If another goal is to encourage personal integrity, then one needs to focus on values clarification, inner moral confusions and conflicts, the importance of choosing values that in fact do support one's life and well-being, the benefits of living congruently with one's convictions, and the pain of self-betrayal.

I shall not elaborate further on these points. I mention them primarily to suggest *a way of thinking* about psychotherapy when the cultivation of self-esteem is a central goal.

The Climate of Therapy

As with parents and teachers, an unrelenting attitude of acceptance and respect is perhaps the first way in which a psychotherapist can contribute to the self-esteem of a client. It is the foundation of useful therapy.

This attitude is conveyed in how we greet clients when they arrive in the office, how we look at them, how we talk, and how we listen. This entails such matters as courtesy, eye contact, being noncondescending and nonmoralistic, listening attentively, being concerned with understanding and with being understood, being appropriately spontaneous, refusing to be cast in the role of omniscient authority, and refusing to believe the client is incapable of growth. The respect is unrelenting, whatever the client's behavior. The message is conveyed: A human being is an entity deserving respect; *you* are an entity deserving respect. A client, for whom being treated in this manner may be a rare or even unique experience, may be stimulated over time to begin to restructure his or her self-concept. Carl Rogers made acceptance and respect the core of his approach to therapy, so powerful did he understand its impact to be.

I recall a client once saying to me, "Looking back over our therapy, I feel that nothing else that happened was quite so impactful as the simple fact that I always felt respected by you. I pulled everything I could to make you despise me and throw me out. I kept trying to make you act like my father. You refused to cooperate. Somehow, I had to deal with that, I had to let that in, which was difficult at first, but as I did the therapy began to take hold."

A therapist is not a cheerleader.

When a client is describing feelings of fear, or pain, or anger, it is not helpful to respond with, "Oh, you shouldn't feel that!" A therapist is not a cheerleader. There is value in expressing feelings without having to deal with criticism, condemnation, sarcasm, distracting questions, or lectures. The process of expression is often intrinsically healing. A therapist who is uncomfortable with strong feelings needs to work on him- or herself. To be able to listen serenely and with empathy is basic to the healing arts. (It is also basic to authentic friendship, to say nothing of love.) When the client's need for emotional expression has been met, then it sometimes can be useful to invite him or her to explore feelings more deeply and examine underlying assumptions that may need to be questioned.

One can subscribe to the merit of acceptance and respect in the abstract, but its implementation, even among well-intentioned therapists, is not always obvious. I am not thinking primarily of such obvious mistakes as resorting to sarcasm, moral condemnation, or other demeaning behavior. I am thinking of the subtler forms of authoritativeness, one-upmanship, "You're doomed without my guidance," and so forth, that put the client in an inferior position and hint at the therapist's omniscience. Psychoanalysis, which took its model from the traditional physician-patient relationship, may be especially vulnerable to this error, but the error can show up in any school of therapy. The error may have less to do with the theoretical orientation of the therapist than with his or her ability to manage personal needs for appreciation and admiration. I like to tell students, "The goal is not to prove that you are brilliant. The goal is to assist clients to discover that *they* are brilliant."

This is one of the reasons I favor experiential learning over explicit teaching (without denying that sometimes explicit teaching can be appropriate). In experiential learning, which often entails the use of psychological exercises, processes, homework assignments, and the like, the client *discovers* relevant realities rather than hears about them from an authority. Autonomy is strengthened in the very nature of the learning process.

Uncovering the "Bright" Side

Most people who seek psychotherapy have as one of their basic goals self-understanding. They want to feel visible to their therapist and they want to gain clearer visibility to themselves.

To many people—and here the influence of traditional psychoanalysis is profound—self-understanding is primarily associated with the uncovering of dark secrets. Freud, the father of psychoanalysis, said somewhere that the difference between psychoanalysis and detective work is that, for the detective, the crime is known and the challenge is to discover the identity of the criminal, whereas to the psychoanalyst, the criminal is known and the challenge is to discover the crime. Even if one takes this as a bit of poetry not to be taken literally, it has rather unpleasant implications. Many clinicians who are not necessarily psychoanalysts share this mind-set. Their professional pride is centered on their ability to lead the client to confront "the dark side" (in Jungian terminology, "the Shadow") and to integrate rather than disown it. This can be a necessary and important project, to be sure. However, a self-esteem-oriented therapy has different priorities—a different emphasis.

There is no need less recognized in most people than the need to contact their unidentified (and possibly disowned) *resources*. This is the need to understand the strengths they do not know they possess, the potentials they have never explored, the capacity for self-healing and self-development they have never summoned. A fundamental distinction among therapists, whatever their theoretical orientation, is whether they think of their task primarily in terms of uncovering assets or shortcomings, virtues or flaws, deficits or resources. Self-esteem-oriented psychotherapy focuses on positives—on the uncovering and activating of strengths—as the highest priority. It deals with negatives of necessity but always in the context of the positive focus and emphasis.

Everyone who has any familiarity with psychology knows about the danger of disowning the murderer within. Far fewer people understand the tragedy of disowning the hero within. In psychotherapy, it is often easy enough to see the part of the individual that is neurotic. The challenge is to see—and mobilize—that part that is healthy.

――――

Everyone who has any familiarity with psychology knows about the danger of disowning the murderer within. Far fewer people understand the tragedy of disowning the hero within.

――――

Sometimes we are simply ignorant of our positive resources. We do not recognize all we are capable of. Sometimes, however, we repress our knowledge. I remember working many years ago with a young woman in a therapy group. She was quite comfortable saying the most outrageously negative (and unjust) things about herself. I asked her, as an experiment, to stand facing the group and say aloud, repeatedly, "The truth is, I'm actually highly intelligent." Her voice choked and at first she could not do it. Then I helped her to say it—and she began to weep. So I gave her the sentence stem: **The bad thing about admitting my intelligence is—**. Here were her first endings:

My family will hate me.

No one in my family is supposed to have a mind.

My sisters and brothers will be jealous.

I won't belong anywhere.

I'll have to take responsibility for my life.

Then I gave her the stem: **If I were to bring my intelligence to bear on my problems—**. Her endings included:

I would know that I'm already responsible for my life whether I admit it or not.

I would see that I'm living in the past.

I would know that I'm not a little girl anymore.

I would see that it's the little girl who's scared, not me the adult.

I would take possession of my life.

Then I gave her the stem: **The frightening thing about admitting my strengths is—**. Her endings included:

No one would feel sorry for me [*laughing*].

I'd move into unfamiliar territory.

I'd have to take a fresh look at my boyfriend.

I'd know nothing is holding me back but me.

I might be alone.

I'd have to learn a new way of living.

Suppose people put expectations on me.

I'd have to learn to assert myself.

It doesn't feel frightening right now!

There are any number of ways skillful therapists put clients in touch with their positive resources, and it is not necessary to explore them here. What is important here is only the basic issue: Is the therapist *primarily* oriented to liabilities or assets? (One cannot always take a therapist's word for it, either, since behavior often differs from professed belief.) One of the secrets of Virginia Satir's great gifts as a family therapist was her conviction that people possessed all the resources they needed to solve their problems, and her ability to transmit that conviction to the people with whom she worked. In terms of producing results, it is one of the most important abilities a psychotherapist can possess.

Survival Strategies

Clients need to understand that humans are, by nature, problem solvers. The solutions we produce, in response to the difficulties and challenges we encounter, aim consciously or subconsciously at filling our needs. Sometimes the means we adopt are impractical and even self-destructive—"neurotic"—but at some level our intention is to take care of ourselves. Even suicide can be understood as a tragic effort at self-care, perhaps escape from intolerable suffering.

When we are young we may disown and repress feelings and emotions that evoke the disapproval of significant others and shake our own equilibrium, and we pay a price in later years in self-alienation, distorted perceptions, and any number of possible symptoms. Yet seen from the perspective of the child, the repression has functional utility; it has survival value; its intention is to make the child able to live more successfully—or at least to minimize pain. Or again, when we are young we may experience a good deal of hurt and rejection and develop a policy, in "self-protection," to reject others first. This policy does not make for a happy life. And yet its intention is not to cause suffering but to reduce it. Survival strategies that do not serve our interests but in fact hurt us, but to which we nonetheless cling like life preservers in a stormy sea, are the ones psychologists label "neurotic." The ones that serve our interests we properly label "good adaptations"—such as learning to walk, speak, think, and earn a living.

Clients can be deeply ashamed of some of their dysfunctional responses to life's challenges. They do not look at their behavior from the perspective of its intended functional utility. They are aware of their timidity or overaggressiveness or avoidance of human intimacy or compulsive sexuality, but not of its roots. They are not in contact with the needs they are blindly trying to address. Their shame and guilt do not make it easier for them to improve their condition, but harder. So one of the ways we can support self-esteem is by educating clients in the idea of survival strategies, helping them see that their worst mistakes can be understood as misguided attempts at self-preservation. Feelings of self-condemnation need to be examined and understood, but after this has been accomplished, their continued existence serves no useful purpose. When they are diminished the client is freer to consider solutions that can better fill their needs. "If it's your own perception that what you do doesn't work, are you willing to look at alternatives you might find more satisfying? Are you willing to experiment with trying something else?"

Integrating Subpersonalities

On a technical level perhaps the two methods that most distinguish my approach are the use of sentence completions, which I have illustrated throughout this book as well as in several of my previous books, and working with subpersonalities, which I turn to now.*

In my discussion of the second pillar of self-esteem, the practice of self-acceptance, I talked about accepting "all the parts" of ourselves, and I mentioned thoughts, emotions, actions, and memories. Yet our "parts" include actual subselves with values, perspectives, and feelings distinctively their own. I am not speaking of "multiple personalities," in the pathological sense. I am speaking of normal constituents of a human psyche, of which most people are unaware. When a psychotherapist wishes to assist in the development of healthy self-esteem, an understanding of the dynamics of subpersonalities is an invaluable tool. This is territory that an individual is not likely to discover on his or her own.

The idea of subpersonalities is almost as old as psychology itself, and some version of it may be found in any number of writers. It expresses the understanding that a monolithic view of the self, in which each individual has one personality and one personality only, with one set of values, perceptions, and responses, is an oversimplification of human reality. But beyond that generalization, there are great differences in how psychologists understand subpersonalities or work with them in psychotherapy.

My wife and colleague, Devers Branden, first persuaded me of the importance of subpersonality work to self-esteem and began developing innovative ways of identifying and integrating these parts several years before I became seriously interested in the subject. Our work reflects the observation that unrecognized or disowned and rejected subselves tend to become sources of conflict, unwanted feelings, and inappropriate behavior. Subselves that are recognized, respected, and integrated into the total personality become sources of energy, emotional richness, increased options, and a more fulfilling sense of identity. The subject is a big one and can only be introduced here.

To begin with the most obvious example: In addition to the adult-self that we all recognize as "who we are," there is within our psyche a child-self—the living presence of the child we once were. As a potential of our

---

* Appendix B contains a thirty-one-week sentence-completion program specifically designed to build self-esteem.

consciousness, a mind-state into which everyone shifts at times, that child's frame of reference and way of responding is an enduring component of our psyche. But we may have repressed that child long ago, repressed his or her feelings, perceptions, needs, responses, out of the misguided notion that "murder" was necessary to grow into adulthood. This recognition led to the conviction that no one could be completely whole who did not reconnect with and create a conscious and benevolent relationship with the child-self. This task is especially important for the attainment of autonomy. I saw that when the task is neglected, the tendency is to look for healing from the outside, from other people, and this never works: the healing that is needed is not between self and others but between adult-self and child-self. A person walking around with painful and lifelong feelings of rejection is unlikely to be aware that the problem has become internalized and that he or she is engaged in *self-rejection*, including the rejection of the child-self by the adult-self, which is why no *external* source of approval ever heals the wound.

First, what do I mean by a "subself" or a "subpersonality"? (The two terms are used synonymously.)

A subself or subpersonality is a dynamic component of an individual's psyche, having a distinctive perspective, value orientation, and "personality" of its own; that may be more or less dominant in the individual's responses at any particular time; that the individual may be more or less conscious of, more or less accepting and benevolent toward; that may be more or less integrated into the individual's total psychological system; and that is capable of growth and change over time. (I call a subself "dynamic" because it actively interacts with other components of the psyche and is not merely a passive repository of attitudes.)

The child-self is the component of the psyche containing the "personality" of the child one once was, with that child's range of values, emotions, needs, and responses; not a generic child or universal archetype, but a specific, historical child, unique to an individual's history and development. (This is very different from "the child ego-state" in Transactional Analysis; TA uses a generic model.)

Nearly two decades ago I gave a self-esteem seminar in which I guided the class through an exercise that involved an imaginary encounter with the child one once was. Afterward, during the break, a woman walked over to me and said, "Do you want to know what I did when I realized that the child sitting under the tree, waiting for me, was my five-year-old self? I created a stream behind the tree, threw the child into it, and drowned her." This was said with a bitter, brittle smile.

What the incident dramatizes is not only that we may be unconscious of any particular subself but that awareness may be instantly accompanied by hostility and rejection. Does it need to be argued that we cannot have healthy self-esteem while despising part of who we are? I have never worked with a depressed personality whose child-self did not feel hated (not merely ignored or rejected) by an older part. In *How to Raise Your Self-Esteem* I offer a number of exercises for identifying and integrating the child-self and the teenage-self (in addition to the work offered in the self-esteem program above).

The teenage-self is the component of the psyche containing the "personality" of the adolescent one once was, with that teenager's range of values, emotions, needs, and responses; not a generic teenager or universal archetype, but a specific, historical one, unique to an individual's history and development.

I have never worked with a depressed personality whose child-self did not feel hated (not merely ignored or rejected) by an older part.

Often, when working with couples on relationship problems, an exploration of the teenage-self is especially useful. This is the subself that often plays an important role in selecting a partner. And this is the mind-state to which we often revert unconsciously during times of relationship difficulty or crisis, as manifested in such withdrawal behaviors as "*I* don't care!" or "No one's going to get to me!" or "Don't tell *me* what to do!"

I recall once treating a couple, both psychotherapists, who came into my office furious at each other. He was forty-one and she was thirty-nine, but they looked like teenagers in their angry defiance of each other. On the way to my office she had said to him that when they arrived he should tell me some particular piece of information; to give her suggestion "authority," she had evidently dropped into an "older" voice, which he heard as the voice of his mother. "Don't tell me what to do!" he snapped. As an adolescent she had experienced "constant" reproaches from her parents, and, dropping into an adolescent mind-state in response to his rebuke, she slammed her fist against his shoulder and shouted, "Don't talk to me that way!" Later, when they were back in their normal adult consciousness, they were mortified at their behavior—"as if we were possessed by demons," one of them said. This is what it can feel like when a subpersonality takes over and we do not understand what is happening. I had helped them pull out of their teenage mind-state by asking them one question: "How old do you feel *right now* and is that the age you need to be to solve this problem?"

The opposite-gender-self is the component of the psyche containing the feminine subpersonality of the male and the masculine subpersonality of the female; not a generic "feminine" or "masculine" or universal archetype, but individual for each man or woman, reflecting aspects of his or her personal development, learning, acculturation, and overall development.

There tends to be a fairly strong correlation between how we relate to the opposite gender in the world and how we relate to the opposite gender within. The man who professes to find women an incomprehensible mystery is almost certainly completely out of touch with the feminine within—just as a woman who professes to find men incomprehensible is out of touch with her masculine side. In therapy I have found that one of the most powerful ways to help men and women become more effective in love relationships is to work with them on their relationship to their opposite-gender-self—making the relationship more conscious, accepting, benevolent, and therefore more integrated into the total personality. Not surprisingly, women are often far more comfortable with the idea that they have an internal masculine side than men are with the idea of an internal feminine side; but neither subself is difficult to demonstrate. (I might mention that none of this has anything to do with homosexuality or bisexuality.)

The mother-self is the component of the psyche containing an internalization of aspects of the personality, perspective, and values of an individual's mother (or other older female "mother figures" who had an influence and impact during childhood). Again, we deal with the individual and the historical, not the generic or universal "Mother." (And again this is very different from TA's generic "parent ego-state." Mother and Father are both parents, but they are very different and should not be treated as a psychological unit; they often send very different messages and have very different attitudes and values.)

Once, stepping into the street with my last client of the day and noticing how chilly it had become, I said to the young man, impulsively and quite untypically, "What! You came out without a sweater?" Before my startled client could reply, I said, "Stop. Don't answer. I didn't say that. My mother said that." We both laughed. For a brief moment, my mother-self had taken over my consciousness.

In more serious ways, of course, this happens all the time. Long after our mother may have died, we play her messages in our head and often imagine they are our own, failing to realize that the voice is hers, not ours, and that it is her perspective, her values, her orientation that we have internalized and allowed to take up residence in our psyche.

The father-self is the component of the psyche containing an internalization of aspects of the personality, perspective, and values of an individual's father (or other older male "father figures" who had an influence and impact during childhood).

I once had a client who, when he was kind and compassionate with his girlfriend, later complained of feeling "guilty" about it, which was a puzzling and unusual reaction. What we learned was that the source of his "guilt" was an unrecognized father-self who sneered at him and said, in effect, "Women are to be used, not treated as persons. What kind of man are you?" The client's struggle became to distinguish his own voice from that of his father-self's.

This list of subpersonalities is not meant to be exhaustive but merely to indicate the ones we work with most often in our practice. What each of these subselves needs from us is understanding, acceptance, respect, and benevolence, and in our therapy we have developed techniques to achieve this result.

A few years ago, Devers identified two other subpersonalities that we find it productive to work with. Technically they are not subpersonalities in quite the same sense as those listed above, but functionally they can be addressed the same way. They are the *outer self* and the *inner self.*

The outer self is the component of the psyche that is expressed through the self we present to the world. Very simply, the outer self is the self other people see. It may be a highly congruent and appropriate vehicle for the expression of the inner self in the world, or it may be a highly armored and defended distortion of the inner self.

The inner self is the self only we can see and experience; the private self; the self as subjectively perceived. (A powerful sentence stem: **If my outer self expressed more of my inner self in the world—** .)

A central aspect of our therapy is *balancing or integrating subpersonalities.* This is a process of working with subselves toward a number of interrelated ends, which include:

1. Learning to recognize a particular subpersonality, to isolate and identify it within the totality of one's experience.
2. Understanding the relationship that exists between the adult

conscious self and this particular subpersonality (for example, conscious, semiconscious, or unconscious, accepting or rejecting, benevolent or hostile).

3. Identifying the salient traits of the subpersonality, such as chief concerns, dominant emotions, characteristic ways of responding.

4. Identifying unmet needs or wants of the subpersonality relative to the adult conscious self (for example, to be heard, listened to, accepted with respect and compassion).

5. Identifying destructive behavior on the part of the subpersonality when important needs and wants are ignored or unmet by the conscious adult-self.

6. Developing a relationship between the adult conscious self and the subpersonality of consciousness, acceptance, respect, benevolence, and open communication.

7. Identifying the relationship existing between a particular subpersonality and the various others in the psyche and resolving any conflicts between them (through dialoguing, sentence-completion work, and mirror work).

Devers developed a particularly effective way to allow clients to have dialogues with their subselves. Mirror work with subpersonalities is a form of psychodrama, entailing an altered state of consciousness, in which the client/subject sits facing a mirror, enters the consciousness (ego state) of a particular subpersonality, and in that state speaks to the adult conscious self seen in the mirror, almost always using sentence completions (for example, **As I sit here looking at you—; One of the ways you treat me as Mother did is—; One of the things I want from you and have never gotten is—; If I felt accepted by you—; If I felt you had compassion for my struggles—**).

We sometimes find that the process of self-acceptance is blocked and we do not know why.

Whether working with a younger self, an opposite-gender-self, or a parent-self toward the end of integration and a greater overall experience of wholeness, the steps are always the same, in principle, and are indicated above. Through this process we convert disowned subselves from sources of turmoil and conflict into positive resources that can energize and enrich us.

Can we become accomplished at the practice of self-acceptance without learning about subpersonalities? Of course. If we learn to accept and respect our internal signals, to be fully present to our own experience, that is what self-esteem asks of us as far as self-acceptance is concerned.

However, we sometimes find that the process of self-acceptance is blocked and we do not know why. Mysterious voices inside our head generate relentless self-criticism. Self-acceptance feels like an ideal we can never fully realize. When this happens, working with subpersonalities can become an avenue to breakthrough.

In psychotherapy subpersonality work can be invaluable, since one of the barriers to growing in self-esteem can be parental voices bombarding the individual with critical and even hostile messages. As therapists we need to know how to turn those negative voices off—and turn an adversarial mother- or father-self into a positive resource.

Skills a Self-Esteem-Oriented Therapist Needs

There are basic skills that every psychotherapist needs to do his or her work effectively: human relationship skills such as building rapport, creating an atmosphere of safety and acceptance, and conveying a perspective of hope and optimism. Then there are the skills a therapist needs to address specific problems, such as sexual difficulties, obsessive-compulsive disorders, or career problems.

If a therapist sees the building of self-esteem as central to his or her work, there are specific issues that need to be addressed. They can be summarized in the form of questions:

By what means do I propose to assist my client in living more consciously?

How will I teach self-acceptance?

How will I facilitate a higher level of self-responsibility?

How will I encourage a higher level of self-assertiveness?

How will I contribute to the client operating at a higher level of purposefulness?

How will I inspire greater integrity in everyday living?

What can I do to nurture autonomy?

How can I contribute to the client's enthusiasm for life?

How can I awaken blocked positive potentials?

How can I assist the client to deal with conflicts and challenges in ways that will extend his or her field of comfort, competence, and mastery?

How do I assist the client in freeing him- or herself from irrational fears?

How do I assist the client in freeing him- or herself from the lingering pain of old wounds and traumas, perhaps originating in childhood?

How can I assist the client to recognize, accept, and integrate denied and disowned aspects of the self?

By the same token, a client wishing to assess his or her own therapy could utilize the standards implicit in these questions to examine a therapeutic approach or the personal progress being made with this approach. Thus: Am I learning to live more consciously? Am I learning greater self-acceptance? Does my therapist's manner of dealing with me contribute to my experience of autonomy and empowerment? And so on.

Fear, Pain, and the Amelioration of Negatives

Irrational fears almost inevitably have a negative effect on our sense of ourselves. Conversely, the elimination of irrational fears causes self-esteem to rise. This is one of the basic tasks of therapy.*

Unhealing pain from the past, because of the sense of debilitation it often provokes and the defenses people typically set against it, repre-

---

* I want to acknowledge the revolutionary work of my colleague, Dr. Roger Callahan, in developing what I regard as a truly ground-breaking technology for reducing or eliminating debilitating fears. Working with a concept of the human energy system whose roots may be traced, via acupuncture, back to Chinese medicine, but for which there is an increasing body of scientific evidence in the West, Callahan's work has profound implications for all the healing arts. The best introduction to his work is his monograph entitled *The Rapid Treatment of Panic, Anxiety, and Agoraphobia*.[1]

sents yet another barrier in the quest for stronger self-esteem.* When we are able to reduce or eliminate the pain of psychological wounds, self-esteem tends to rise.

———

When we eliminate negatives, we clear the way for the emergence of positives, and when we cultivate positives, negatives often weaken or disappear.

———

In working with the issues itemized in the above questions, we constantly move back and forth between what I call the "positive" issues (for example, learning to live more consciously) and the "negative" ones (for example, eliminating irrational fears). They are interwoven at every point. It is worth isolating them conceptually for purposes of discussion and analysis, but in reality they do not operate in isolation. When we eliminate negatives, we clear the way for the emergence of positives, and when we cultivate positives, negatives often weaken or disappear.

In recent years significant breakthroughs in psychopharmacology have been achieved, with implications for the amelioration of some "negatives," particularly among the severely disturbed, the origins of whose problems is surmised to be biochemical imbalances. Many men and women have been enabled to function in the world who could not do so before. But this field is not without controversy. Opponents of the claims made by enthusiasts assert that they are often grossly exaggerated, are not supported by reviews of the research, and that the dangerous side effects of some of these psychopharmacological agents are denied or minimized.† I have treated clients before and after their anxiety, depression, or obsessive-compulsive reactions were reduced or eliminated (or masked?) by chemical agents, but what has always struck me is that their fundamental self-esteem problems (and personality structure) remained, quite apart from whether they "felt" better or not. However, one of the therapeutic benefits of their medication, in addition to the alleviation of

---

* I am not in a position to offer a blanket endorsement for every claim Callahan might make about his therapy, but I have personally been able to duplicate extraordinary results in treating fear, pain, and the emotional aftermath of trauma, as have other colleagues.

† For a critique of pharmacologically oriented psychiatry, see *Toxic Psychiatry* by Peter R. Breggan (New York: St. Martin's Press, 1991).

suffering, is that it sometimes made them more capable of participating in psychotherapy. The bad news is that sometimes it facilitated their flights from real problems, the solutions for which demanded more of them than the ingestion of a pill.

Methodology evolves and we will continue to discover new ways to achieve our goals in therapy. My primary focus in this chapter is with the question of what our goals need to be. I have wanted to convey basic guiding principles for a self-esteem-based approach.

The Therapy of the Future

As consciousness of the importance of self-esteem spreads through our culture, it is a foregone conclusion that more psychotherapists will be asked by their clients, "How can I grow in self-esteem?" There will be increasing demand for a technology specifically addressed to this issue. But first, there must be an understanding of what, precisely, self-esteem is, *and what its healthy emergence depends on.*

For example, there is an approach to self-esteem that thinks primarily in terms of assisting the client to grow in practical efficacy—that is, to acquire new skills. This is an important aspect of self-esteem therapy, to be sure, but it is only an aspect. If the client is living hypocritically and dishonestly, new skills will not fill the void in his or her sense of worth. Or, if the client has internalized the hypercritical voice of Mother or Father (represented by a mother-self or a father-self), a feeling of basic inadequacy or worthlessness can coexist with high achievement. Or, if the client thinks of competence and worth only in terms of specific knowledge and skills, but not the underlying mental processes that make them possible, a deep feeling of inefficacy can coexist with any number of acquired abilities. Regarding this last point: When we say that self-efficacy is trust in one's competence to cope with the basic challenges of life, we are anchoring this component of self-esteem not in specific knowledge or skills *but in one's ability to think, make decisions, learn, and persevere in the face of difficulties,* which are matters of process, not content. An effective self-esteem therapy has to be process focused, but it has to be more than that. It has to be comprehensive enough to address not only issues of competence but also of worth—self-respect: confidence that one deserves love, success, and happiness.

Another tradition has it that self-esteem is the "reflected appraisals" of significant others. Then a therapist might logically tell the client, "You must learn how to make yourself likable to other people." In reality, however, few therapists would make this statement; nor would they say, "Through therapy you will learn how to manipulate people so expertly that the overwhelming majority will have no choice but to like you—and then you will have self-esteem!" And yet, if one really believes that self-esteem is a gift from others, why wouldn't one say it? The answer, I suspect, is that no matter how "other directed" one may be theoretically, somewhere there is the implicit knowledge that the approval each of us needs is from within. When we are children, we are dependent on others for the satisfaction of most of our needs. Some children are more independent than others, but no child can have the level of independence possible to an adult. As we mature, we become "self-supporting" in more areas, including self-esteem. If we develop properly, we transfer the source of approval from the world to ourselves; we shift from the external to the internal. But if one does not understand the nature and roots of adult self-esteem, but thinks in terms of "reflected appraisals," one is at a severe disadvantage when it comes to putting theory into effective practice.

If we develop properly, we transfer the source of approval from the world to ourselves; we shift from the external to the internal.

Some psychotherapists identify self-esteem exclusively with self-acceptance and treat it in effect as a birthright, with no further effort required of the individual. This approach conveys a very limited view of what self-esteem is and requires. Important as self-acceptance is, the client will be left to wonder why it does not satisfy the hunger for something more—some height the client may yearn for but have no inkling of how to reach, and no guidance.

For these reasons, I recommend that a person seeking professional assistance in raising self-esteem, which is an eminently worthy and admirable undertaking, would do well to interview a prospective therapist and ask these questions:

What do you understand "self-esteem" to mean?

What do you think healthy self-esteem depends on?

What will we do together that will have a positive effect on my self-esteem?

What are your reasons for thinking so?

Any conscientious professional will respect these questions.

17

Self-Esteem and Culture

One way to deepen our understanding of the themes with which this book has been concerned is to look at self-esteem as it relates to and is affected by culture.

Let us begin by considering the idea of self-esteem itself. It is not an idea—let alone an ideal—one finds in all cultures. It emerged in the West only recently and is still far from well understood.

In medieval times, "self" as we understand the idea still lay sleeping in the human psyche. The basic mind-set was tribal, not individualistic. Each person was born into a distinct and unchangeable place in the social order. With very rare exceptions, one did not choose an occupation but rather was cast by circumstances of birth into the role of peasant, artisan, or knight—or the wife of one. One's sense of security derived, not from one's achievements, but from seeing oneself as an integral part of "the natural order," which was presumed to be ordained by God. Subject to the vicissitudes of war, famines, and plagues, one was more or less guaranteed a livelihood, determined by tradition. There was very little competition, just as there was very little economic freedom—or any other kind of freedom. In such an environment, with so little outlet for an independent, self-assertive mind, self-esteem—when and to the extent it existed—could not manifest itself through superior economic adaptiveness. There were occasions when it was life endangering: it could lead its possessor to the torture rack and the stake. The Dark and Middle Ages did not value self-assertion; did not understand individuality; could not conceive self-responsibility; had no grasp of the "Rights of Man" or the modern idea of political freedom; could not imagine innovativeness as a way of life; did not grasp the relation of mind, intelligence, and creativity to survival; had no place for self-esteem (which does not mean it did not exist).

Our idea of "the individual," as an autonomous, self-determining unit, able to think independently and bearing responsibility for his or her existence, emerged from several historical developments: the Renaissance in the fifteenth century, the Reformation in the sixteenth, and the Enlightenment in the eighteenth—and their two offspring, the Industrial Revolution and capitalism. Self-esteem, as we think about the concept today, has its roots in the post-Renaissance emerging culture of individualism. This is true of any number of ideals that we (and increasingly people in other countries) have come to admire, such as the freedom to marry for love, a belief in the right to the pursuit of happiness, a hope that work can be not only a source of sustenance but also of self-expression and self-fulfillment. Not long ago these values were regarded as very "Western," very "American"—and now more and more of the world is embracing them. These values reflect human needs.

Self-esteem as a psychological reality existed in human consciousness thousands of years before it emerged as an explicit idea. Now that it has emerged, the challenge is to understand it.

The Need for Self-Esteem Is Not "Cultural"

Every human being, whatever the network of customs and values in which he or she grows up, is obliged to act to satisfy and fulfill basic needs. We do not always and automatically feel competent in facing this challenge. Yet all human beings need an experience of competence (which I call self-efficacy) if they are to possess a fundamental sense of security and empowerment. Without it, they cannot respond appropriately. We do not always and automatically feel worthy of love, respect, happiness. Yet all human beings need an experience of worth (self-respect) if they are to take proper care of themselves, protect their legitimate interests, gain some enjoyment from their efforts, and (when possible) stand up against those who would harm or exploit them. Without it, again they cannot act appropriately in their own best interests. The root of the need for self-esteem is *biological:* it pertains to survival and continued efficacious functioning.

The need is inherent in human nature; it is not an invention of Western culture.

The Universality of Self-Esteem Issues

Living Consciously. For every organism that possesses it, conscious-ness is an imperative of effective adaptation. The distinctive *human* form of consciousness is conceptual: our survival, well-being, and skillful adaptation depend on our ability to think—on the appropriate use of mind. Whether one is mending a fishing net or debugging a computer program, tracking an animal or designing a skyscraper, negotiating with an enemy or seeking to resolve a dispute with one's spouse—in all cases, one can bring a higher level of consciousness to the occasion or a lower. One can choose to see or not to see (or anywhere between). But reality is reality and is not wiped out by self-elected blindness. The higher the level of consciousness one brings to what one is doing, the more effec-tive and in control one feels—and the more successful one's efforts.

---

*The root of the need for self-esteem is biological:
it pertains to survival and continued
efficacious functioning.*

In any context where consciousness is needed, operating consciously benefits self-esteem, and operating (relatively) unconsciously wounds self-esteem. The importance of living consciously is grounded not in culture but in reality.

Self-Acceptance. When individuals deny and disown their experience, when they reject their thoughts, feelings, or behavior as "not me," when they induce unconsciousness of their inner life, their intention is self-protection. They are trying to maintain their equilibrium and defend their view of themselves. The intention is to serve "self-esteem." But the result is to harm self-esteem. Self-esteem requires self-acceptance; it is not served by self-rejection. This truth stands apart from any question of whether the beliefs of a given culture do or do not encourage self-acceptance. A highly authoritarian society, for example, might encour-age neglect and even disparagement of the individual's inner life. This does not mean that self-acceptance is merely a cultural bias with no justification in human nature. It means that some cultures may hold values that are inimical to human well-being. Cultures are not equal in the psychological benefits they confer on their members.

Self-Responsibility. No one can feel empowered, no one can feel competent to cope with life's challenges, who does not take responsibility for his or her choices and actions. No one can feel efficacious who does not take responsibility for the attainment of his or her desires. Self-responsibility is essential to the experience of inner strength. When we look to others to provide us with happiness or fulfillment or self-esteem, we relinquish control over our life. There is no social environment in which these observations become untrue.

Not all cultures value self-responsibility equally. This does not alter the fact that where we see responsibility and the willingness to be accountable, we see a healthier, more robust sense of self—a biologically more adaptive organism.

As for teamwork, group activity, and the like, the self-responsible person can function effectively with others precisely because he or she *is willing to be accountable.* Such a person is not a dependent nor a parasite nor an exploiter. Self-responsibility does not mean one does everything oneself; it means that when one acts in concert with others, one carries one's own weight. Does it need to be argued that a society whose members value this attitude is stronger and better equipped for survival than a society whose members do not?

Self-Assertiveness. Self-assertiveness is the practice of honoring one's needs, wants, values, and judgments, and seeking appropriate forms of their expression in reality. Not all cultures value self-assertiveness equally. And some forms of appropriate self-expression may differ from place to place—for example, the words one uses, or the tone of voice in which one speaks, or the gestures one makes. But to the extent that a culture suppresses the natural impulse to self-assertion and self-expression, it blocks creativity, stifles individuality, and sets itself against the requirements of self-esteem. Nazi Germany and Soviet Russia, to name two examples in this century, ruthlessly punished self-assertiveness; in these countries, it was a cultural disvalue. They were not societies in which human life could flourish. Other cultures punish self-assertiveness and self-expression in less extreme and violent ways (sometimes in very gentle ways). Hawaiian children may be lovingly enjoined, "Remain among the clumps of grasses and do not elevate yourself."[1] Just the same, self-effacement as a basic pattern of being is inimical to self-esteem—and to the life force.

To the extent that a culture suppresses the natural impulse to self-assertion and self-expression, it blocks creativity, stifles individuality, and sets itself against the requirements of self-esteem.

Self-expression is natural; self-suppression is not. Children do not need to be educated into self-assertion; authoritarian societies do need to socialize them into self-surrender. That some children may come into this world more naturally self-assertive than others does not contradict this observation. When fear is absent, self-assertiveness is the natural condition of human beings. What people may have to learn is comfort with and respect for the self-assertiveness of others. This is clearly an imperative of cooperation. Cooperation is not a "middle ground" between self-assertiveness and self-suppression, but the intelligent exercise of self-interest in a social context—which *does* have to be learned.

Living Purposefully. The idea of living purposefully can be misinterpreted to mean that all of one's life is given over to long-term productive goals. Our purposes can include many things besides productive work: raising a family, enjoying a love affair or a marriage, pursuing a hobby, developing one's body through exercise or one's spirit through study and meditation. Understood correctly, there is nothing intrinsically "Western" about a strong goal orientation. When Buddha set out in search of enlightenment, was he not moved by a passionate purpose? I am confident that even among Polynesians, some men and women are more purposeful than others.

In discussing self-esteem, I use words like "efficacy," "competence," "achievement," "success." In our culture there might be a tendency to understand these ideas in exclusively materialistic terms; I intend no such implication. They are meant metaphysically or ontologically, not merely economically. Without disparaging the value of material attainments (which are, after all, necessities of survival), we can appreciate that these ideas embrace the total spectrum of human experience, from the mundane to the spiritual.

The question is: Is our life and well-being better served by organizing our energies with relation to specific (short- and long-term) purposes, or are they better served by living from day to day, reacting to events rather than choosing one's own direction, passively drifting at the whim of impulse and circumstance? If one holds to the Aristotelian perspective, as I do, that a proper human life is one in which we seek the fullest exercise of our distinctive powers, then the answer is obvious. In passivity neither our reason nor our passion nor our creativity nor our imagination fulfill themselves. We only half live our existence. This perspective may be Western, but I believe it is arguably superior to the alternative.

If human life and happiness are the standard, not all cultural traditions are equal. In Africa, for example, there are societies in which it is normal and accepted practice to mutilate the genitals of young females. An ancient tradition in India led millions of widows to be burned alive. If we object to these practices, I doubt that anyone will wish to raise the charge of "cultural imperialism."

We will want to keep this in mind as our discussion of self-esteem and culture proceeds.

Personal Integrity. The practice of integrity consists of having principles of behavior and being true to them. It means keeping one's word, honoring one's commitments, being faithful to one's promises. Since I have never heard this virtue disparaged as a "cultural artifact," since it is esteemed in every society I know of—even in the underworld there is the idea of "honor among thieves"—I think it is obvious that this virtue is deeper than any "cultural bias." It reflects an implicit awareness held by everyone about life.

The betrayal of one's convictions wounds self-esteem. This is decreed not by culture but by reality—that is, by our nature.

I stressed early in the book that self-esteem is neither comparative nor competitive. It has nothing to do with striving to make oneself superior to others. A Hawaiian psychologist asked me, "Aren't you teaching people to elevate themselves above others?" I answered that the work had nothing to do with others, in the sense he imagined: it had to do with our relationship with ourselves—and with reality. Raised in a culture in which not the individual but the group is primary, he had difficulty understanding this; his whole orientation was to the social collective.

"When gathered in a bucket, the crabs on top will always keep the others from getting out," he insisted. "It's not good to be too great." "In the first place," I answered, "I don't see human society as a bucket of crabs, and in the second place, what happens to children of extraordinary talent or ability in your world?" He said that as he understood self-esteem, it could only be the security of belonging—of being well integrated into a network of relationships. Was that different, I wanted to know, from trying to base self-esteem on being liked and approved of? He countered that I was "phobic" about dependency.

If we have a genuine need to experience our powers and worth, then more is required than the comfort of "belonging." This is not to argue against the value of "relationships." But if a culture places relationships first, above autonomy and authenticity, it leads the individual to self-alienation: to be "connected" is more important than to know who I am and to be who I am. The tribalist may wish to assert that being "connected" *is* more important, *is* the higher value, but that is not a license to equate it with self-esteem. Let that kind of gratification be called something else. Otherwise, we are trapped in an eternal Tower of Babel.

If human life and happiness are the standard,
not all cultural traditions are equal.

When I discussed these issues with a Hawaiian educator who was eager to introduce better self-esteem principles into the school system, she said, "No matter what our skills or talents, so many of us here have a major self-esteem problem. We feel inferior and we're afraid we'll never catch up. Our children suffer from demoralization."

All this leads naturally to the question: What is the effect of different cultures, and different cultural values, on self-esteem?

The Influence of Culture

Every society contains a network of values, beliefs, and assumptions, not all of which are named explicitly but which nonetheless are part of the human environment. Indeed, ideas that are not identified overtly but are held and conveyed tacitly can be harder to call into question—precisely because they are absorbed by a process that largely bypasses the conscious mind. Everyone possesses what might be called a "cultural unconscious"—a set of implicit beliefs about nature, reality, human beings, man-woman relationships, good and evil—that reflect the knowledge, understanding, and values of a historical time and place. I do not mean that there are no differences among people within a given culture in their beliefs at this level. Nor do I mean that no one holds any of these beliefs consciously or that no one challenges any of them. I mean only that at least some of these beliefs tend to reside in every psyche in a given society, and without ever being the subject of explicit awareness.

It is not possible for anyone, even the most independent, to make *every* premise conscious or to subject *every* premise to critical scrutiny. Even great innovators who challenge and overthrow paradigms in one area of reality may accept uncritically the implicit assumptions reigning in other areas. What impresses us about a mind like Aristotle's, for instance, is the wide number of fields to which he brought the power of his extraordinarily original intellect. Yet even Aristotle was in many respects a man of his time and place. None of us can entirely escape the influence of our social environment.

Consider, as illustration, the view of women that has dominated human history.

---

*Some version of woman-as-inferior is part of the
"cultural unconscious" of just about every
society we know of.*

In almost every part of the world and throughout virtually all the centuries behind us, women have been regarded, and been taught to regard themselves, as the inferior of men. Some version of woman-as-inferior is part of the "cultural unconscious" of just about every society we know of—and in the "cultural *conscious*" as well. Woman's second-class status is a pronounced aspect of every brand of religious fundamentalism—be it Jewish, Christian, Islamic, or Hindu. Therefore, it is at its most virulent in societies dominated by religious fundamentalism, such as modern Iran.

In Christianity, and not only among fundamentalists, it was held (and often is still held) that woman's relationship to man should be as man's relationship to God. Obedience, in this view, is a woman's cardinal virtue (after "purity," no doubt). I once made the mistake, in therapy with a female client, of associating this idea with "medieval Christianity." She looked at me with astonishment and said sadly, "Are you kidding? I heard it from our minister last Sunday—and from my husband on Monday." When her husband learned of our discussion, he insisted that she discontinue therapy. Woman-as-inferior is not an idea that supports female self-esteem. Can anyone doubt that it has had a tragic effect on most women's view of themselves? Even among many modern American women who consider themselves thoroughly "emancipated," it is not difficult to detect the pernicious influence of this view.

There is a corresponding widely held idea about men's value that is detrimental to male self-esteem.

In most cultures men are socialized to identify personal worth with earning ability, with being "a good provider." If, traditionally, women "owe" men obedience, then "owe" women financial support (and physical protection). If a woman loses her job and cannot find another, she has an economic problem, to be sure, but she does not feel diminished as a woman. Men often feel emasculated. In hard times, women do not commit suicide because they cannot find work; men often do—because men have been trained to identify self-esteem with earning ability.

Now it could be argued that there is rational justification for tying self-esteem to earning ability. Does not self-esteem have to do with being equal to the challenges of life? Then is not the ability to earn a living essential? There are at least two things to be said about this. First, if a person is unable to earn a living because of his (or her) own choices and policies—unconsciousness, passivity, irresponsibility—then that inability is a reflection on self-esteem. But if the problem is the result of factors beyond the individual's control, such as an economic depression, then it is wrong to make the problem the occasion of self-blame. Self-esteem properly pertains only to issues open to our volitional choice. Second, note that the emphasis usually is not on earning ability as such, but on being *a good provider.* Men are judged, and are encouraged to judge themselves, by how well they can financially *take care of others.* Men are socialized to be "servants" fully as much as women; only the *forms* of culturally encouraged servitude are different.* If a man cannot support a woman, he tends to lose stature in her eyes and in his own. It would take unusual independence and self-esteem to challenge this culturally induced attitude and to ask "*Why* is this the gauge of my value as a man?"

---

* For an excellent discussion of "men's story," see Warren Farrell's *The Myth of Male Power* (New York: Simon & Schuster, 1993).

The Tribal Mentality

Throughout human history, most societies and cultures have been dominated by the tribal mentality. This was true in primitive times, in the Middle Ages, and in socialist (and some nonsocialist) countries in the twentieth century. Japan is a contemporary example of a nonsocialist nation still heavily tribal in its cultural orientation, although it may now be in the process of becoming less so.

The essence of the tribal mentality is that it makes the tribe as such the supreme good and denigrates the importance of the individual. It tends to view individuals as interchangeable units and to ignore or minimize the significance of differences between one human being and another. At its extreme, it sees the individual as hardly existing except in the network of tribal relationships; the individual by him- or herself is nothing.

Plato, the father of collectivism, captures the essence of this perspective in the *Laws*, when he states, "My law will be made with a general view of the best interests of society at large . . . as I rightly hold the single person and his affairs as of minor importance." He speaks enthusiastically of "the habit of never so much as thinking to do one single act apart from one's fellows, of making life, to the very uttermost, an unbroken concert, society, and community of all with all." In ancient times, we think of this vision as embodied in the militaristic society of Sparta. In modern times, its monuments were Nazi Germany and the Soviet Union. Between the ancient and the modern, we think of the feudal civilization of the Middle Ages, in which each person was defined by his or her place in the social hierarchy, apart from which personal identity could hardly be said to exist.

The essence of the tribal mentality is that it makes the tribe as such the supreme good and denigrates the importance of the individual.

Tribal societies can be totalitarian but they need not be. They can be relatively free. Control of the individual can be more cultural than political, although the political is always a factor. What I wish to point out here is that the tribal premise is intrinsically anti-self-esteem.

It is a premise and an orientation that disempowers the individual qua individual. Its implicit message is: You don't count. By yourself, you are nothing. Only as part of us can you be something. Thus, any society, to the extent that it is dominated by the tribal premise, is inherently unsupportive of self-esteem and more: it is actively inimical. In such a society the individual is socialized to hold him- or herself in low esteem relative to the group. Self-assertiveness is suppressed (except through highly ritualized channels). Pride tends to be labeled a vice. Self-sacrifice is enjoined.

Some years ago, in *The Psychology of Romantic Love*, I wrote about the lack of importance attached to emotional attachments in primitive societies. Love, as a celebration of two "selves" in union, was an utterly incomprehensible idea. I argued in that book that romantic love, rationally understood, requires self-esteem as its context—and that both ideas, romantic love and self-esteem, are foreign to the tribal orientation.

Anthropological studies of primitive tribes still in existence tell us a good deal about early forms of the tribal mentality and its perspective on what we call "individuality." Here is a rather amusing illustration provided by Morton M. Hunt in *The Natural History of Love:*

> By and large, the clanship structure and social life of most primitive societies provide wholesale intimacy and a broad distribution of affection; . . . most primitive peoples fail to see any great difference between individuals, and hence do not become involved in unique connections in the Western fashion; any number of trained observers have commented on the ease of their detachment from love objects, and their candid belief in the interchangeability of loves. Dr. Audrey Richards, an anthropologist who lived among the Bemba of Northern Rhodesia in the 1930s, once related to a group of them an English folk-fable about a young prince who climbed glass mountains, crossed chasms, and fought dragons, all to obtain the hand of the maiden he loved. The Bemba were plainly bewildered, but remained silent. Finally an old chief spoke up, voicing the feelings of all present in the simplest of questions: "Why not take another girl?" he asked.

Margaret Mead's well-known study of the Samoans shows likewise that deep emotional attachments between individuals are very foreign to such societies' psychology and pattern of living.[2] While sexual promiscuity and a short duration of sexual relationships are sanctioned and encouraged, any tendency to form strong emotional bonds between individuals is actively discouraged. If love is self-expression and self-celebration, as well as celebration of the other, think of the self-esteem implications of the Samoan orientation—or of its spiritual equivalent in contemporary "sex clubs" in New York City.

In the mores regulating sexual activity in primitive cultures, one often encounters a fear of, even an antagonism toward, sexual attachments that grow out of (what we call) love. Indeed, sexual activity often appears acceptable to most when the feelings that prompt it are superficial. "In the Trobriand islands, for instance," writes G. Rattray Taylor:

> Adults do not mind if children engage in sexual play and attempt precociously to perform the sexual act; as adolescents, they may sleep with one another, provided only that they are not in love with one another. If they fall in love, the sexual act becomes forbidden, and for lovers to sleep together would outrage decency.[3]

Love, if it occurs, is sometimes more severely regulated than sex. (Of course, in many instances there is not even a word for "love" in any sense approximating our own.) Passionate individual attachments are seen as threatening to tribal values and tribal authority. Again, think of the implications for self-esteem.

One encounters the tribal mentality again in the technologically advanced society of George Orwell's *1984*, where the full power and authority of a totalitarian state is aimed at crushing the self-assertive individualism of romantic love. The contempt of twentieth-century dictatorships for a citizen's desire to have "a personal life," the characterization of such a desire as "petty bourgeois selfishness," is too well known to require documentation. Modern dictatorships may have a better grasp of individuality than did primitive tribes, but the result is that the hostility is more virulent. When I attended the First International Conference on Self-Esteem in Norway in 1990, a Soviet scholar remarked, "As Americans, you can't possibly grasp the extent to which the idea of self-esteem is absent in our country. It's not understood. And if it were, it would be condemned as politically subversive."

What is interesting about modern Japan is that it is a semifree society whose tradition is tribal and authoritarian while containing within itself some liberal forces thrusting toward greater individualism and freedom from the constraints of old ways. Here is Jonathan Rauch commenting on the "older" aspect of Japanese culture:

> There is a disturbing side of Japan: a traditional, preliberal side. The baseball teams often train their players to the point of pain and exhaus-

tion on the grounds that this will build strength of spirit. In high school hazings, underclassmen are humiliated and bullied on the understanding that they will get their own turn at bullying when they become upperclassmen. In the ever-present Japanese seniority systems, the young suffer and pay their dues and learn to endure and accept and later inflict the same. The bully-worshipping portion of Japan is only one sector of the rich and diverse Japanese moral geography. Yet I was not in Japan a week before this sector had drawn my attention and seduced me with its vaguely fascist magnetism. . . . As it happened, I had been recently reading Plato, and when I saw the traditional Japanese values—strength through suffering, strength through hierarchy, strength through individual submersion in the group—I recognized what I beheld. . . . No one would have admired the traditional Japanese values more than Plato, who would have seen in them the gleaming Sparta of his dreams.[4]

Some years ago I had a Japanese teacher of aikido as a psychotherapy client. He had moved from Japan to California at the age of twenty-two. He said, "Japan is changing, sure, but the weight of tradition is still very heavy. The idea of self-esteem barely exists, and it's really something else there, not what you write about, not what I understand and want for myself. There, it's all tied up with a group thing—family, the company, you know, not really the individual. I saw my friends struggling with the issue, not knowing how to put it into words. I came to the States because I like the greater individualism. A lot of people are crazy here, you know, really mixed up—but still, I think there's a better chance to develop self-esteem here."

My point is not that the Japanese culture in its entirety is unsupportive of self-esteem. The culture is far too diverse and contains too many conflicting values for any such proposition. The elements alluded to above are indeed inimical to self-esteem. There is much in Japanese culture that discourages autonomy, as is generally true of tribal cultures. But there are other elements whose psychological effects are positive. A high regard for knowledge and learning. An understanding of the importance of being fully accountable for one's actions and commitments. A loving pride in work well done. In cultures of high diversity, it is more useful to think of the implications for self-esteem of specific beliefs or values rather than of the culture as a whole.

What one can say as a generalization is that tribal cultures discount individuality and encourage dependency and to this extent may be characterized as unfriendly to self-esteem.

The Religious Mentality

In California, when educators introduced self-esteem curricula into the schools, the most fervent opponents were Christian fundamentalists. They denounce such programs as "self-worship." They argue that self-esteem alienates children from God.

I recall, many years ago, a Carmelite nun speaking of her training. "We were taught that the enemy to be annihilated, the barrier between ourselves and Divinity, was the self. Eyes cast down—not to see too much. Emotions suppressed—not to feel too much. A life of prayers and service—not to think too much. Above all, obedience—not to question."

Throughout history, wherever religion has been state enforced, consciousness has been punished. For the sin of thinking, men and women have been tortured and executed. This is why the American idea of the absolute separation of Church and State was of such historic significance: it forbade any religious group to use the machinery of government to persecute those who thought or believed differently.

Throughout history, wherever religion has been state enforced, consciousness has been punished.

When beliefs are arrived at not by a process of reason but by faith and alleged revelation—when there are no objective criteria of knowledge to appeal to—those who think differently are often perceived by believers as a threat, a danger, capable of spreading the disease of nonbelief to others. For example, consider the typical religious response to atheism. If one has arrived at belief in God through some authentic personal experience, one would imagine that an appropriate response to those not similarly advantaged would be compassion. Instead, more often than not, the response is hatred. Why? The answer can only be that the atheist is experienced by the believer as a threat. Yet if the believer truly feels not only that God exists but that God is on his or her side, then it is the atheist, not the believer, who should receive kindness and sympathy, having lacked the good fortune to be touched by the experience of Divinity. (As it happens, the Bible sets the precedent for this lack of benevolence; we are told Jesus threatened those who did not believe he was the son of God with an eternity of torment. And in the Koran, Mohammed is no more merciful toward nonbelievers. Religious support for cruelty toward those who don't agree with one has a long history.)

Of course the issue is deeper than theism versus atheism. For thousands of years men have killed other men in the name of different notions of God. Terrible religious wars were between people all of whom called themselves Christians.

Historically, not only has traditional religion generally set itself in opposition to science, it has also condemned most personal mysticism—because the mystic claims direct, unmediated experience of God, unrouted through religious authority. For the traditional religionist, the mystic who operates outside the orbit of the church is too much of an "individualist."

My purpose here is not an examination of the impact of religion as such, but only religious authoritarianism as it manifests itself in a given culture. If there are religions or specific religious teachings that encourage the individual to value him- or herself and that support intellectual openness and independent thinking, then they are outside the scope of this discussion. My focus here is on the effects for self-esteem of cultures (or subcultures) in which religious authoritarianism dominates, in which belief is commanded and dissent is regarded as sin. In such situations, living consciously, self-responsibly, and self-assertively is proscribed.

It would be a mistake to let one's thinking on this point stop at Islam or Roman Catholicism. Luther and Calvin were no friendlier to the independent mind than was the pope.

If, in any culture, children are taught, "We are all equally unworthy in the sight of God"—

If, in any culture, children are taught, "You are born in sin and are sinful by nature"—

If children are given a message that amounts to "Don't think, don't question, *believe*"—

If children are given a message that amounts to "Who are you to place your mind above that of the priest, the minister, the rabbi?"—

If children are told, "If you have value it is not because of anything you have done or could ever do, it is only because God loves you"—

If children are told, "Submission to what you cannot understand is the beginning of morality"—

If children are instructed, "Do not be 'willful,' self-assertiveness is the sin of pride"—

If children are instructed, "Never think that you belong to yourself "—

If children are informed, "In any clash between your judgment and that of your religious authorities, it is your authorities you must believe"—

If children are informed, "Self-sacrifice is the foremost virtue and noblest duty"—

—then *consider what will be the likely consequences for the practice of living consciously, or the practice of self-assertiveness, or any of the other pillars of healthy self-esteem.*

In any culture, subculture, or family in which belief is valued above thought, and self-surrender is valued above self-expression, and conformity is valued above integrity, those who preserve their self-esteem are likely to be heroic exceptions.

In my experience, what makes discussions of the impact of religious teachings difficult is the high degree of individual interpretation of what they mean. I have been told on occasion that none of the teachings given above really mean what it sounds like it means. Many Christians I have talked to assure me that they personally know what Jesus Christ *really* meant but that, alas, millions of other Christians don't.

What is inarguable, however, is that whenever and wherever religion of any kind (Christian or non-Christian) has been backed by the power of the state, consciousness, independence, and self-assertiveness have been punished, sometimes with appalling cruelty. This is the simple fact at which one must look in weighing the cultural/psychological impact on individuals of the religious authoritarian orientation. This does not mean that all religious ideas are necessarily mistaken. But it does mean that if one looks from a historical perspective at one culture after another, one cannot claim that the influence of religion in general has been salutary for self-esteem.

The subject of religion tends to provoke strong passions. To some readers, almost every sentence in this section may be incendiary. My colleagues in the self-esteem movement are understandably eager to persuade people that there are no conflicts between the self-esteem agenda and the precepts of conventional religion. In discussions with religious critics, I myself have sometimes asked, "If you believe that we are the children of God, isn't it blasphemy to suggest that we not love ourselves?" And yet, the question remains: If the fundamentalists have gone on the warpath about the introduction of self-esteem programs in the schools because they believe such programs are incompatible with traditional religion, is it possible they are not mistaken? That is a question that must be faced.

If, as is my hope, the six pillars will one day be taught to schoolchildren, well—has any religious orthodoxy ever wanted a people fully committed to the practice of living consciously? And will boys and girls (and men and women) of high self-esteem accept Protestant theologian Paul Tillich's assertion that everyone is equally unworthy in the sight of God?

The American Culture

The United States of America is a culture with the greatest number of subcultures of any country in the world. It is a society characterized by an extraordinary diversity of values and beliefs in virtually every sphere of life. And yet, if we understand that we will be speaking only of dominant trends to which there are any number of countervailing forces, there is a sense in which we may legitimately speak of "American culture."

What was so historically extraordinary about the creation of the United States of America was its conscious rejection of the tribal premise. The Declaration of Independence proclaimed the revolutionary doctrine of individual, inalienable rights and asserted that the government exists for the individual, not the individual for the government. Although our political leaders have betrayed this vision many ways and many times, it still contains the essence of what the abstraction—*America*—stands for. Freedom. Individualism. The right to the pursuit of happiness. Self-ownership. The individual as an end in him- or herself, not a means to the ends of others; not the property of family or church or state or society. These ideas were radical at the time they were proclaimed, and I do not believe they are fully understood or accepted yet; not by most people.

―――

What was so historically extraordinary about the creation of the United States of America was its conscious rejection of the tribal premise.

―――

Many of the Founding Fathers were Deists. They saw God as a force that had created the universe and then largely withdrew from human affairs. They were keenly aware of the evil that resulted when any particular religion gained access to the machinery of government and thereby acquired power to enforce its views. As men of the Enlightenment, they tended to be suspicious of the clergy. George Washington said explicitly that the United States was not to be identified as "a Christian nation." Freedom of conscience was integral to the American tradition from the beginning.

To this day, as Harold Bloom observes in *The American Religion*, the American's relationship to his or her God is a highly personal one, unmediated by any group or authority.[5] It is an encounter that takes place in the context of utter spiritual aloneness. This is quite unlike what one tends to find elsewhere in the world. It reflects the individualism at the heart of the American experience. The majority of Americans, according to Bloom, are convinced that God loves them in a highly personal way. He contrasts this perspective with Spinoza's observation in his *Ethics* that whoever loved God truly should not expect to be loved by God in return. Americans tend to see themselves as the chosen people.

At the core of the American tradition was the fact that this country was born as a frontier nation where nothing was given and everything had to be created. Self-discipline and hard work were highly esteemed cultural values. There was a strong theme of community and mutual aid, to be sure, but not as substitutes for self-reliance and self-responsibility. Independent people helped one another when they could, but ultimately everyone was expected to carry his or her own weight.

In nineteenth-century America, people were not educated in "the psychology of entitlement." They were not encouraged to believe that they were born with a claim on the work, energy, and resources of others. This last was a cultural shift that occurred in the twentieth century.

This generalized account of traditional American culture leaves out a good deal. It does not, for instance, address the institution of slavery, the treatment of black Americans as second-class citizens, or legal discrimination against women, who only acquired the right to vote in this century. Just the same, we can say that to the extent the American vision was actualized, it did a good deal to encourage healthy self-esteem. It encouraged human beings to believe in themselves and in their possibilities.

At the same time, a culture is made of people—and people inevitably carry the past with them. Americans may have repudiated the tribal premise politically, but they or their ancestors came from countries dominated by the tribal mentality, which often continued to influence them culturally and psychologically. They may in some instances have come to these shores to escape religious prejudice and persecution, but many of them carried the mind-set of religious authoritarianism with them. They brought old ways of thinking about race, religion, and gender into the New World. Conflicting cultural values, present from the beginning, continue to this day. In our present culture, pro-self-esteem forces and anti-self-esteem forces collide constantly.

The twentieth century witnessed a shift in cultural values in the United States, and predominately the shift has not supported higher self-esteem but has encouraged the opposite.

I am thinking of the ideas I was taught in college and university, during the 1950s, when epistemological agnosticism (not to say nihilism) joined hands with moral relativism, which joined hands with Marxism. Together with millions of other students, I was informed that:

The mind is powerless to know reality as it really is; ultimately, mind is impotent.

The senses are unreliable and untrustworthy; "everything is an illusion."

Principles of logic are "mere conventions."

Principles of ethics are mere "expressions of feelings," with no basis in reason or reality.

No rational code of moral values is possible.

Since all behavior is determined by factors over which one has no control, no one deserves credit for any achievement.

Since all behavior is determined by factors over which one has no control, no one should be held responsible for any wrongdoing.

When crimes are committed, "society," never the individual, is the culprit (except for crimes committed by businessmen, in which case only the most severe punishment is appropriate).

Everyone has an equal claim on whatever goods or services exist—notions of the "earned" and "unearned" are reactionary and antisocial.

Political and economic freedom have had their chance and have failed, and the future belongs to state ownership and management of the economy, which will produce paradise on earth.

I thought of these ideas and of the professors who taught them in the spring of 1992 as I sat watching on television the riots in South-Central Los Angeles. When a looter was asked by a journalist, "Didn't you realize that the stores you looted and destroyed today wouldn't be there for you tomorrow," the looter answered, "No, I never thought of that." Well, who would have ever taught him it was important to learn how to think, when "advantaged children" aren't taught it either? When I saw a group of men drag a helpless man out of his truck and beat him almost to death, I heard the voice of my professors saying, "If you find this morally objectionable, that's just your emotional bias. There is no right or wrong behavior." When I saw men and women laughing gleefully while dragging TV sets and other household goods out of looted stores, I thought of the professors who taught, "No one is responsible for anything he or she does (except the greedy capitalists who own the stores and deserve whatever trouble they get)." I thought how perfectly the ideas of my professors had been translated into cultural reality. Ideas do matter and do have consequences.

If mind is impotent and knowledge is superstition, why *should* a course on "the great thinkers of the Western world" be rated as more important than a course on modern rock music? Why *should* a student exert the effort of attending a course in mathematics when he or she can get credit for a course on tennis?

If there are no objective principles of behavior, and if no one is responsible for his or her actions, then why *shouldn't* business executives defraud customers and clients? Why *shouldn't* bankers embezzle or misappropriate customers' funds? Why *shouldn't* our political leaders lie to us, betray us in secret deals, withhold from us the information we need to make intelligent choices?

If the "earned" and the "unearned" are old-fashioned, reactionary ideas, why *shouldn't* people loot whatever they feel like looting? Why is working for a living superior to stealing?

Ideas do matter and do have consequences.

What has emerged in the second half of this century is a culture that in many respects reflects the ideas that were taught for decades in the philosophy departments of the leading universities of our nation, passed to other departments, and passed into the world. They became the "received wisdom" of our leading intellectuals. They surfaced in editorial pages, television programs, movies, and comic strips. These ideas are irrational, they cannot be sustained, and there are a growing number of thinkers who oppose them. Still, they are read and heard everywhere, with the exception of the eulogizing of Marxism; empirical evidence has blasted socialism into the junk-heap of history. The ideas are deadly for civilization, deadly for our future, and deadly for self-esteem.

The American culture is a battleground between the values of self-responsibility and the values of entitlement. This is not the only cultural conflict we can see around us, but it is the one most relevant to self-esteem. It is also at the root of many of the others.

We are social beings who realize our humanity fully only in the context of community. The values of our community can inspire the best in us or the worst. A culture that values mind, intellect, knowledge, and understanding promotes self-esteem; a culture that denigrates mind undermines self-esteem. A culture in which human beings are held accountable for their actions supports self-esteem; a culture in which no one is held accountable for anything breeds demoralization and self-contempt. A culture that prizes self-responsibility fosters self-esteem; a culture in which people are encouraged to see themselves as victims fosters dependency, passivity, and the mentality of entitlement. The evidence for these observations is all around us.

The American culture is a battleground between the values of self-responsibility and the values of entitlement.

There will always be independent men and women who will fight for their autonomy and dignity even in the most corrupt and corrupting culture—just as there are children who come out of nightmare childhoods with their self-esteem undestroyed. But a world that values consciousness, self-acceptance, self-responsibility, self-assertiveness, purposefulness, and integrity will not preach values inimical to them or pass laws that discourage or penalize their exercise. For example, children will not be taught to regard themselves as sinful, obedience will not be rewarded more than intelligent questioning, students will not be taught reason is a superstition, girls will not be told femininity equals submissiveness, self-sacrifice will not be eulogized while productive achievement is met with indifference, welfare systems will not penalize the choice to work, and regulatory agencies will not treat producers as criminals.

Some awareness of these realities is reflected in the fact that those who are genuinely concerned with the problems of the underclass in

America are thinking increasingly about the importance of teaching cognitive skills, the values of the work ethic, self-responsibility, interpersonal competence, the pride of ownership—and objective standards of performance. The philosophy of victimhood has not worked, as is evidenced by the steady worsening of social problems under several decades of that perspective. We do not help people out of poverty by telling them the responsibility is "the world's" and that they themselves are powerless and that nothing need be expected of them.

Christopher Lasch is not a champion of individualism, and he has been a vocal critic of the self-esteem movement, which makes his observations on this issue interesting:

> Is it really necessary to point out, at this late date, that public policies based on a therapeutic model of the state have failed miserably, over and over again? Far from promoting self-respect, they have created a nation of dependents. They have given rise to a cult of the victim in which entitlements are based on the display of accumulated injuries inflicted by an uncaring society. The politics of "compassion" degrades both the victims, by reducing them to objects of pity, and their would-be benefactors, who find it easier to pity their fellow citizens than to hold them up to impersonal standards, the attainment of which would make them respected. Compassion has become the human face of contempt.[6]

In our discussion of living purposefully, I spoke about paying attention to outcomes. If our actions and programs do not produce the results intended and promised, then it is our basic premises we need to check. It has been rightly noted that "doing more of what doesn't work, doesn't work." A culture of self-esteem is a culture of accountability, which means of self-responsibility. There is no other way for human beings to prosper or to live benevolently with one another.

In Chapter 12, "The Philosophy of Self-Esteem," I discussed the premises that support self-esteem in that they support and encourage the six pillars. A culture in which these premises are dominant, are woven into the fabric of child-rearing, education, art, and organizational life, will be a high-self-esteem culture. To the extent that the opposite of these premises are dominant we will see a culture inimical to self-esteem. My point is not pragmatism: I am not saying we should subscribe to these ideas because they support self-esteem. I am saying that because these ideas are in alignment with reality, they are in alignment with and supportive of self-esteem.

The focus of this book is psychological, not philosophical, and so I have expressed these ideas in a very personal way, as beliefs exist in an individual consciousness. But if the reader senses that in its implications this book is almost as much a work of philosophy as of psychology, he or she will not be mistaken.

The Individual and Society

We all live in a sea of messages concerning the nature of our value and the standards by which we should judge it. The more independent we are, the more critically we examine these messages. The challenge is often to recognize them for what they are—other people's ideas and beliefs that may or may not have merit. The challenge, in other words, is not to take the assumptions of one's culture as a given, as "reality," but to realize that assumptions can be questioned. As a boy growing up, I am sure I benefited from the fact that my father's favorite saying (after the Gershwin song, I imagine) was, "It ain't necessarily so."

Cultures do not encourage the questioning of their own premises. One of the meanings of living consciously has to do with one's awareness that other people's beliefs are just that, their beliefs, and not necessarily ultimate truth. This does not mean that living consciously expresses itself in skepticism. It expresses itself in critical thinking.

The challenge is not to take the assumptions of one's culture as a given, as "reality," but to realize that assumptions can be questioned.

There are tensions between the agenda of a society and that of any individual that may be inevitable. Societies are primarily concerned with their own survival and perpetuation. They tend to encourage the values that are perceived as serving that end. These values may have nothing to do with the growth needs or personal aspirations of individuals. For example, a militaristic nation or tribe, in adversarial relationships with other nations or tribes, tends to value warrior virtues: aggressiveness, indifference to pain, absolute obedience to authorities, and so on. But this does not mean that from the standpoint of an individual, his interests are served by identifying masculinity or worth with those particular traits, even though he will be encouraged or pressured to do so. He may set a different agenda of his own, which his culture may label "selfish," such as the life of a scholar. In holding to his own standards, in his eyes he manifests integrity; his society may brand him as disloyal or narrow and petty in his vision. Or again, a society may identify its interests with a large and growing population, in which case women will be encouraged to believe there is no glory comparable to motherhood and no other standard of true femininity. Yet an individual woman may see her life another way; her values may lead her toward a career that precludes or postpones motherhood, and she may or may not have the independence to judge her life by her own standards and to understand womanhood very differently from her mother, her minister, or her contemporaries (who, again, may brand her as "selfish").

The average person tends to judge him- or herself by the values prevalent in his social environment, as transmitted by family members, political and religious leaders, teachers, newspaper and television editorials, and popular art such as movies. These values may or may not be rational and may or may not answer to the needs of the individual.

I am sometimes asked if a person cannot achieve genuine self-esteem by conforming and living up to cultural norms that he or she may never have thought about, let alone questioned, and that do not necessarily make a good deal of sense. Is not the safety and security of belonging with and to the group a form of self-esteem? Does not group validation and support lead to an experience of true self-worth? The error here is in equating any feeling of safety or comfort with self-esteem. Conformity is not self-efficacy; popularity is not self-respect. Whatever its gratifications, a sense of belonging is not equal to trust in my mind or confidence in my ability to master the challenges of life. The fact that others esteem me is no guarantee I will esteem myself.

———

Genuine self-esteem is what we feel about ourselves when everything is not all right.

———

If I live a life of unthinking routine, with no challenges or crises, I may be able to evade for a while the fact that what I possess is not self-esteem but pseudo self-esteem. When everything is all right, everything is all right, but that is not how we determine the presence of self-esteem. Genuine self-esteem is what we feel about ourselves when everything is *not* all right. This means, when we are challenged by the unexpected, when others disagree with us, when we are flung back on our own resources, when the cocoon of the group can no longer insulate us from the tasks and risks of life, when we must think, choose, decide, and act *and no one is guiding us or applauding us.* At such moments our deepest premises reveal themselves.

One of the biggest lies we were ever told is that it is "easy" to be selfish and that self-sacrifice takes spiritual strength. People sacrifice themselves in a thousand ways every day. This is their tragedy. To honor the self—to honor mind, judgment, values, and convictions—is the ultimate act of courage. Observe how rare it is. But it is what self-esteem asks of us.

18

Conclusion:
The Seventh Pillar of
Self-Esteem

Early in this book I said the need for self-esteem is a summons to the hero within us. Although what this means is threaded through our entire discussion, let us make it fully explicit.

It means a willingness—and a will—to live the six practices when to do so may not be easy. We may need to overcome inertia, face down fears, confront pain, or stand alone in loyalty to our own judgment, even against those we love.

No matter how nurturing our environment, rationality, self-responsibility, and integrity are never automatic; they always represent an achievement. We are free to think or to avoid thinking, free to expand consciousness or to contract it, free to move toward reality or to withdraw from it. The six pillars all entail choice.

Living consciously requires an *effort*. Generating and sustaining awareness is *work*. Every time we choose to raise the level of our consciousness, we act against inertia. We pit ourselves against entropy, the tendency of everything in the universe to run down toward chaos. In electing to think, we strive to create an island of order and clarity within ourselves.

The first enemy of self-esteem we may need to overcome is *laziness* (which may be the name we give to the forces of inertia and entropy as they manifest psychologically). "Laziness" is not a term we ordinarily encounter in books on psychology. And yet, is anyone unaware that sometimes we fail ourselves for no reason other than the disinclination to generate the effort of an appropriate response? (In *The Psychology of Self-Esteem*, I called this phenomenon "antieffort.") Sometimes, of course, laziness is abetted by fatigue; but not necessarily. Sometimes we are just lazy; meaning we do not challenge inertia, we do not choose to awaken.

The other dragon we may need to slay is the impulse to *avoid discomfort*. Living consciously may obligate us to confront our fears; it may bring us into contact with unresolved pain. Self-acceptance may require that we make real to ourselves thoughts, feelings, or actions that disturb our equilibrium; it may shake up our "official" self-concept. Self-responsibility obliges us to face our ultimate aloneness; it demands that we relinquish fantasies of a rescuer. Self-assertiveness entails the courage to be authentic, with no guarantee of how others will respond; it means that we risk being ourselves. Living purposefully pulls us out of passivity into the demanding life of high focus; it requires that we be self-generators. Living with integrity demands that we choose our values and stand by them, whether this is pleasant and whether others share our convictions; there are times when it demands hard choices.

Taking the long view, it is easy to see that high-self-esteem people are happier than low-self-esteem people. Self-esteem is the best predictor of happiness we have. But in the short term, self-esteem requires the willingness to endure discomfort when that is what one's spiritual growth entails.

If one of our top priorities is to avoid discomfort, if we make this a higher value than our self-regard, then under pressure we will abandon the six practices precisely when we need them most.

The desire to avoid discomfort is not, per se, a vice. But when surrendering to it blinds us to important realities and leads us away from necessary actions, it results in tragedy.

Here is the basic pattern: First, we avoid what we need to look at because we do not want to feel pain. Then our avoidance produces further problems for us, which we also do not want to look at because they evoke pain. Then the new avoidance produces additional problems we do not care to examine—and so on. Layer of avoidance is piled on layer of avoidance, disowned pain on disowned pain. This is the condition of most adults.

Here is the reversal of the basic pattern: First, we decide that our self-esteem and our happiness matter more than short-term discomfort or pain. We take baby steps at being more conscious, self-accepting, responsible, and so on. We notice that when we do this we like ourselves more. This inspires us to push on and attempt to go farther. We become more truthful with ourselves and others. Self-esteem rises. We take on harder assignments. We feel a little tougher, a little more resourceful. It becomes easier to confront discomfiting emotions and threatening situations; we feel we have more assets with which to cope. We become more self-assertive. We feel stronger. We are building the spiritual equivalent of a muscle. Experiencing ourselves as more powerful, we see difficulties in more realistic perspective. We may never be entirely free of fear or pain, but they have lessened immeasurably, and we are not intimidated by them. Integrity feels less threatening and more natural.

If the process were entirely easy, if there was nothing hard about it at any point, if perseverance and courage were never needed—*everyone* would have good self-esteem. But a life without effort, struggle, or suffering is an infant's dream.

Neither struggle nor pain has intrinsic value. When they can be avoided with no harmful consequences, they should be. A good psychotherapist works to make the process of growth no more difficult than it needs to be. When I examine my own development as a therapist over the past three decades, I see that one of my goals has been to make self-examination, self-confrontation, and the building of self-esteem as unstressful as possible. The evolution of my approach and technique has had this intention from the beginning.

One of the ways this is accomplished is by helping people see that doing what is difficult but necessary need not be "a big thing." We do not have to catastrophize fear or discomfort. We can accept them as part of life, face them and deal with them as best we can, and keep moving in the direction of our best possibilities.

But always, will is needed. Perseverance is needed. Courage is needed.

The energy for this commitment can only come from the love we have for our own life.

This love is the beginning of virtue. It is the launching pad for our highest and noblest aspirations. It is the motive power that drives the six pillars. It is the seventh pillar of self-esteem.

APPENDIX A:

Critique of Other
Definitions of Self-Esteem

To set my definition of self-esteem in context, I want to comment on a few representative definitions that have been proposed.

The "father" of American psychology is William James, and in his *Principles of Psychology*, originally published in 1890, we find the earliest attempt I know of to define self-esteem:

> I, who for the time have staked my all on being a psychologist, am mortified if others know much more psychology than I. But I am contented to wallow in the grossest ignorance of Greek. My deficiencies there give me no sense of personal humiliation at all. Had I "pretensions" to be a linguist, it would have been just the reverse. . . . With no attempt there can be no failure; with no failure no humiliation. So our self-feeling in this world depends entirely on what we *back* ourselves to be and do. It is determined by the ratio of our actualities to our supposed potentialities; a fraction of which our pretensions are the denominator and the numerator our success: thus,
>
> $$\text{Self-esteem} = \frac{\text{Success}}{\text{Pretensions}}$$
>
> Such a fraction may be increased as well by diminishing the denominator as by increasing the numerator.

I said in my Introduction that whoever speaks about self-esteem inescapably speaks about himself. The first thing James is telling us about himself is that he bases his self-esteem on how well he compares to others in his chosen field. If no one else can match his expertise, his self-esteem is satisfied; if someone else surpasses him, his self-esteem is devastated. He is telling us that in a sense he is placing his self-esteem at the mercy of others. In his professional life, this gives him a vested interest in being surrounded by inferiors; it gives him reason to fear talent rather than welcome, admire, and take pleasure in it. This is not a formula for healthy self-esteem but a prescription for anxiety. To tie our self-esteem to any factor outside our volitional control, such as the choices or actions of others, is to invite anguish. That so many people judge themselves just this way is their tragedy.

If "self-esteem equals success divided by pretensions," then, as James points out, self-esteem can equally be protected by increasing one's success or lowering one's pretensions. This means that a person who aspires to nothing, neither in work nor in character, and achieves it, and a person of high accomplishment and high character, are equals in self-esteem. I do not believe that this is an idea at which anyone could have arrived by paying attention to the real world. People with aspirations so low that they meet them mindlessly and effortlessly are not conspicuous for their psychological well-being.

How well we live up to our personal standards and values (which James unfortunately calls "pretensions") clearly has a bearing on our self-esteem. The value of James's discussion is that it draws attention to this fact. But it is a fact that cannot properly be understood in a vacuum, as if the *content* of our standards and values were irrelevant and nothing more were involved than the neutral formula James proposes. Literally, his formula is less a definition of self-esteem than a statement concerning how he believes the level of self-esteem is determined not in some unfortunate individuals but in everyone.

One of the best books written on self-esteem is Stanley Coopersmith's *The Antecedents of Self-Esteem.* His research on the contribution of parents remains invaluable. He writes:

> By self-esteem we refer to the evaluation that the individual makes and customarily maintains with regard to himself: it expresses an attitude of approval or disapproval, and indicates the extent to which the individual believes himself to be capable, significant, successful, and worthy. In short, self-esteem is a *personal* judgment of worthiness that is expressed in the attitudes the individual holds toward himself.

Relative to James, this formulation represents a great step forward. It speaks much more directly to what our experience of self-esteem is. Yet there are questions it raises and leaves unanswered.

"Capable" of what? All of us are capable in some areas and not in others. Capable relative to whatever we undertake? Then must any lack of adequate competence diminish self-esteem? I do not think Coopersmith would want to suggest this, but the implication is left hanging.

"Significant"—what does this mean? Significant in what way? Significant in the eyes of others? Which others? Significant by what standards?

"Successful"—does this mean worldly success? Financial success? Career success? Social success? Success concerning what? Note he is not saying that self-esteem contains the idea that success (in principle) is *appropriate;* he is saying that self-esteem contains the idea of *seeing oneself as successful*—which is entirely different and troublesome in its implications.

"Worthy"—of what? Happiness? Money? Love? Anything the individual desires? My sense is that Coopersmith would mean by "worthy" pretty much what I spell out above in my own definition, but he does not say so.

Another definition is offered by Richard L. Bednar, M. Gawain Wells, and Scott R. Peterson in their book *Self-Esteem: Paradoxes and Innovations in Clinical Theory and Practice*:

> Parenthetically, we define self-esteem as a subjective and enduring sense of realistic self-approval. It reflects how the individual views and values the self at the most fundamental levels of psychological experiencing. . . . Fundamentally, then, self-esteem is an enduring and affective sense of personal value based on accurate self-perception.

"Approval"—concerning what? Everything about the self from physical appearance to actions to intellectual functioning? We are not told. "Views and values the self"—concerning what issues or criteria? "An enduring and affective sense of personal value"—*what does this mean?* One the other hand, what I like in this formulation is the observation that genuine self-esteem is reality based.

One of the most widely publicized definitions of self-esteem is given in *Toward a State of Esteem: The Final Report of the California Task Force to Promote Self and Personal and Social Responsibility*:

Self-esteem is defined as: "Appreciating my own worth and importance and having the character to be accountable for myself and to act responsibly toward others."

In this definition, we find the same lack of specificity as in the other definitions—"worth and importance" *concerning what?* There is another problem with the task force statement: inserting into the definition what is obviously meant to be a basic *source* of healthy self-esteem (that is, being accountable for oneself and acting responsibly toward others). A definition of a psychological state is meant to tell us what a state *is*, not how one gets there. Did the people who offered this definition want us to understand that if we don't act responsibly toward others we won't possess healthy self-esteem? If so, they are probably right, but is that part of the definition—or is it a different issue? (Almost certainly such a definition is influenced by "political" rather than scientific considerations—to reassure people that champions of self-esteem are not fostering petty, irresponsible "selfishness.")

Finally, there are those in the self-esteem movement who announce that "self-esteem means 'I am capable and lovable.' "

Again we must ask, "Capable" of what? I am a great skier, a brilliant lawyer, and a first-rate chef. However, I don't feel competent to assess independently the moral values my mother taught me. I feel, Who am I to know? In such a case, am I "capable"? Do I have self-esteem?

As to "lovable"—yes, feeling lovable is one of the characteristics of healthy self-esteem. So is feeling worthy of happiness and success. Is feeling lovable more important? Evidently, since the other two items are not mentioned. *By what reasoning?*

I shall not belabor the point by offering additional examples that would only reflect variations of the same difficulties.

APPENDIX B:

A Sentence-Completion Exercise for Building Self-Esteem

I want to share with the reader a thirty-one-week sentence-completion program I developed specifically to build self-esteem. Some fairly complex theoretical ideas are embedded in these stems and in their progression, which cannot be appreciated without experience in doing the exercise.

We have already seen the powerful role that sentence-completion work can play in facilitating self-understanding and personal development. The program offered here aims at facilitating understanding of the six pillars and their application to daily life. The reader will note that theme threading through the entire exercise. The issues raised in the program are explored in the course of therapy in many different ways and from many different angles; the client's endings invariably suggest additional pathways of needed attention. What follows is the generic version, which itself keeps evolving and being revised.

To make the program complete and self-contained, I have had to restate some points made earlier. Some stems introduced previously are brought together here, along with new ones, and organized in a particular structure that is intended to lead the individual to a progressive awakening: to increased self-understanding and a strengthening of self-esteem.

It is as if half of this section were written in invisible ink—which becomes visible only over time, as one works with the stems and studies the patterns in one's endings. I hope the program will be studied with that realization in mind.

The Program

When working with sentence completion on your own, you can use a notebook, typewriter, or computer. (An acceptable alternative is to do the sentence completions into a tape recorder, in which case you keep repeating the stem into a recorder, each time completing it with a difference ending, and play the work back later to reflect on it.)

WEEK 1
First thing in the morning, before proceeding to the day's business, sit and write the following stem:

If I bring more awareness to my life today—

Then, as rapidly as possible, without pausing for reflection, write as many endings for that sentence as you can in two or three minutes (never fewer than six and ten is enough). Do not worry if your endings are literally true, or make sense, or are "profound." Write *anything*, but write *something*.

Then, go on to the next stem:

If I take more responsibility for my choices and actions today—

Then:

If I pay more attention to how I deal with people today—

Then:

If I boost my energy level by 5 percent today—

When you are finished, proceed with your day's business.

Do this exercise every day, Monday through Friday for the first week, always before the start of the day's business.

Naturally there will be many repetitions. But also, new endings will inevitably occur. Time spent meditating on these endings "stokes" the creative unconscious to generate connections and insights and to propel growth. When we intensify awareness, we tend to evoke a need for action that expresses our psychological state.

Sometime each weekend, reread what you have written for the week, then do a minimum of six endings for this stem:

If any of what I wrote this week is true, it might be helpful if I—

This facilitates translation of new learnings into action. Continue this practice throughout the program on the weekend.

In doing this work, the ideal is to empty your mind of any expectations concerning what will happen or what is "supposed" to happen. Do not impose any demands on the situation. Do the exercise, go about your day's activities, take a little time to meditate on your endings when you can, and merely notice any differences in how you feel or are inclined to act.

Remember. Your endings must be a grammatical completion of the sentence—and if your mind goes absolutely empty, *invent* an ending, but do not allow yourself to stop with the thought that you cannot do this exercise.

An average session should not take longer than ten minutes. If it takes much longer, you are "thinking" (rehearsing, calculating) too much. Think *after* the exercise, but not during it.

Never do less than six endings for a stem.

WEEK 2
If I bring 5 percent more awareness to my important relationships—
If I bring 5 percent more awareness to my insecurities—
If I bring 5 percent more awareness to my deepest needs and wants—
If I bring 5 percent more awareness to my emotions—

WEEK 3
If I treat listening as a creative act—
If I notice how people are affected by the quality of my listening—
If I bring more awareness to my dealings with people today—
If I commit to dealing with people fairly and benevolently—

WEEK 4
If I bring a higher level of self-esteem to my activities today—
If I bring a higher level of self-esteem to my dealings with people today—
If I am 5 percent more self-accepting today—
If I am self-accepting even when I make mistakes—
If I am self-accepting even when I feel confused and overwhelmed—

WEEK 5
If I am more accepting of my body—
If I deny and disown my body—
If I deny or disown my conflicts—
If I am more accepting of all the parts of me—

WEEK 6
If I wanted to raise my self-esteem today, I could—
If I am more accepting of my feelings—
If I deny and disown my feelings—
If I am more accepting of my thoughts—
If I deny and disown my thoughts—

WEEK 7
If I am more accepting of my fears—
If I deny and disown my fears—
If I were more accepting of my pain—
If I deny and disown my pain—

WEEK 8
If I am more accepting of my anger—
If I deny and disown my anger—
If I am more accepting of my sexuality—
If I deny and disown my sexuality—

WEEK 9
If I am more accepting of my excitement—
If I deny and disown my excitement—
If I am more accepting of my intelligence—
If I deny and disown my intelligence—

WEEK 10
If I am more accepting of my joy—
If I deny and disown my joy—
If I bring more awareness to all the parts of me—
As I learn to accept all of who I am—

WEEK 11
Self-responsibility to me means—
If I take 5 percent more responsibility for my life and well-being—

If I avoid responsibility for my life and well-being—
If I take 5 percent more responsibility for the attainment of my goals—
If I avoid responsibility for the attainment of my goals—

WEEK 12
If I take 5 percent more responsibility for the success of my relationships—
Sometimes I keep myself passive when I—
Sometimes I make myself helpless when I—
I am becoming aware—

WEEK 13
If I take 5 percent more responsibility for my standard of living—
If I take 5 percent more responsibility for my choice of companions—
If I take 5 percent more responsibility for my personal happiness—
If I take 5 percent more responsibility for the level of my self-esteem—

WEEK 14
Self-assertiveness to me means—
If I lived 5 percent more assertively today—
If I treat my thoughts and feelings with respect today—
If I treat my wants with respect today—

WEEK 15
If (when I was young) someone had told me my wants really mattered—
If (when I was young) I had been taught to honor my own life—
If I treat my life as unimportant—
If I were willing to say yes when I want to say yes and no when I want to say no—
If I were willing to let people hear the music inside me—
If I were to express 5 percent more of who I am—

WEEK 16
Living purposefully to me means—
If I bring 5 percent more purposefulness into my life—
If I operate 5 percent more purposefully at work—
If I operate 5 percent more purposefully in my relationships—
If I operate 5 percent more purposefully in marriage—
[if applicable]

WEEK 17
If I operate 5 percent more purposefully with my children —
[if applicable]
If I were 5 percent more purposeful about my deepest yearnings —
If I take more responsibility for fulfilling my wants —
If I make my happiness a conscious goal —

WEEK 18
Integrity to me means —
If I look at instances where I find full integrity difficult —
If I bring 5 percent more integrity into my life —
If I bring 5 percent more integrity to my work —

WEEK 19
If I bring 5 percent more integrity to my relationships —
If I remain loyal to the values I believe are right —
If I refuse to live by values I do not respect —
If I treat my self-respect as a high priority —

WEEK 20
If the child in me could speak, he/she would say —
If the teenager I once was still exists inside me —
If my teenage-self could speak he/she would say —
At the thought of reaching back to help my child-self —
At the thought of reaching back to help my teenage-self —
If I could make friends with my younger selves —

Note: For a more detailed discussion of how to work with integrating your younger selves, please consult *How to Raise Your Self-Esteem*

WEEK 21
If my child-self felt accepted by me —
If my teenage-self felt I was on his/her side —
If my younger selves felt I had compassion for their struggles —
If I could hold my child-self in my arms —
If I could hold my teenage-self in my arms —
If I had the courage and compassion to embrace and love my younger selves —

WEEK 22
Sometimes my child-self feels rejected by me when I—
Sometimes my teenage-self feels rejected by me when I—
One of the things my child-self needs from me and rarely gets is—
One of the things my teenage-self needs from me and hasn't gotten
is—
One of the ways my child-self gets back at me for rejecting him/her
is—
One of the ways my teenage-self gets back at me for rejecting him/her
is—

WEEK 23
At the thought of giving my child-self what he/she needs from me—
At the thought of giving my teenage-self what he/she needs from me—
If my child-self and I were to fall in love—
If my teenage-self and I were to fall in love—

WEEK 24
If I accept that my child-self may need time to learn to trust me—
If I accept that my teenage-self may need time to learn to trust me—
As I come to understand that my child-self and my teenage-self are
both part of me—
I am becoming aware—

WEEK 25
Sometimes when I am afraid I—
Sometimes when I am hurt I—
Sometimes when I am angry I—
An effective way to handle fear might be to—
An effective way to handle hurt might be to—
An effective way to handle anger might be to—

WEEK 26
Sometimes when I am excited I—
Sometimes when I am turned on sexually I—
Sometimes when I experience strong feelings I—
If I make friends with my excitement—
If I make friends with my sexuality—
As I grow more comfortable with the full range of my emotions—

WEEK 27
If I think about becoming better friends with my child-self—
If I think about becoming better friends with my teenage-self—
As my younger selves become more comfortable with me—
As I create a safe space for my child-self—
As I create a safe space for my teenage-self—

WEEK 28
Mother gave me a view of myself as—
Father gave me a view of myself as—
Mother speaks through my voice when I tell myself—
Father speaks through my voice when I tell myself—

WEEK 29
If I bring 5 percent more awareness to my relationship with my mother—
If I bring 5 percent more awareness to my relationship with my father—
If I look at my mother and father realistically—
If I reflect on the level of awareness I bring to my relationship to my mother—
If I reflect on the level of awareness I bring to my relationship with my father—

WEEK 30
At the thought of being free of Mother, psychologically—
At the thought of being free of Father, psychologically—
At the thought of belonging fully to myself—
If my life really does belong to me—
If I really am capable of independent survival—

WEEK 31
If I bring 5 percent more awareness to my life—
If I am 5 percent more self-accepting—
If I bring 5 percent more self-responsibility to my life—
If I operate 5 percent more self-assertively—
If I live my life 5 percent more purposefully—
If I bring 5 percent more integrity to my life—
If I breathe deeply and allow myself to experience what self-esteem feels like—

Let us imagine that you have now completed this thirty-one-week program—once. If you have found it helpful, do it again. It will be a new experience for you. Some of my clients go through this program three or four times, always with new results, always with growth in self-esteem.

APPENDIX C:

Recommendations for Further Study

The central focus of my work has been the study of self-esteem, its role in human life, and, most particularly, its impact on work and love. If you have found the work you have just read of value, then the following works are suggested for further reading.

The Psychology of Self-Esteem. This is my first major theoretical exploration and overview of the entire field. Unlike my later books, it puts heavy emphasis on the philosophical foundations of my work. It deals with such questions as: What is the meaning—and justification—of the idea of free will? What is the relation of reason and emotion? How do rationality and integrity relate to self-esteem? Which moral values support self-esteem and which undermine it? Why is self-esteem the key to motivation?

Breaking Free. This is an exploration of the childhood origins of negative self-concepts, dramatized through a series of vignettes taken from my clinical practice. Through these stories we see in what ways adults can adversely affect the development of a child's self-esteem. Indirectly, therefore, the book is a primer on the art of child-rearing.

The Disowned Self. This book examines the painful and widespread problem of self-alienation, in which the individual is out of touch with his or her inner world, and indicates pathways to recovery. This book has proven especially helpful for adult children of dysfunctional families. It takes a fresh look at the relation of reason and emotion that goes beyond my earlier treatment of the subject in its scope and depth. Demonstrating how and why self-acceptance is essential to healthy self-esteem, it points the way to the harmonious integration of thought and feeling.

The Psychology of Romantic Love. In this book I explore the nature and meaning of romantic love, its difference from other kinds of love, its historical development, and its special challenges in the modern world. It addresses such questions as: What is love? Why is love born? Why does it sometimes flourish? Why does it sometimes die?

What Love Asks of Us. Originally published as *The Romantic Love Question-and-Answer Book,* this revised and expanded edition, written with my wife and colleague, Devers Branden, addresses the questions we hear most often from those struggling with the practical challenges of making love work. It covers a wide range of topics, from the importance of autonomy in relationships, to the art of effective communication, to conflict-resolution skills, to dealing with jealousy and infidelity, to coping with the special challenges of children and in-laws, to surviving the loss of love.

Honoring the Self. Again returning to the nature of self-esteem and its role in our existence, this book is less philosophical than *The Psychology of Self-Esteem* and more developmental in its focus. It looks at how the self emerges, evolves, and moves through progressively higher stages of individuation. It explores what adults can do to raise the level of their own self-esteem. It examines the psychology of guilt. It addresses the relationship between self-esteem and productive work. It upholds a morality of enlightened self-interest and challenges the traditional notion that self-sacrifice is the essence of virtue.

If You Could Hear What I Cannot Say. This is a workbook. It teaches the fundamentals of my sentence-completion technique and how it can be used by a person working alone for self-exploration, self-understanding, self-healing, and personal growth.

The Art of Self-Discovery. This book carries further the work of the preceding volume on sentence completion and self-exploration. Originally published as *To See What I See and Know What I Know,* this revised and expanded edition also provides counselors and psychotherapists with tools to be utilized in their own clinical practice.

How to Raise Your Self-Esteem. The purpose here is to provide the reader with specific strategies for building self-esteem. The discussion is more concrete than in my earlier writings, more action oriented. It is addressed equally to people working on their own development and to parents, teachers, and psychotherapists who are invited to experiment with the techniques.

Judgment Day: My Years with Ayn Rand. This investigative memoir tells the story of my personal and intellectual development, including the rises and falls and rises of my own self-esteem, through my relationship with three women, of which the centerpiece is my relationship with novelist-philosopher Ayn Rand (*The Fountainhead, Atlas Shrugged*). It describes the extraordinary contexts in which I came upon some of my most important psychological ideas, including my first understanding, at the age of twenty-four, of the supreme importance of self-esteem to human well-being.

The Power of Self-Esteem. A brief distillation of my key ideas in this field, this book is intended as a basic introduction.

Through the Branden Institute for Self-Esteem in Los Angeles, we offer psychotherapy and family counseling; conduct ongoing self-esteem groups; give lectures, seminars and workshops; do management consulting; create self-esteem/high-performance programs for organizations; and offer telephone counseling with individual and corporate clients.

For information, write to:

> The Branden Institute for Self-Esteem
> P.O. Box 2609
> Beverly Hills, California 90213
> Telephone: (310) 274-6361   Fax: (310) 271-6808

THE SIX PILLARS OF SELF-ESTEEM

The Weekend Seminar

For information on dates and locations for The Six Pillars of Self-Esteem weekend seminars, contact:

> The Continuing Education Institute
> 1079 Morse Blvd.
> Winter Park, Florida 32789
> Telephone: 1-800-531-2208

References

Chapter 1:
Self-Esteem: The Immune System of Consciousness

[1] L. E. Sandelands, J. Brockner, and M. A. Glynn (1988) "If at first you don't succeed, try again: Effects of Persistence-performance contingencies, ego-involvement, and self-esteem on task-performance." *Journal of Applied Psychology,* 73, 208–216.

[2] E. Paul Torrance. *The Creative Child and Adult Quarterly,* VIII, 1983.

[3] Abraham Maslow. *Toward a Psychology of Being.* New York: Van Nostrand Reinhold, 1968.

[4] *Fortune,* December 17, 1990.

[5] T. George Harris. *The Era of Conscious Choice.* Encyclopedia Britannica Book of the Year, 1973.

Chapter 5:
The Focus on Action

[1] See, for instance, *The Invulnerable Child,* a collection of studies edited by E. James Anthony and Bertram J. Cohler. New York: The Guilford Press, 1987.

Chapter 13:
Nurturing a Child's Self-Esteem

[1] For detailed discussions of this principle, see the books of Haim Ginott: *Between Parent and Child; Between Parent and Teenager;* and *Teacher and Child.* All are published by Avon.

Chapter 14:
Self-Esteem in the Schools

[1] Personal communication with Robert Reasoner.

[2] George Land and Beth Jarman. *Breakpoint and Beyond.* New York: Harper Business, 1992.

[3] Jane Bluestein. *21st Century Discipline.* Jefferson City, Mo.: Scholastic Inc., 1988.

[4] Robert Reasoner. *Building Self-Esteem: A Comprehensive Program for Schools,* rev. ed. Palo Alto: Consulting Psychologists Press, 1992.

[5] Ibid.

[6] Ibid.

[7] Personal communication with Kenneth Miller.

[8] Jane Bluestein. *21st Century Discipline.* Jefferson City, Mo.: Scholastic Inc., 1988.

[9] Howard Gardner. *The Unschooled Mind: How Children Think and How Schools Should Teach.* New York: Basic Books, 1992.

[10] Howard Gardner. "What Parents Can Do to Help Their Kids Learn Better." *Bottom Line,* June 1992.

[11] "Shortchanging Girls, Shortchanging America." American Association of University Women, 1991.

[12] For information about Constance Dembrowsky's program *Personal and Social Responsibility,* contact the Institute for Effective Skill Development, P.O. Box 880, La Luz, NM 88337.

Chapter 15:
Self-Esteem and Work

[1] Quoted in *The Economist,* December 1, 1990.

[2] See my *Honoring the Self.* New York: Bantam Books, 1984.

[3] Michael Dertouzos, Richard K. Lester, Robert M. Solow, and the MIT Commission on Industrial Productivity. *Made in America.* Cambridge: MIT Press, 1989.

[4] Charles Garfield. *Second to None.* Homewood, Ill.: Business One Irwin, 1992.

[5] Warren Bennis. *On Becoming a Leader.* New York: Addison-Wesley, 1989.

Chapter 16:
Self-Esteem and Psychotherapy

[1] For information about Dr. Callahan's work, including how to obtain this monograph, write to: 45350 Vista Santa Rosa, Indian Wells, CA 92210.

Chapter 17:
Self-Esteem and Culture

[1] Mary Kawena Puku'i. *'Olelo No'eau*. Honolulu: Bishop Museum Press, 1985.

[2] Margaret Mead. *Coming of Age in Samoa*. New York: New American Library, 1949.

[3] G. Rattray Taylor. *Sex in History*. New York: Harper Torchbooks, 1973.

[4] Jonathan Rauch. "A Search for the Soul of Japan." *Los Angeles Times Magazine,* March 8, 1992.

[5] Harold Bloom. *The American Religion*. New York: Simon & Schuster, 1992.

[6] Christopher Lasch. "In Defense of Shame." *The New Republic,* August 10, 1992.

Acknowledgments

I wish to express my appreciation to my editor, Toni Burbank, for the energy and enthusiasm she brought to this project and for many helpful suggestions.

Thanks also to my literary agent, Nat Sobel, for his unstinting support and dedication.

And finally, my love and gratitude to my wife, Devers, for her excitement about the book, the stimulation of our discussions about it, and the provocative ideas she often provided.

Index